NEW

D0380225

THE INDEPENDENT WOMAN'S GUIDE TO

EUROPE

THE INDEPENDENT WOMAN'S GUIDE TO
EUROPE

LINDA WHITE

Fulcrum Publishing
Golden, Colorado

Copyright © 1991 Linda Sanders White

An earlier version of this book was published in 1987 by Inbal Travel Information, Tel Aviv, Israel.

Book Design by Ann E. Green
Cover Illustration by Gary Kelley © 1990

All Rights Reserved

Library of Congress Cataloging-in-Publication Data

White, Linda, 1946–
    The independent woman's guide to Europe / Linda White.
        p.   cm.
    Includes bibliographical references and index.
    ISBN 1-55591-087-4 (pbk.)
    1. Europe—Description and travel—1971– —Guide-books. 2. Single women—Travel—Europe. I. Title.
D909.W534 1991
914.04'559—dc20   90-85223
                                                                   CIP

Printed in the United States of America

10   9   8   7   6   5   4   3   2

Fulcrum Publishing
350 Indiana Street, Suite 350
Golden, CO 80401

To Muh, for letting me go

CONTENTS

8

9

10

11

12

Practical Matters

Acknowledgments

Grateful acknowledgment is made to Joe Weisel and to Faye and Kent Prince for reading and criticizing the manuscript, to Faye for "how to do" and to the national tourist offices for answering my many questions. I owe special thanks to Betsy Armstrong for wanting to publish my book and for making many helpful suggestions. Thanks, too, to Carmel Huestis for shepherding the book through its final stages.

As I was working on this book, exciting events began to unfold in Eastern Europe. These events have already changed the face of Europe, forcing us to toss out the old clichés about the East Bloc. In fact, changes are taking place so swiftly that anything written one day is liable to be outdated the next. I have tried to anticipate changes whenever possible; I ask the reader's indulgence if I have anticipated wrongly.

At the time of the book's second printing, countries were splitting up, gasoline coupons and money-exchange requirements were becoming a thing of the past, and visas were either not required or issued free at borders to Americans (the most prominent exception is Russia). Tipping in Western goods (such as perfume or pantyhose) is still sometimes appreciated, but hard currency is appreciated more. War wiped out the former Yugoslavia's tourist industry, one of its main sources of income. However, the northwest corner, now the Republic of Slovenia, is peaceful—fighting only against heavy odds to make a tourism comeback.

These are exciting times for traveling in Eastern Europe, and it is the thesis of this book that the best traveler is the informed traveler. For example, those who realize the extent of food shortages in Russia are less likely to complain about the monotony of meals there. Before going East, inform yourself about the current situation and be prepared to find it changed by the time you arrive.

Any errors in this book are my own; I would appreciate corrections, updates or simply hearing of others' travel experiences.

INTRODUCTION

My job is to travel; almost always I travel alone. Life is a series of planes and trains, of highways stretching as Turkey blends into Spain blurs into Flanders ferries over to England. Three days here, ten days there; packing and unpacking, checking in and out of hotels so often that I can seldom remember my room number.

This book is a distillation of my experiences living and traveling in Europe for the past ten years. It is designed especially for women who wish to see Europe without having to suffer the "sheep syndrome" of group tours. It does not speak so much of what to see (many good books can tell you that), but of *how to do*. It is not a listing of hotels and restaurants that welcome women as independent individuals, nor is it a listing of "women's" activities. It is a guide to show you *how to* choose hotels and restaurants, *how to* find activities that interest you. It gives you a framework to build on, brief pictures of European life for you to use in creating your own montage. Being travel-wise, like being street-wise, can take the anxiety out of your trip.

Traveling alone has its problems. No one is there to hold the table at the restaurant while you go to the toilet, or to keep an eye on the luggage while you dash over to ask a question at the airport information booth. But traveling alone also has its rewards, allowing you to travel at your own pace and do the things you want to do. Life can be easier when you share the adventure of Europe with a friend, but the stress of travel puts friendship to the acid test. Make a short "trial run" together before you decide to make a long trip together. Everyone has her own style of traveling, and friends who travel together must have compatible styles!

Even the liberated woman suffers anxiety when setting out for foreign shores. Almost all single travelers know fear—an icy finger that touches your wrist at the sudden realization that you are alone in a strange land. The unfamiliar is the most fearsome. The sensible thing to do is to find out as much as possible about where you are going before you get there. That means more than where to find the museums, more than which restaurant is "in" this year. It means learning the customs of the place, learning how the local people will react to you, learning travel manners—you are, after all, the guest.

How you travel is just as important as where you travel, and it is especially important for women alone. Women's liberation has not reached the whole world: in places, the lone woman is regarded by both men and women either as predator (looking for a man) or as prey (easy to attack). It is in these places that you must not make an error of judgment and you must not leave your words and actions open to misinterpretation. Learning *how* to travel may mean rethinking your attitudes, reshaping your behavior. It certainly means being able to act and taking responsibility for your actions.

Travel is a very personal thing. Backpacker or businesswoman, certain rules apply, and certain experiences will be the same. The difference lies in the way you approach them. Travel is a total experience, more than sightseeing. It cannot be passive; if you sit and wait for things to happen, they seldom do. Seek out activities that you enjoy. Learn to talk to people—stock questions sometimes elicit surprising answers. The real traveler is open-minded, ready to see and hear and feel and experience something new. She grows as she goes along.

I offer this book with the assumption that you, the reader, want to become an explorer of the spirit as well as of the place—that you welcome things that are different instead of seeking things that are the same—that you will build the confidence you need to travel alone and will let travel prove that you are indeed an independent woman.

1

LIFE IS EASIER FOR THE LOCALS

How *Not* to Look Like a Tourist

"How did they know we're Americans?" asked the woman in the red polyester pantsuit. "We hadn't said a word." Clothes, cameras, guidebooks and luggage are the least subtle advertisements that you are a stranger in town. American clothing and hairstyles, as well as mannerisms, stand out in Europe.

Why not let people know at once that you are a tourist? Because the local population gets better service in shops and restaurants. They are, after all, the steady customers. Local women command more respect from local men. Tourists are the natural first targets for propositions and worse. In some places, touts swarm around tourists like flies.

It is impossible to "go native" completely, but you can fit in. Modifying your appearance is the easiest way to play the chameleon. But you can't travel without luggage, you need a guidebook and you probably want a camera. So what can you do?

Guidebooks and Cameras

I am waiting for the day when all guidebooks will be loose-leaf so I can remove the sections I want to take with me. Meanwhile, I use a razor blade to slice out the sections I need, clip the pages together, and slip them back between the book covers when I return. Guidebooks not only show that you are a tourist, they also are heavy. Read as many as possible *before* you go and carry only the essential with you.

You can pick up leaflets at the local tourist offices to use on the spot. If you want to keep them, mail them home to yourself. You can also find guidebooks along the way that are not available at home. Check the souvenir shops and bookstores for local picture- and guidebooks. Many are translated into English.

Among tourists in Europe, the Americans and the Japanese seem to vie to see who can carry the most photographic equipment. Keep your camera inconspicuous; a big handbag is better than an extra camera bag. At the most, you need one camera and a couple of lenses; a mini-camera is best unless you need professional quality.

Consider postcards as an alternative to lugging photo apparatus. If you collect stamps, all the better—mail postcards to yourself. The cards will also help you relive the trip when you get home.

Dress

To blend with the crowd, dress for the country you are visiting. This may mean wearing a skirt instead of jeans or lengthening your short skirts, so plan your wardrobe carefully before you go.

Avoid tight jeans and shorts if you plan to travel outside beach resort areas, especially in southern and eastern countries. You may earn an obvious frown if you visit a cathedral in shorts—if you are allowed in at all. In Italy, for example, women are not allowed into churches if they are wearing sundresses, so carry a large scarf or jacket to drape over your shoulders.

When you are selecting your travel wardrobe, keep in mind the importance of pockets. You need them for telephone and tip change, for maps, for keys, for keeping your hands warm in winter, maybe even for a small flashlight. The more deep pockets you have, the better.

It's also a good idea to "break in" all your clothes—not just your shoes—before you set out. Try different combinations so you can mix and match with confidence. Make sure your clothes aren't too loose or too tight for comfort, that they hold their shape with hard wear and that they are suitable with the shoes you are taking. Many hotels don't provide full-length mirrors, so check the appearance of each outfit and each variation before you leave home.

Europe is the fashion trend-setter for the Western world. You might like to bring along a minimum of clothes and go shopping. To get an idea of the fashions, look at the people in the streets as well as at the fashion magazines. The punk look is still "in" in Britain and Germany, but the leaders in chic fashion are the Italians and French. You can't go wrong if you dress as they do.

If the big-name designers are beyond your means, there are ways to dress beautifully on a budget. Second-hand clothing shops are becoming more and more popular in the big cities, and many of them specialize in high fashion. This is where the movie and TV stars and other trend-setters dispose of things they have worn just a few times. With a little luck, you'll find a terrific outfit in your size at a fraction of its original price.

In Paris, a number of shops selling last season's designer models can be found on the rue d'Alésia; take the Métro to the Alésia stop on the edge of town. Check the English-language bookstores for up-to-date shoppers' guides, which list factory outlets, second-hand shops and other money savers.

The farther south and east you travel, the more conservative women's dress becomes. In prime tourist areas, almost all types of dress (and undress) are accepted from tourists even if not acceptable for the locals, but if you venture off the beaten track—say, into eastern Turkey—short skirts and bare shoulders can invite disdain or downright hostility. In poorer regions, especially in rural areas, women dress mostly in black. Muslim women all over Europe may cover their hair with scarves.

Traditional folk costume is daily wear in many places. You see dirndls in Austria, knee britches in Bavaria, tartans in Scotland. In Germany, it is not surprising to meet a chimney sweep outfitted in black, complete with top hat (shake his hand for luck). *Zimmermen* (carpenters) in their distinctive silver-buttoned suits still travel around the country for jobs. In other places, costumes are donned only for festivals or by shopkeepers and waitresses/waiters in self-conscious tourist towns.

If you are tempted to buy a costume (a dirndl is perfectly reasonable in Salzburg), consider how it will look at home. Clothes, like wine, may not travel well, though some do. Lodencloth coats, for example, are among the most practical on earth. Lightweight and water-repellent, they are usually styled classically for comfort.

What's the Weather?

Unless you are very lucky, you will need a coat or sweater, raincoat and boots in Europe. A group of tourists with visions of sunny Spain came to Madrid one May with only shorts and sundresses. They did not know that Madrid is high and cool and that May in Europe is still far from summer. The sellers of heavy fishermen's sweaters did a good day's business with that group. In bad weather, fashion takes a back seat to creature comfort. Don't be surprised if you see women in snow-covered cities wearing mink coats and moonboots.

I have shivered on Malta and been rain-dampened in the Canary Islands. Forget the romance of the song: April in Paris can be miserable if you aren't properly dressed. Always bring a sweater and an umbrella.

Before packing your bags, consult a globe or an atlas to determine the exact location of where you are going. The latitude of a country will help you determine what kind of weather to expect. For example, Frankfurt, Germany—the center of Central Europe—lies farther north than any place in the continental United States. Rome is on approximately the same latitude as New York City; St. Louis matches up with Lisbon. If you come from the deep South, the climate you are used to is nearer to North African than European.

Consider the altitude of where you are going and the proximity of lakes and the sea. If you are traveling in the mountains, you may find some of the sunniest skies in Europe. Yes, you can ski in a bikini on the glaciers in summer, but you need a jacket when the sun goes down. Lake and ocean breezes can be chilly, too. At continental Europe's southwesternmost tip of land, Cape St. Vincent, Portugal, a cool wind blows in August, although on the beaches not far away you can bask in a swimsuit.

The winds of Europe have names, such as the *Mistrael* or the *Yugo*. One of the winds you are most likely to meet is the *Föhn*, which is most strongly felt north of the Alps, in the Alpine valleys of the Rhine, the Inn and the Salzach rivers. The *Föhn* is caused by a deep barometric depression passing along the north slope of the Alps, and it is a dry, burning wind that clears the atmosphere beautifully. However, it sets everyone's nerves on edge. It is blamed for everything from avalanches to forest fires, and it is a fact that schools in Innsbruck give no exams when the *Föhn* is blowing. It has even been used as a defense in a murder trial!

Once in Europe, you can find out about weather, road and skiing or swimming conditions by phoning weather services, automobile clubs or, in some cases, tourist offices. A number of radio stations include this information in regular broadcasts. However, these reports are seldom in English, so unless you speak the language you may find it best to inquire at your hotel.

Feet First

Comfortable shoes are an important part of your wardrobe. People look at your face before they look at your feet, and it is easier to smile when your feet don't hurt.

Be kind to your feet when you are sightseeing: cobblestones are hell on high heels and are extremely slippery when wet or icy—and you'd be surprised how many streets and courtyards are cobblestone.

Choose low heels, thick soles and good arch supports. You need them for standing long hours on stone floors of museums (a sure way to get a backache if your shoes are wrong), as well as for scrambling over castle ruins. Running shoes are far and away the most popular among tourists these days.

You need closed toes and heels for cool, rainy weather; sandals are only good for hot summer weather. Europeans usually walk, and they expect you to do the same—in rain or snow or hot sun. Never take shoes that have not been broken in.

For winter, you need boots, preferably waterproof. It is easy to ruin dress boots, especially in areas where the snow or ice is salted. Salt marks will not come off. Boots and shoes should be treated periodically with water-repellent spray or polish, but heavy rain and snow may penetrate, nevertheless.

Shoes are heavy to carry, but you need at least two pairs of walking shoes. Slippers are a luxury to allow yourself for a rest at the end of a day of walking or as a respite on long journeys. Change to slippers on long train rides or transatlantic flights—you will arrive at your destination much less tired.

Attending dress functions in foul weather can present a problem. In Moscow, women bring dress shoes to the ballet in plastic bags, change and check their boots at the coat-check stand. In Stockholm, women bring their high heels in soft cloth pouches. The principle is the same.

Stockings are hot in summer but do very little to keep you warm in winter. Consider socks instead; fashion colors and designs often look fine with sportswear. Woolen pantyhose are better for dress-up. I find stockings with a garter belt more practical than nylon pantyhose. A run in one stocking doesn't mean I have to throw the whole pair away, and I always keep a spare stocking in my handbag.

Packing

Every guidebook repeats—travel light! A mound of luggage marks you as an amateur traveler and becomes a tremendous burden. Bring along less than you can carry, because you will add things along the way.

You always need fewer clothes than you think you will. No matter how little I pack, I always end up with a blouse or dress that I haven't worn. However, you do need insurance—a change of clothes for when you dribble lobster sauce on your blouse or a little boy jumps in a mud puddle and splatters you from head to foot, on a weekend, when the cleaners are closed.

Bring one outfit that lets you dress to the teeth. If you spend days in jeans, it gives you a lift to have a classy night on the town. But don't go loaded down with diamonds. Expensive jewelry is another burden, especially if hotel safes are not available.

Below is a suggested basic travel wardrobe. It assumes that you will layer and coordinate. Layering is a practical matter. A day that starts out chilly may turn hot in the noon sun, then cool again with an afternoon shower. Central European weather is fickle. You need a sweater, vest or jacket to put on and take off. Don't be shy about crawling out of a pullover at the dinner table or when you enter a theater.

Basic Travel Wardrobe

1 pair heavy-duty slacks or jeans
1 pair slacks or skirt that can be dressed up
3 blouses
1 sweater
1 dress or suit
1 jacket or raincoat
2 pairs walking shoes
1 pair high heels (optional)
1 nightgown or pajamas
1 robe (can double as beach robe)
1 pair slippers
1 swimsuit (optional—many hotels have indoor pools or you may want to visit a spa)
3 changes stockings, socks and underwear
1 large scarf
   umbrella

Vary the materials according to the season and destination. Bring cotton, linen or light woolens for summer, heavy woolens for winter. Natural fibers are more attractive and more comfortable, too. Don't worry about a few honest wrinkles.

In summer in the South, a sundress with a light jacket is enough; in winter, substitute a suit. A trip into the mountains or to the Far North in winter requires ski clothes, preferably padded. In winter, also, you need a warm coat. Bring along thermal underwear for long periods out of doors, but for indoors you may find silk longjohns ideal for adding warmth without bulk. You need a hat or cap in winter, one without a wide brim for windy weather.

That's enough. Don't be tempted to bring more. One week's supply of clothing will get you through three months. Keep the clothes clean—undies and socks can be rinsed out. Almost every hotel room has a sink.

Luggage

Now that you are ready to pack, consider the value of luggage wheels and shoulder straps. Built-in wheels are less clumsy than the strap-on type, but a sturdy luggage carrier can hold two bags. Don't waste your money on a flimsy set of wheels; they won't make it past the first railway station.

Dress bags are hard to handle unless they fold. Backpacks are popular, but I find shoulder bags more convenient and easier to get to. Have you ever been hit in the face by a backpack when the person to whom it was attached suddenly turned around?

The size of your luggage is important. Giant suitcases are tempting if you are thinking of getting everything into one bag. However, they have several drawbacks. Big baggage may not fit into luggage lockers, under train seats or on overhead luggage racks in trains. Besides, when they are full they are very heavy. Even bags with wheels have to be lifted sometimes—onto trains, onto (and worse, off of) luggage racks—and carried up steps.

One piece of hand luggage is essential. Pack the absolute necessities in it: makeup, a change of underwear and stockings, medication, guidebook, reading material—all the things you need in case the rest of your luggage goes astray. Keep it with you; never check it on planes or trains.

Consider the kind of transportation you will be using. Obviously you can carry more in a car than you can on a train or bus. But remember, most European cars are smaller than American cars and may have less luggage space than you think they will. Most airports and railway stations provide free luggage carts. At peak hours, however, they may be hard to come by.

Make use of left-luggage facilities at airports and railway stations. Stow your luggage while you are looking for a room or if you must check out of your hotel in the morning and your train doesn't leave until evening. Or just use them for storage by packing up the things you don't need at the moment and taking only the essentials to the hotel. If you have a few hours between trains, park your luggage and explore.

Some places have done away with luggage lockers because of bomb threats, but they are still available in many locations. When using lockers, pay attention to the time limit. Normally, the locker limit is twenty-four to seventy-two hours. Insert coins for the first twenty-four hours, close the locker and take the key. If you exceed twenty-four hours, you must add extra coins for the extra time used before the door will open. If you exceed the maximum limit, your luggage will be removed and placed in left-luggage.

At peak times, all the luggage lockers may be full. Although lockers cost less than left-luggage, you can waste valuable time waiting for an empty one. It may be worthwhile to check your luggage at the window. At the Milan Railway Station, among other places, you may be asked to open your luggage for a security check when you use left-luggage.

Major airports and railway stations have round-the-clock left-luggage service, but smaller ones close at night. Before storing your bags, make sure the window will be open when you need to retrieve them. Allow plenty of time for waiting in line when you return.

If you don't want to carry your luggage on the train, it is possible to check it just as on planes. However, unless you take it to the station early, it may not go on the same train you do. Sometimes, it can take a day or two to catch up with you.

Home Away from Home

Tourists are easily recognized by the blank stare of exhaustion that comes after a certain period of time on the road. Don't be too ambitious, trying to start at one end of the Continent and get to the other in a couple of weeks. This can be so exhausting that you don't know what you have seen.

A better way to travel is to choose a central location, perhaps a room in a private home, as a base and explore limited areas from there. This gives you the freedom to make day trips or short overnight trips without having to take all your luggage along. Many hotels will store luggage against your return, but it is more comfortable not to have to pack up.

On an extended trip, you need a nest, a feeling of having a home. A small establishment can give you the safety of a family more than a big hotel can. Make friends with the landlady; tell her where you are going and about how long you will be gone. If you are delayed, let her know. For a woman alone, the fact that you know someone and that someone knows where you are gives an extra measure of security.

On a long trip, you may want to shift this central spot two or three times in the course of your travels. Inexpensive (as little as $15 a night) bed-and-breakfast accommodations are available throughout Europe. Tourist offices have lists of them.

2

HOTELS, RESTAURANTS AND SECOND-CLASS SERVICE

Some restaurants seat single women at the tiny table by the kitchen. Some hotel clerks claim to have no more single rooms. The end of the day seems to be the worst time for a woman traveling alone.

The better restaurants and hotels are believed to be the most polite to single women, but that is not always the case. In Maastricht, the Netherlands, I had dinner at an elegant restaurant seated at a table for two beside the window. I lingered over several courses, enjoying the passing scene and the conversations going on around me. But when I ordered coffee and cognac, the maître d' asked if I would mind taking it at the bar. A couple had just come in and wanted my table. A bit incensed—the back dining room had not been opened and there were plenty of tables there—I nevertheless shifted to a barstool. My wonderful evening had been marred. With hindsight and experience, I know I should have said, "Yes, I do mind." After all, I was paying for the services of the restaurant.

I have also learned to be firm about my seating arrangements in the first place. Unless the restaurant is very crowded, I ask for a better table if I do not like the one to which I am shown. Be firm, but be polite. A smile goes a long way.

Of course, many restaurants allow you to choose your own seat, and you should not be shy about sharing a table. That is common practice in Europe, except in the most exclusive restaurants. Simply ask if the seat is free. Even if you don't speak the language, look inquiringly and smile. Sometimes the seat is being saved, but usually the answer is "Please, have a seat."

Occasionally, a single woman will not be seated at all. This has happened to me only once, at a restaurant in Prague, and I remain mystified as to why I was refused entry. Earlier the same day, I had spent a pleasant hour in the city's best beerhall before I realized I was the only woman present.

Within the past few years, it has become difficult for tourists of either sex to reserve tables in France. The problem has been Americans who make reservations at several restaurants and do not bother to cancel the extra reservations once they've decided where they want to eat. Be sure to cancel your reservation as early as possible if you can't make it.

As for hotels, singles are sometimes relegated to the rooms under the eaves. It has always seemed unfair that two people traveling together can spend the night much more cheaply than a single traveler. In France and Italy, the difference in price between a single and a double room is sometimes no more than the cost of a second breakfast. The price difference is wider in other countries, but it is a rare hotel that rents a single room at half the price of a double. However, in the past few years some progress has been made on the singles front.

A *Friends' Circle of Single Travelers*, the brainchild of Barbara Harms-Wichmann of Hamburg, Germany, has been operating since 1987 to improve the prospects of single travelers. The nonprofit organization has compiled a listing of hotels in Germany "with sympathy for the single traveler." Most of these hotels have agreed to do away with the single-room supplement.

In addition, the organization has gone international with its *We Travel Together* (WTT) program. This program is a contact point for travelers who want to get to know the local people. For example, WTT puts Americans in touch with English-speaking Germans who are happy to share a trip.

Ms. Harms-Wichmann notes that single women are traveling more and more and that the most active are women between thirty and fifty years old, followed closely by the fifty-to-seventy age group.

Gudrun Klein, a German woman, has begun a service called *konnex* which is building up a network of apartments, guest houses and small hotels where women can feel at home. At publication time, she offered accommodation in France (especially Provence), Austria, Luxembourg, Great Britain and Ireland, as well as in the United States. A few travel agencies, too, have sprung up in Germany for single and women travelers.

The *Frauen-Reisebörse* (Women's Travel Exchange), the first women-only travel agency in Germany, was opened in 1987 by Hannelore Vierrath-Lewitzki in Cologne. It helps women find traveling companions who share their interests—and the expenses. Those who travel often can buy a year's membership in the exchange; those who are taking only one trip pay a smaller fee. So far, not only Germans but also women from a number of surrounding countries have used the agency's services, and shortly after the Berlin Wall fell, East German women began to participate.

Frauen auf Reisen in Hamburg and *Frauen Unterwegs* in Berlin plan study and adventure tours for women only. *Hoffmann Reisen*, a Munich travel agency, has a selection of tours for women only. *Single Travel* in Rodgau, near Frankfurt a.M., organizes tours for singles of both sexes, providing private rooms for everyone in the group—but the trips are usually limited to the off or shoulder seasons because of the difficulty in getting enough single rooms at peak times. (See "Practical Matters: Women's Hotels, Cafes, Centers, Groups and Travel Agencies.") Hotels and resorts sometimes offer specials for singles during the low season. The region of Upper Austria has introduced year-round "solo" sports packages.

Finding a Room

I know people who would not dream of visiting Europe without reserving rooms far in advance for each night of their stay. I find such a method of travel too restrictive.

Ideally, book the first few nights in advance. This will get you over jet-lag, organized and in condition to cope with finding lodging on the spot. If you are arriving in the morning, it is a good idea to arrange for early check-in; normally hotel rooms are not ready before about 2:00 P.M. If you plan to arrive later than 6:00 P.M., on the other hand, inform the hotel to make sure your room will be held. If you are delayed en route, telephone the hotel with your new arrival time.

You might be more comfortable making a reservation for your last night, as well, especially if you want to be near your point of departure. This is a good way to avoid end-of-journey stress and to give yourself the time you need to relax and get yourself organized for the trip home.

Reservations are necessary, too, in crowded cities during trade fairs or large festivals and in resorts in high season. As a rule, the tourist season runs Easter to October, with July and August the peak months. Of course, sunny islands and ski resorts have high season in winter. In beach areas, the majority of the hotels close down completely in winter, and in the mountains, many hotels close between the winter ski season and the summer hiking season. In resorts with high rates of one- or two-week package bookings, it is difficult to find a room for just one or two nights.

Rather than make reservations, however, I prefer to go to a town, have a look around and then decide on a hotel. When I do this, I find that the ideal time to arrive is 3:00 or 4:00 P.M., but certainly no later than 6:00 P.M. The early arrival gets the room; if none is available, there's time to move on to the next town. Bed-and-breakfast houses put signs out front announcing "room free." Hotels may post "booked up" signs on their doors to avoid wasting time—yours and theirs.

Local tourist information offices can help. Many of them have room-booking services: tell them what you want (price range, whether you want private bath and toilet) and they will find a room for you (either in a hotel or private home) and give you directions for getting there. Sometimes the service is free, sometimes there is a nominal fee, usually equal to a couple of dollars. Most tourist offices will give you a list of accommodations if you prefer to do the telephoning yourself. If the tourist office is closed, you may find listings of hotels posted nearby.

In places (the Stockholm Airport, for example) a free telephone connection is provided to certain hotels—usually the higher priced ones. In Zurich, Switzerland, a map in the main railway station shows some hotel locations; push the button next to a hotel description and the exact location lights up on the map. A toll-free telephone to the hotels is also provided.

In large cities and prime tourist spots, information offices are open long hours and on weekends. In small towns, they usually close for lunch, and they operate on abbreviated schedules—if at all—in the low season. Most information offices are located in or near railway stations, airports and city centers. Some are found along major highways. Switzerland has a network of tiny roadside stands where travelers can book rooms.

Hotel chains and cooperative groups will make reservations without charge for other hotels in their groups. Catalogs list the hotels by country and city; you'll find a copy in your room. Big American hotel chains attract tour groups and business travelers. You are not likely to get to know the locals if you stay there. They, and other national chains, are fairly standard the world over.

I prefer the smaller hotels and bed-and-breakfast accommodations for atmosphere. Smaller hotels lend a more secure feeling for a woman alone (unless you go to the luxury end of the scale) because service is of necessity more personal and the staff is more likely to notice your comings and goings.

If you want the best of both worlds—the reputation of a chain standing behind a charming small hotel or guest house—several such associations exist in Europe. Among them are Romantik Hotels, Gast im Schloss (Guest in a Castle), Logis et Auberges (Lodgings and Inns) in France, Relais & Chateau (Post Houses and Castles), CountrySide Sweden, Ring Hotels Deutschland, Best Western and Tourisme Vert (rural France).

In most cases, the hotels belonging to these groups are run by the owners, are small and pride themselves on friendliness. Their restaurants serve local specialties. Of the ones I have used (and I have sampled each group), all have been as polite to a single woman as to couples. The rooms range from comfortable to superb.

Youth hostels are another alternative for the single traveler. Except in Bavaria (in southern Germany), there is no maximum age limit on who can stay in the hostels, although those under thirty have priority. The minimum age is fourteen for persons traveling without an adult. A Youth Hostel Card is required. (See "Practical Matters: Youth Hostels.") Be aware that hostels may close early in the evening, leaving you locked out with your luggage inside. Check the closing time before going out. Other alternatives are mountain chalets or bare-basic mountain huts, colleges and universities that rent dormitory rooms in summer, cabins (especially in Scandinavia), farm houses, self-catering apartments and converted mills.

Then there are the national hotels: the *pousadas* in Portugal, the *paradors* in Spain and the *kro* in Denmark. They may be run by the government or may be members of a loosely knit association, but they specialize in local atmosphere and food. The number of days you can spend in a *pousada* or *parador* may be limited. In Portugal, private inns called *estalagems* provide similar accommodation without a time limit.

Europe has few women-only hotels, and most of them are designed for groups wishing to hold cultural programs or seminars. (See "Practical Matters: Women's Hotels, Cafes, Centers, Groups and Travel Agencies.") Children are welcome—boys up to a limited age, sometimes six but not older than twelve. In the past couple of years, however, women-only hotels have opened in London, Berlin and Schleswig, Germany. They are designed for women: cheerful colors, large baths, well-lighted full-length mirrors, hair dryers and tampons provided. But more important, they are safety conscious, being located close to public transportation and providing entry intercoms and safety locks. A few hotels have introduced women-only floors, along with no-smoking rooms.

It is a long way from being universal, but hotels are beginning to train their personnel how to treat women guests. Desk clerks give you the key face down so that no one can see your room number, and they do not announce the number for all the lobby to hear. They give women rooms near the elevator, saving the long walk down dimly lit hallways. However, it is still rare to find hotels that provide peepholes on the room doors or chains—and even such comforts as skirt hangers and full-length mirrors.

Hotels specializing in business guests are promoting women's rooms as well as executive rooms, with amenities women need rather than oversized robes hanging behind the bathroom doors and cabinets stocked with aftershave. Of course, these things are found primarily in luxury hotels, which brings up the question of choosing the category of hotel you want.

What do those stars in the guidebook or on the hotel door mean? To a great extent, it depends on who gives them. Tourist offices or hotel associations control the standards, and while the official ratings throughout Europe are similar, standards do vary from country to country. A three-star hotel in Spain is seldom comparable to a three-star hotel in Switzerland. Find out what amenities the hotel provides. When consulting guidebooks and pamphlets, notice whether the ratings are independent or whether the guide is recommending its advertisers.

Ask to see the room before you take it, and if it isn't suitable, ask for another one. It is easy to misjudge a hotel by its façade. In France, a charming lobby doesn't necessarily mean charming rooms. It is not unusual for a well-run two-star hotel to be more comfortable than an indifferently run three-star. Ask the price of each room you see; it may vary by location in the building. You pay less if you don't mind a room over the disco, garbage cans or delivery door.

The trend in European hotels is toward toilets and baths in every room, but many still have rooms without private facilities. Sometimes the use of the bath down the hall is free, sometimes there is a small charge. In any case, tip the chambermaid who brings the towels and unlocks the door. Usually there will be a toilet and bath on each floor.

If you insist on a private bath and toilet, be sure to ask for both. A room with a bath sometimes has no toilet. French baths almost always include a bidet; I thought once I'd found a French hotel without a bidet, but discovered a "pull-out" model under the sink. British and Russian baths often include wonderful heated towel bars.

Breakfast may be included in the price of the room, especially in small hotels and guest houses, but always inquire. It is not included in Iceland, seldom in Italy, and less and less frequently in France. Sometimes, continental breakfast is included but eggs, meat and juice cost extra. Many small hotels have no restaurant but nevertheless provide breakfast.

When you register, you must give your passport number; sometimes you will be asked to leave your passport at the desk. You will get it back later in the day or the next morning, except in some East European countries, where it is kept at the desk until you check out. In the Soviet Union, you may get a hotel pass, which you leave with the hall matron when you pick up your key; give her your key when you leave the hotel and get your pass back. It's something like living in a women's dorm at college in the 1950s.

Large luxury hotels are going with the trend toward computerized card "keys," but many others retain the huge, heavy keyrings. In most cases, leave your key at the desk when you go out, but if you plan to be out late, ask for a key to the front door. Small hotels and guest houses lock up for the night. If you don't have a key, you must ring for the night porter and wait on the dark steps until he wakes and asks enough questions to ascertain that you really belong there and should be allowed in.

Many hotels do not leave the entry and hall lights on all night. The light switch is on a timer, allowing you several minutes to get to your room or to the toilet before the light goes off. Most of the switches glow, but make a mental note of where they are in case you get caught in the dark. A small flashlight is helpful in such cases.

Prepaid vouchers for hotels and restaurants help you stay within your budget and save you the worry of carrying so much cash. Travel agents can make reservations, collect your money and give you vouchers for your room. The main trouble with this is that you are tied to a schedule, having already paid for everything. Also, travel agents tend to deal with luxury- to high-middle-priced hotels. The quaint, cozy, inexpensive hotels may not subscribe to a voucher system.

However, in some countries, tourist offices cooperate with hotels and restaurants to provide voucher systems that require little preplanning and include smaller establishments. Generally, you reserve the first night when you buy the vouchers, then make reservations from one hotel to the next. For example, Denmark has a KroCheck, good at any of sixty-six country inns. (See "Practical Matters: Hotel and Restaurant Voucher Plans.")

Tipping

Perhaps one reason women receive second-class service is that they have the undeserved reputation of being poor tippers. (Through long-standing observations, I have noticed that women in general are more generous than men.) Tipping is important in almost every country. The exceptions are Iceland, where tips are considered insulting, and the Scandinavian countries and Switzerland, where waiters and waitresses, at least, seldom expect tips.

European restaurants usually include taxes and service charges in the price; the menu card notes whether service is included in the price of each dish or added onto the final bill. If it doesn't say, ask. Either way, simply round off the amount to the next whole number, and add a bit more if the service was especially good. For example, a bill in Germany amounting to 13.50 marks could be rounded off to 14 marks. Tell this to the waiter or waitress when you pay, rather than leave the money on the table.

It is easy to remember to tip at restaurants, in taxis, at the hairdressers, but don't forget the chambermaid. (See "Practical Matters: Tipping.") Use your discretion in judging what the service deserves. Tip in the currency of the country you are in. If you must tip in dollars, use bills only. American coins cannot be exchanged for other currencies and are therefore useless. In the past, hard currency (that is, Western currency) was appreciated in East Bloc countries—and such items as nylons, scarves and small bottles of perfume also made nice tips. This will probably hold true for the next few years, until their economies adjust, but as this side of Europe integrates more and more into a total Europe, such practices will become outmoded.

3

I'S OKAY TO TALK TO STRANGERS

A Little Language Goes a Long Way

Travel is more than sightseeing; it is an opportunity to meet people with varying viewpoints and to exchange ideas. Admittedly, this opportunity can be intimidating for women traveling alone, but it is not impossible and is seldom dangerous.

I once fell into conversation with an elderly gentleman on a train to Vienna. He was going directly there while I planned to stop first for a couple of days in Linz. In Linz we said good-bye and I thought no more of it, but when I arrived in Vienna, Herr X was waiting for me on the railway platform.

He introduced me to his family and for the next three days they showed me their city and even invited me to their home. They gave me insights into European life and thinking that no guidebook or museum could, and we remained friends.

That episode was pleasant, though not all are. Women traveling alone are vulnerable, but not as much as you may fear. Use common sense: you can talk with people without giving your name and phone number. You may want to give only your first name, or if you are really paranoid, use a pseudonym. If you seriously want to fend off suitors, wear a wedding ring—note that Europeans usually wear the wedding band on the right hand.

Meeting the People

Don't hesitate to initiate conversations, even if you fall back on the standard questions: Where are you from? Where are you going? Where is the museum? Many Europeans welcome a chance to practice their English. Even when they speak no English at all, they are willing to help. If you ask directions, not only will they direct you—often they will walk with you to make sure you don't get lost.

Asking directions is one good way to begin a conversation. Photographing is another, since it is courteous to ask permission before you photograph someone. Muslims will probably refuse, because to reproduce the human figure is taboo, but often the person will be flattered and eager to talk. In Turkey and Yugoslavia, especially, most people will ask for a copy of the photo, and you may end up with a sheaf of illegible addresses (Europeans form their letters a bit differently from ours). It's a good idea to rewrite the address in your own handwriting while the person looks on and corrects.

Trains, in my opinion, are the best places to meet people. Sitting in silence in a compartment with three or four others on a long journey is almost impossible. More than once in my experiences, a party atmosphere has prevailed, with people sharing the lunches they brought along.

Cafes and restaurants are also excellent spots to strike up conversations. The practice of sharing tables is a good ice-breaker. I have spent entire afternoons talking to a variety of people for the price of one cup of coffee.

Above all, don't lock yourself in your room at night. So much of the good life of Europe is nightlife—concerts, theater, folklore performances. Many cities publish English-language weekly or monthly entertainment listings, and the hotel concierge can direct you to the type of entertainment you want.

European cities have a huge choice of events. On any given night, you can find operas, theater of all sorts, concerts from classical to heavy metal, variety shows, or poetry readings. Even villages have a fair selection of cultural events.

Sample the local bars, cafes and restaurants. Don't be afraid to trust your instinct. Just walk into a place that catches your eye. You can walk back out again if it isn't right; red-lights and rowdy bars are easy to recognize. Live entertainment is a regular feature at many bars and restaurants, either with or without dancing. Ask at the hotel for directions to the nightlife quarters, where you'll have a choice of restaurants and clubs.

If you are shy about a night on the town alone, take a nightclub tour. They are available in most big cities and seldom need to be booked more than a day in advance. Some cities have cafes and cultural centers for women only. (See "Practical Matters: Women's Hotels, Cafes, Centers, Groups and Travel Agencies.") Listings will be in the local alternative press.

Do You Speak English?

In countries where waiters have command of five languages, it can be embarrassing to speak only one. Nevertheless, it is not necessary to be fluent in another language to make yourself understood. To try to speak another person's language is a gesture of good will. That person generally responds by helping you. Learn the basics: please, thank you, yes, no. Learn the numbers for prices, telling time, railway track numbers, addresses. Learn to say "I don't understand" and "Do you speak English?" You can get into heaps of trouble if you just nod your head to everything. Sign language is always useful. Point at what you want to buy, wave your map and say "museum," rub the thumb and forefinger together to ask for the price or the bill.

Universal symbols are invaluable for helping you find the way around airports, train stations and cities. (See "Practical Matters: International Information Signs.") The stylized *i* denotes "information" all over Europe, even when it carries a local touch—such as the Brussels sign celebrating the city mascot, the Manneken Pis.

The usual i for information

The Brussels i for information

Toilet and WC are almost universally understood. Don't use euphemisms. No one will understand you if you ask for the restroom, powder room, john, loo (except in Britain) or little girl's sandbox. The bathroom is *not* the toilet; it is the place where you take a bath. 00 is often the sign for toilet and pictures of a man or woman on the door may help. When I first moved to Germany, I had no trouble sorting out *Damen* and *Herren* on the toilet doors, but I was at a loss the first time I saw *Er* and *Sie* used as Americans use *His* and *Hers.*

I feel illiterate when I don't understand the local language, but knowing a little can be dangerous; you can stumble into double entendres and sexual implications without realizing you have made a mistake until weeks later. Pronunciation makes a difference, too. The word *bus* as pronounced in English means fornication in Hungarian: to be safe in Hungary, say *autobus* (pronounced *awtoboos*).

At a German post office, I noticed a sign beside a stack of address forms that said, *"Hamstern verboten!"* Why, I wondered, was it expressly forbidden to send hamsters through the mail, when there was no mention of gerbils or white mice. I asked a friend. The expression means to take more of something than you need, exactly the way we say "to squirrel away"!

And once at a restaurant, a friend who smokes asked the waitress for matches. Imagine her surprise when the waitress returned with a plate of herring. *Matjes,* pronounced *matches,* is a popular first course in Germany.

However, I admit to enjoying just a little knowledge of French. I speak enough to order meals, get hotel rooms, ask directions. But I'm afraid if I learn it better, it will lose some of its magic. I prefer a *rendezvous* to a meeting, and somehow it is more romantic to be called *"mon chèri"* than "my dear."

Even in Britain, you may come smack against words and usages that you don't understand. A British-American dictionary is good for laughs, but it is also a practical guide. It's handy to know basic British expressions (lift for elevator, flat for apartment) even outside the British Isles, since a great many Continentals have learned Oxford English.

In Romance and Germanic languages, it is not too difficult to figure out certain basic words. Practice reading billboards and advertisements—they are usually easiest and the illustrations help. Words in many languages are similar to English: *police, polizei, polis, polizia, policija, politie*—but in Hungarian, *rendörseg:* the language has different roots.

When you travel in countries with a different alphabet, you may run into problems. If you plan to visit Bulgaria, southeastern Yugoslavia or the Soviet Union, familiarize yourself with the Cyrillic alphabet. If you are going to Greece, learn the Greek alphabet. It takes a little of the mystery out of the writing.

The Slavic tongues may present difficulties, and without a doubt Hungarian, Finnish and Turkish will throw foreigners into utter confusion. If you travel in a country with a difficult or little-known language, find out what other languages are also spoken. In Turkey and Yugoslavia, it is easy to get around in German; in Portugal, you'll do fine with English.

A small dictionary is worth its weight. In fact, I prefer a dictionary to a phrasebook. In a pinch, nouns and verbs will see you through without the connective tissue of adjectives and adverbs. I get terribly frustrated when I practice a phrasebook question until I have it perfect, then get a reply in English, but it is equally frustrating to be answered in a spate of explanations that is impossible to understand.

Whether you choose phrasebook or dictionary, keep it beside you until you feel confident without it. Computer translators are nice toys, but not yet practical. It takes more time to run through the dictionary electronically than to flip pages. Many words in the computer are variations on roots, taking up space that could be better used for words not in the program.

Know which language is spoken where. A colleague asked me if she could get around easily in Portugal without Spanish. In fact, she would do *better* without it, because the Portuguese resent the fact that their country is so often mistaken for part of Spain. Minority groups in every country hold onto their own languages: you find Hungarian-speaking villages in Romania, Albanian-speaking pockets in southern Italy.

Knowing schoolbook language is good grounding for travel, but it doesn't get you through the colloquialisms and dialects. The dialects of Europe are rich and varied and sometimes all but impossible to understand. In the Alps, the dialect will vary from village to village and valley to valley. The Parisian ear can detect a provincial accent spoken in a whisper across a banquet hall. The *plattdeutsch* of northern Germany shows more than a little English influence. Swiss German bears hardly any resemblance to *hochdeutsch* (high German); although it is a dialect, it sounds like a different language altogether.

Even if you master the dialects, you'll sometimes find that vocabulary and grammar alone are not enough. You need to step inside the mentality that a language reflects. That's why some expressions simply do not translate. An excellent book teaching the Russian language in the context of Russian culture has been written by Genevra Gerhart *(The Russian's World: Life and Language).* We need these for every language!

Most Europeans speak more than one language. The Dutch learn five languages in school. The Swiss shopkeeper may say, *"Merci viel mals,"* and the customer may reply, *"Merci ... ciao,"* so mixed are their four national languages. Yugoslavia has three national tongues—Serbo-Croatian, Slovenian and Macedonian (using the Cyrillic alphabet). By law, English has been taught since World War II in West German schools, just as Russian was required in East Bloc countries.

English is the language of business circles and international airports. It is often the common language of internationally mixed groups. It is spoken in the larger hotels, restaurants and shops in every country. Of course, it is not always spoken perfectly. Sometimes, translations into English are amusing. Mushrooms appear on many a menu as *fungus;* don't let it turn you off—they are wonderful. One French menu listed frog paws for frogs' legs. A Swedish brochure noted, "The largest bridge was sailed on and demolished by a ship. This turned out to be a catastrophe." People may speak a stilted schoolbook English, using outmoded words and phrases. "See you later, alligator" and "last not least" are great favorites in Germany.

Pronunciation can be a problem, too. Even though the Latin alphabet is basically the same everywhere, the pronunciation of the letters varies and diacritical marks influence the way letters sound. Generally, the vowels *a, e, i, o, u* are pronounced *ah, a, e, o, oo.* The Germans make a conscientious concession to our *w,* which they pronounce *v,* so when they move into English they overcompensate and *valley* often comes out *walley.* Once I telephoned a restaurant for reservations. When I arrived, my table was clearly marked with a card that said *"Vait."* It can be great fun, but before you criticize, think— can you do as well in their language?

Keeping Informed

There is no need to feel cut off from the English-speaking world in Europe. English-language newspapers are available almost every-where, albeit in out-of-the-way spots they may arrive a day or a week late. Long before Eastern Europe's borders opened, American and British publications were sold on Budapest newsstands. Yugoslavia always carried such newspapers and magazines, though they were limited in the off-season—a cost-cutting measure rather than a matter of censorship. Small villages in southern France, off the beaten track in Bulgaria and tiny islands in Greece probably won't have

English-language periodicals at all. Take along some reading material and buy the newspapers when you return to the main thoroughfares.

The American newspapers most commonly found on the Continent are the *International Herald Tribune* and the *Wall Street Journal*, which have European editions, and *USA Today*. The weekly news magazines are available, as are many specialty magazines—business, electronics, automotive, etc. British publications are available in even greater numbers. You can find them at international newsstands in cities, at airports and railway stations. Large hotels also have a selection.

English-language newspapers or magazines also may be published locally. The *Bulletin* in Brussels is one. Another is the *Daily News* of Budapest, published in combination with the *Neueste Nachrichten* in German; each language gets four pages. Paris has several English-language journals: *Passion, City, Speakeasy*.

If you have a radio, you may be able to tune in to AFN, the American Forces Radio and Television Network, which has affiliate stations in several West European countries. AFN television broadcasts require a special converter for the TV set, which a number of hotels in Germany have installed on their televisions. The Canadian and British Forces also broadcast in Germany.

With a shortwave radio, you can pick up all sorts of English programs, from the BBC to Radio Moscow. At least one station in most countries gives the news in English once or twice a day, although in some countries this is limited to high season. Many cities have English-speaking theaters, and in a number of countries movies and television interviews are broadcast in their original language. (See "Practical Matters: Keeping in Touch in English.")

Weights and Measures

A language easily learned but often overlooked is the language of measures. Continental Europe speaks of kilos instead of pounds, centimeters instead of inches, liters instead of quarts, Celsius instead of Fahrenheit, kilometers instead of miles. Great Britain, on the other hand, uses the imperial gallon, which contains a quart more than the American gallon. The British also compute weight in stone—one stone equals fourteen pounds. They measure road distance in miles.

Sometimes you'll run across unusual local usages of weights. In Vienna, food is priced in *dekagrams,* ten-gram units. If you want to buy a kilo, ask for 100 *deka.*

For casual travel, approximate conversions are all you will need and they are quick to make. A kilo equals about two pounds, an inch is made up of about 2.5 centimeters, a liter is about a quart—so there are about four liters to a gallon. To convert kilometers to miles, multiply by six-tenths (100 kilometers is about 60 miles).

The most difficult conversion is Celsius (or centigrade) to Fahrenheit. Zero degrees Celsius is freezing; 10 degrees C is 50 degrees F; 20 degrees C is 68 degrees F; 30 degrees C is hot. To convert Celsius to Fahrenheit, double the Celsius reading, subtract 10 percent and add 32 to the answer. For example, 15 degrees C doubled is 30; subtract 10 percent, or 3 degrees, to get 27; add 32. The temperature is 59 degrees F.

*   *   *

A last word about language: speak softly. American voices carry. One night in a small restaurant the waiter delivered this note to the table where three American women were enjoying an evening of food, wine and conversation. "I find your tongue very interesting, your melodic American sounds attractive but somewhat eerie, your presence extremely conclusive, your absolutely over-the-Atlantic attitude non-Canadian, your German *je-ne-sais-quoi* not quite Quebec. So—would you like a drink?"

4

KNOW WHERE YOU ARE —

And Where You Come From

A good traveler does her homework before she leaves home. She learns about where she will visit—history, culture, politics, as well as sights to see. Especially now, since the Iron Curtain crumbled and Eastern Europe is moving into the European mainstream, you need to know something about what is happening here.

You also need to know what is happening on your own doorstep. Europeans are curious and they ask serious questions: about the environment, crime or unemployment. Do some thinking. Be prepared to discuss current events and forget the old saw "avoid discussing politics."

As you travel across Europe, events from history books begin to fall into place. You see how the Turkish invasions of several hundred years ago affected the entire Continent, even bringing coffee to Vienna. You see the scars of World War II—for example, the bombed-out Kaiser Wilhelm Church, which stands unrestored on West Berlin's main thoroughfare as a testament to the destruction of war. You hear people speak with familiarity of the long-reigning Hapsburgs, and indeed, the family is still around.

Before you leave home, read as much as you can about where you are going. At the very least, choose a guidebook that contains a capsule survey of history and social customs. Better, read a selection of guidebooks, travelogs, newspaper and magazine articles. National tourist offices have a wealth of brochures about their countries, most of which are free for the asking. Such brochures can supply everything from maps to short histories to explanations of the public transportation system, as well as information about sights to see.

Once you arrive, listen to the radio and watch television. Look at the local newspapers, which many cafes provide for their customers. You will find them on wooden sticks hanging from hooks or tucked into special niches. Even if you do not speak the language, you can pick up some information this way by looking at the pictures. You'll probably recognize many words that are similar to English, and you will know names of people and places.

Places and Names

Know which country is which. Americans sometimes confuse Sweden and Switzerland, or call a Scotsman or Welshman an Englishman. (Remember, the Scots are Scottish, not Scotch as in whiskey.) A friend in the tourist business told me of a tour he conducted for a group of Americans. They visited the Netherlands, Belgium and Scandinavia. When the tour was over, he asked, "What was your favorite city in the Netherlands?" A woman in the front row eagerly answered, "Copenhagen!"

Be aware of the differences in spelling of European place names. This can be especially confusing in trying to read road maps and in knowing where your rail ticket tells you to change trains. How many Americans have missed seeing Florence because they didn't get off the train at *Fierenze!*

There is no Cologne in Germany—it's *Köln.* Some Anglicized variations are not so marked: for example, *Nürnberg* in German is Nuremberg to us. In Belgium, most cities have two names, the French and the Flemish. It's *Bruges* or *Brugge,* depending on whether you are in Wallonia or Flanders; *Bruxelles* or *Brussel, Antwerpen* or *Anvers, Mons* or *Bergen, Liege* or *Luik, Gent* or *Gand.*

The Alsace region of France, which has changed hands more than once, is full of German *heims, hauses* and *hoffens.* Some atlases still use the Germanic names of towns and rivers in Czechoslovakia, the result of forced Germanization under the Hapsburgs in the seventeenth century. I once wrote about the *Vltava* River, which flows through the center of Prague (*Praha* in Czech), only to be "corrected" by a reader who told me the river is the *Moldau.* If that isn't confusing enough, the transliteration from other alphabets into the Latin creates a plethora of variables. For example, *Moscow* in English is *Moskau* in German.

In Europe, as in the United States, several towns within a country have the same name. Sometimes they are distinguished by adding the region or the name of a river to show their location. For example, Frankfurt am Main (shortened to Frankfurt a.M.) is Frankfurt on the Main River to distinguish it from Frankfurt on the Oder River. Expect a number of cities in Eastern Europe to change their names in the near future: the original name *Chemnitz* has been restored to what was for over forty years Karl-Marx-Stadt. Street names are also being changed.

Paris is *Paris* to English speakers and to the French, though it is pronounced differently by each, but it is *Parigi* to the Italians. The Baltic is the *Ostsee* to Germans; the Mediterranean is the *Mittelmeer.* Likewise, countries don't call themselves by their Anglicized names. They are *Deutschland, Sverige, Österreich, España, Suomi* (Germany, Sweden, Austria, Spain, Finland, respectively). Before you leave home, get two good maps—one in English and one in the language of the country you will visit—and study them carefully. Pay special attention to the place-name variations.

Finding Yourself

Know where you are staying. Keep a map of the area in your pocket or purse, along with cab fare and change for the telephone and toilet. Keep your hotel name, address and telephone number written down in case you forget it, or to show to the taxi driver if he seems not to understand your pronunciation. Most hotels give you a room card with this important information on it when you check in. Otherwise, pick up the hotel's brochure or business card. Don't write down your room number, however, and be cautious about telling anyone where you are staying. You could end up with telephone calls all night.

Telephoning

Learn how to use the telephone. Phone systems in every country have their little quirks. When dialing out-of-country in France and Belgium, you must pause between the country code and the individual number. In Sweden, the 0 is at the top of the dial. At public phones in Britain, the coin won't drop and complete the connection until the party on the other end answers and a beep sounds. In some countries, you must press a button to complete the connection.

Emergency phone numbers may be posted in phone booths, but public phones don't always work. (Surprisingly often in clockwork Germany, phones seem to have indigestion and spit out your change.) In some places, public phone booths contain emergency switches unconnected to the phone, and in others the operator can be reached without putting coins into the phone.

It is almost always cheaper to telephone from a public phone or from the post office or telephone exchange than from a hotel. Exorbitant surcharges added to phone calls by some hotels have raised a public outcry. As a result, AT&T introduced Teleplan, which has since been upgraded to Teleplan-Plus, and—even better—USA Direct calling cards. (See "Practical Matters: Telephone Codes.")

If you think you prefer the convenience of telephoning from your hotel despite the price, look first at the rate card or ask what the hotel surcharge is. Note that prices may be quoted in units (increments of a few seconds) rather than in minutes. As of this writing, it costs nearly $2 per minute to phone from Germany to the United States—not including hotel surcharge—and there is no reduction for night-time calls.

Some public phones take coins; a few take tokens purchased at shops or kiosks. In Italy, where coins are always in short supply, telephone tokens (*gettoni*) are often given as change at shops. Coin phones are also available now in Italy, so the tokens may soon disappear.

Telephone cards are becoming popular in a number of countries. In Paris, it is hardly possible to find a coin phone anymore, and the trend is moving swiftly into the French provinces. This can create a real problem if you arrive in a village when the post office (which sells the cards) is closed.

Germany, too, has introduced card phones, though they usually stand side-by-side with coin phones. In both France and Germany, the cards are available in two different prices. In France, the digital instructions flash on in French only but in Germany you can press a button to choose English, French or German.

Post office or telephone exchange phones are best for long-distance calls because you don't have to feed in change but pay when you have finished. This is excellent when you need a receipt, too. Go to the telephone section, tell the clerk where you want to call, and you will be assigned a booth. Even small-town post offices have one or two booths, and in cities they have a dozen or more. When you complete the call, go back to the clerk to pay.

At times, a deposit may be required before you place the call. In the West, you can usually dial for yourself, but it is not uncommon in some countries for the telephone clerk to place the call, a process that can run into hours. When the call comes through, the clerk tells you in which booth you can take it.

Some restaurants and small hotels will allow you to use their private phones. These may be kept locked and outfitted with a unit counter to calculate the cost of your call. If you use a friend's telephone, remember that there are charges for local as well as long-distance calls on private phones.

Making collect calls can be difficult. In some places, U.S. telephone credit cards can be used, but don't count on it. If necessary, make a quick call home, give the number where you can be reached, and ask someone to call you back. Not all public phones can receive calls, however. Those that can are usually marked with a picture of a ringing bell. Also, some public phones are for in-country calls only, while others function for both local and international calls. A sign on the phone booth door indicates which is which.

The direct-dial system in Europe is efficient. (See "Practical Matters: Telephone Codes.") However, at present the phone lines in Eastern Europe are overloaded and you may have to dial again and again to get your call through. To reach Hungary, save yourself time and frustration by sending a telex or telegram. Telex and telefax facilities are available at many post offices and hotels throughout Europe.

Most large cities have all-night post offices that are also open on weekends and holidays. Many post offices have telefax and telex service, as well as telephone cabins. However, in a few places the telephone services are located in separate telephone exchange offices.

The Post

Postage stamps are available in some countries only at the post office; in others, they may be sold at kiosks or tobacconists. Usually, but not always, hotels will have stamps, though sometimes they don't know what denomination is required for your letter. Tiny Andorra has two post offices, the French and the Spanish, and prints stamps for both the French and Spanish mail. Letter boxes on the streets come in pairs; be sure you use the right one for the stamps you have.

Send letters and postcards airmail from everywhere unless you want to arrive home before they do. Anything not marked airmail goes by ship. At the post office, various services—banking, general delivery, money exchange, as well as stamp sales—are provided, and not all services are provided at all windows. Try to figure out where stamps are being sold to avoid standing in a long line only to discover when you reach the window that you are in the bill-payment line.

If you plan to use general delivery during your travels, letters to you should be marked *poste restante*. Before you leave home, find out from your travel agent or the national tourist office how to use such services. For example, Intourist runs the most reliable general delivery service in the Soviet Union.

Money Matters

As the countries of the European Economic Community move toward their closer union in 1992–1993, the question of a uniform currency remains unresolved. Whether or not a "Euro currency" becomes viable, a number of different currencies will remain in use on the Continent.

Understand the local money and be able to make quick calculations. A pocket calculator is a boon, but it is conspicuous, and it seems to have a penchant for the bottom of your purse. So learn to make conversions in your head. For example, if the conversion rate is 2.95 to the dollar, divide by three and note that the amount is a little more: something that costs 12 of the local currency would cost slightly more than $4.

Know the value of the local currency so that you don't give embarrassingly small or outrageously large tips. It's an easy slip to make as you move from country to country. In England, a 1-pound tip would be more than generous for a bellboy carrying one suitcase, because a pound is worth more than a dollar. In Spain, a 1-peseta tip would be insulting; it is worth less than an American penny.

Don't refer to the local currency as "play money" or "Monopoly money" or to your own money as "real money." Europeans find American money dull—all one color—and difficult to distinguish among the denominations because all bills are the same size. European money is colorful, and the size varies by denomination. Some countries even have touch-coded bills to help the blind.

Since bills in European countries are large, it is a good idea to invest in a wallet that they fit, one that has several compartments to keep various currencies separated. Once I carried money from France and Germany tucked together: I couldn't understand why a German clerk refused to accept my money until I realized I was trying to pay with francs. I solved this problem by buying a waiter's wallet—a five-sectioned expandable affair available in European shops that sell work clothes and uniforms.

It remains to be seen when black-market money-changers will disappear from the East European countries. Beware if you deal with them; such dealings are not only illegal, they subject you to the tricks of the trade. Some changers will give you bills long since out of circulation; others will give you one genuine bill wrapped around a wad of newspaper. Shortly after the Yugoslav dinar reform went into effect, dealers in Budapest began passing dinar bills to tourists who didn't know that forints—not dinars—are the currency of Hungary and that the dinar was worth only a tiny fraction of the forint. The exchange rate offered on the street may sound tempting, but if the dealer cheats you, you have no redress. Never make money-changes in dark alleys or in places where the changer can disappear quickly.

To counter the black market, some East European countries offer a bonus on hard-currency exchanges. Keep exchange and purchase receipts in these countries; they may be checked when you leave. Poland has effectively wiped out the currency black market by taking a deep breath and making the black market rate the official rate of exchange. Many countries limit the amount of local currency that can be taken in or out, and some require a declaration of any currency brought in. (See "Practical Matters: Currency Regulations.")

Traveler's checks are accepted in many places, but don't expect to be able to use them at street markets. It's a good idea to have an emergency store of cash in small bills. Credit cards are becoming more and more popular in Europe, but are by no means universal. VISA and MasterCard (along with its European version, Eurocard) are the most widely accepted, with more than four million establishments worldwide taking each. American Express counts more than one million businesses throughout the world, and it has about 1,200 offices offering financial services. Diners Club has 650,000 business participants. Carte Blanche is also accepted in Europe.

Most tourist shops, large stores, expensive restaurants and major hotels accept a variety of credit cards, but the smaller establishments seldom honor them. I was having dinner at my favorite "local" in Salzburg when an American couple sat down at the next table. It was obvious from their conversation that they were driving through Europe and had just crossed the border. When the bill came, the man pulled out his credit card.

"Sorry," said the waitress. "We don't take credit cards." The couple had no Austrian schillings. They were surprised that the restaurant would not let them pay in dollars. The manager was called; there was much head-scratching and repetition of explanations. There seemed to be nothing else to do, so I offered to change their dollars.

On another occasion, a woman complained bitterly because she wanted to buy aspirin in Bruges and the clerk refused to accept dollars. It didn't seem to occur to her what would happen if she tried to pay for aspirin in Kansas City with Belgian francs.

If at all possible, change some money before you go or immediately upon entering a country. (If you are traveling from France to Germany, you can buy German marks while still in France, and so on.) Should you be caught at mealtime without the local currency, most expressway rest houses accept other currencies. If you want to use your credit card, ask if the establishment will accept it before you order. U.S. banks sell small packets of foreign currency for travelers. It's not a bad idea to buy a "starter" before you leave home, to familiarize yourself with the money and to use for taxi fare and tips before you get settled and find a bank.

Small change is the biggest problem when you first arrive in a country. When you buy currency outside a country, you get only bills, but you also will need coins—for telephones, bus ticket automats, tips. Break a bill or two as soon as you arrive, even if it means buying a newspaper or a cup of coffee. Many shops refuse just to give change.

Money can be changed at most European banks and at many post offices (look for the designated windows). Change offices operate extra-long hours and weekends at airports, major railway stations and major highway border crossings. Private change offices and some banks charge hefty fees. If you arrive on a weekend or after hours and think you could get a better rate later, change just enough money to see you through until regular banking hours.

Guidebooks advise shopping around for the best exchange rate, but this can waste valuable time. Take a look at just a few places: the rate doesn't vary much from bank to bank. The important thing to consider is the fee charged for the transaction. If it is not posted, ask before you put your money down.

I prefer to change money at the post offices in France, because they charge no extra fee, while many of the banks charge large fees.

Private change offices that skim off large fees operate around Victoria Station in London, so check the costs carefully before changing money in that area.

In many high tourist-traffic areas, changing money is a quick process: put your money down, the clerk figures the rate and gives you your change. Sometimes, however, the clerk painstakingly fills out a form with your name and address and requires you to show your passport.

Money-changing automats are beginning to appear in Europe: there is one at the main railway station in Frankfurt, Germany, that gives German marks for French francs, British pounds, U.S. dollars or Swiss francs. Not all automats accept dollars, however.

In the West, most hotels give lower rates than banks, but East European hotels have traditionally given the official exchange rate. However, this is already changing in several East European countries. Fairly often, hotels run low of cash on weekends and holidays and refuse to change money. Many will change money only for their own guests.

Exchange rates are usually better for traveler's checks than for cash. That is because banks must go to the expense of physically sending cash back to its country of origin. However, it may come out about the same if you have paid a fee for the checks. The universal 1 percent traveler's check fee is sometimes waived for preferred bank customers or credit card holders. Members of AAA in the United States can buy American Express traveler's checks without paying the fee.

You may get a better exchange rate on purchases by using a credit card than by paying cash. It all depends on whether your currency is rising or falling. Credit card charges have nothing to do with the rate on the day of purchase. You get the rate of the day the transaction is processed. If the dollar is rising, you may save a bit by using your credit card; if it is falling—change money quickly and pay cash! MasterCard, Diners Club and American Express all charge 1 percent over the wholesale bank rate, which is better than the retail rate. VISA charges a one-quarter of a percent more than the wholesale rate.

Consumer laws in the United States protect American travelers when tour operators or airlines default, and the major credit card firms have refund policies for such cases. If your trip is canceled by the tour operator or if an airline goes bankrupt leaving you with an unuseable ticket, and if you have charged these things on your credit card, contact the issuing bank and ask for a refund.

If you plan to make an extended trip to Europe, or if you are there on business, a European bank account can be helpful. Most European banking is done with drafts rather than with checks. However, the Eurocheck is widely accepted. It can be written in about three dozen currencies, no matter where your account is. It is accepted at banks and shops in twenty-two countries and at banks only in another sixteen. It takes three months' active bank account to get the checks and the accompanying card.

The amount guaranteed by a bank for one Eurocheck is the equivalent of about $200 in local currency, and many businesses refuse to accept a check for more than that amount. If your purchase is larger, they ask you to write several checks. Eurochecks are accepted at the discretion of the shop owner. Many gasoline stations also accept them for a small surcharge. A European bank account and its accompanying check card also allow you to use the handy twenty-four-hour cash automats, which are extremely popular.

Personal checks on your bank back home won't do you much good unless you have a credit card that allows you to cash a check at one of the issuing firm's offices. These offices are found in major European cities. Ask for a list of them from your credit card company before you leave home. Occasionally, however, you will find a shop that will accept your dollar check—usually with a sizeable surcharge added to cover the expenses of the bank transaction. Banks require considerable time and take out large fees for cashing checks in other currencies.

If you carry cash, make sure your bills are in good condition. I once ended up in southern Yugoslavia with nothing but a $100 bill—and it had a torn corner. The banks refused to accept it. I could not change money until I got back to Belgrade. Since that time, I carry nothing larger than a $20 bill and make sure the bills are clean and whole, but not crispy new.

Small bills and small denomination traveler's checks are invaluable for short stops or last-minute costs when leaving a country—for breakfast in Vienna when you are waiting for the train to Budapest, for overweight charges at the Lisbon Airport or for a gift that you put off buying until the last minute. You don't want to change lots of money for small expenses and be left with a handful of currency that must be changed back into dollars—probably at a loss.

The bits and pieces of currency that you have left can be spent in the duty-free shop before you leave for home. Duty-frees accept a large number of currencies and will let you pay with several different leftovers. It is impossible to arrange a perfect fit between your time and money, so don't miss your plane trying to get rid of every bit of change. Those coins make excellent souvenirs or good starters for your next trip to Europe.

5

CUSTOMS AND IDIOSYNCRASIES

Travel is stressful and tiring; the constant barrage of new situations leads to a short temper and general crankiness. A group tour I once made, Christmas in Italy, certainly reflected none of the good will of the season. In fact, it was characterized by pushing, shoving, toe-stomping and many complaints to the tour guide and hotel management.

If a local resident is snappish when you ask a perfectly reasonable question, he or she may have just dealt with such a group. In high season, especially, tempers shorten for both tourists and locals. Remember, the residents see the same reactions and hear the same *clichés* from tourists *ad nauseam*.

An understanding of the customs of the country you are visiting and the mentality of its people can smooth your path immeasurably. Here are a few random guidelines, of necessity only a small selection. Keep your eyes and ears open and face the fact that when in Rome, unless you find a custom violently objectionable, life is easier if you do as the Romans do. Mealtime etiquette is discussed in the next chapter. Men often enter restaurants first, though more and more frequently individuals work out between themselves who goes ahead.

Some restaurants, especially the rest houses along the expressways, have introduced no-smoking sections. Militant nonsmokers are rare in Europe, however; despite the exorbitant price of cigarettes, smoking is the rule rather than the exception. Trains and planes, of course, have smoking and no-smoking sections, and smoking is generally not allowed on city public transportation. There has been a crackdown on both smoking and drinking in the Soviet Union; Leningrad has become a "nonsmoking city"—in philosophy, if not in practice.

Europeans (especially those in the North) are slow to invite new acquaintances into their homes, but they are sincere when they do. They seldom say, "Come to see me sometime," without actually setting a date. When you visit a private home, it is polite to bring a hostess gift. A bottle of wine or bouquet of flowers is almost always acceptable, but even here there are pitfalls. In Portugal, wine is not advisable because it is cheap and most people have well-stocked cellars. In France, give wine only to close friends and be sure it is good wine. If you bring wine, expect it to be put aside, not opened at once for the guests. Before you give alcohol in Muslim areas, make sure it will be welcome: many Muslims do not drink. But in the Scandinavian countries, hard liquor makes an excellent gift because it is so expensive there.

Flower bouquets need not be large; sometimes a single stem or a flowering branch is enough. It is customary to put an odd number of flowers (but not thirteen) into bouquets in France, Italy, Poland and Yugoslavia. They should be presented wrapped in some countries, unwrapped in others; ask the florist about the local custom.

Be careful with red roses—they signify romantic love. Avoid chrysanthemums, lilies, dahlias and all white flowers because they are funeral flowers. In Norway, don't give even a Christmas wreath for the same reason. Carnations are Mother's Day flowers in Austria, funeral flowers in Sweden. Potted plants are acceptable in Greece.

In Eastern Europe, fresh fruit, especially if it is out of season, and chocolate have long been highly prized as hostess gifts. However, within a few years these things will probably not be so rare or expensive there and you can fall back on the standard gifts.

You might prefer to pack a few "typically American" items to give your friends, something made in your hometown, perhaps. Portugal is the only country where you need not bring a hostess gift, but do reciprocate by inviting the family out for a meal.

If you are speaking a foreign language, be careful to use the formal forms of address until a relationship is firmly established. This means avoiding first names and using the formal "you" until you are invited to use the informal expression. In many countries, this involves quite a little ceremony: in Germany, friends intertwine right arms and drink to *brüderschaft* (brotherhood)—even women. After this, they are on a first-name basis and say *du* instead of *sie* for "you." The invitation customarily comes from the older person or the person of higher social position.

Austrians, Germans and Swiss address any woman over twenty as *frau,* whether she is married or not. They also use all titles when addressing a person, such as Frau Dr. Weiss. It is not unusual to hear someone referred to as Dr. Dr., denoting two doctor's degrees. In some countries, a person's last name may come first on business cards, addresses and in verbal reference. You may notice this on streets named for people, too—in Budapest, for example.

People shake hands much more frequently in Europe than in the United States, and a woman can hardly go wrong if she offers her hand first. Shake hands every time you meet and again when you say good-bye. Between good friends, light kisses on the cheek are usual. The number of kisses varies from place to place; Parisians always make it three. An Austrian man will raise a woman's hand to his lips and say, *"Kuss die hand."* Romanians actually do kiss the hand. When you enter a shop, the personnel will greet you. Return the greeting before asking for what you want.

Americans may be confused by the numbering of floors in European buildings. Except in the U.S.S.R., the ground floor in Europe is the American first floor. Thus, our second floor is the European first floor.

Likewise, dates can be confusing: the European sequence is usually day, month, year. A date written 12.1.1991 would be January 12, rather than December 1. To avoid confusion, write out the month. Also, notice that Europeans cross the numeral seven; otherwise, it may be mistaken for a one. Europeans form their letters differently from ours, so you may have a hard time reading some handwriting. The thumb is used to indicate the number one. If you hold up your forefinger at a bar to say you want another drink, you may find that you have ordered two.

Don't be surprised if, even in the dead of winter, you find the windows of your room open after the maid has been in to clean.

Europeans are great believers in fresh air. Many windows and doors tilt out from the top for ventilation, as well as open fully. A lever adjusts them to whichever position you prefer. In the mountains and Far North, double windows are common.

You are expected to dress warmly, even indoors, because heating is expensive. Sometimes the heat will be turned off during the day, and if you travel in spring or autumn you may find the furnace has been turned off or not yet started up, even though you are in the middle of a cold spell. An exception is the Soviet Union, where buildings are almost always overheated.

As an antidote to the cold, the Europeans have down-stuffed quilts (often called *duvets*) to sleep under. They are wonderfully cuddly, and because they breathe and because Central Europe has many chilly nights, they can be used almost year-round. With them, you need no other cover, not even a top sheet. They take most of the work out of making the bed.

You know spring is on the way in Germany when you see people standing on the expressway overpasses watching the traffic go by. People on foot, on bicycles or on horseback stop to look. I once saw a couple with deck chairs set up beside the bridge railing. It was like sighting the year's first robin.

Men on the Continent carry handbags, a practical way to prevent bulging pockets. They range from small bags with wrist straps to large shoulder bags, always styled for masculinity.

Few shops in Europe provide brown paper bags—they use plastic. Some shops charge a few pennies for the bags. It's a good idea to carry one or two in your purse in case you want to make a purchase. You still sometimes see a string bag, but in most places these have given way to plastic. In the East, purchases are wrapped with paper and string; the clerks are adept at tying little handles. In the markets, folded newspaper or brown paper cones hold fruit and vegetables.

Primarily in the East, but occasionally elsewhere, you make your selection at the shop counter, then go to the cashier to pay and bring back your receipt to the original clerk to collect your merchandise. Patience. In the Soviet Union, the abacus is still very much in use, often preferred over the cash register that sits on the counter. Clerks can add on the abacus as fast as a computer, it seems.

At markets or small greengrocer's, don't handle the produce. I picked up an apple once and was escorted out of the shop by the nape of my neck. Tell the shopkeeper what you want and he or she makes the selection. Once you get used to this method of shopping, it presents no problem—and where else can you buy half a cucumber!

The Germans have a definite preference for dogs, the Italians for cats. Trains and streetcars have fares for pets; dogs are allowed in most restaurants and hotels, and many a house cat can be seen curled up on bars.

Prostitution is legal in much of Europe, though it is more or less restricted to certain areas of town. Gigolos seem to be fewer in number than prostitutes, but if one approaches you, he will probably show you his health certificate as part of his pitch. Condom automats are beginning to appear in women's public toilets and outside pharmacies.

Germans are painstakingly clean (most people sweep their side-walks every Saturday), but the Swiss are even neater. If you throw a gum wrapper on the ground, don't be surprised if someone takes you to task. "Doggie pooper-scoopers" are sold from vending machines in some public parks. The big cities are the dirtiest: London, Amsterdam, Berlin.

Shop hours vary greatly from country to country. It can be disconcerting to be ready for a Saturday of shopping only to find that everything closes by 1:00 P.M. Conversely, in some countries shops may remain open on Saturday and close Monday morning. In southern countries and in small villages everywhere, stores close one to three hours for lunch.

Late-night and Sunday shopping in some countries is limited to airports and railway stations, to souvenir shops and to pharmacies. Pharmacies in each town take turns being on-call nights and week-ends; the shops post the name of the on-duty shop in their windows, or there will be a listing in the local newspaper. (See "Practical Matters: Opening Hours.")

Be careful how you wave in Greece: the out-turned palm is an insult. Don't pour wine with your left hand in southern Italy. If you nod in Bulgaria, you are saying "no"; if you shake your head, you are saying "yes." Take a bathtub plug with you to Bulgaria and Yugoslavia—otherwise you may have to improvise to soak in the bath (sitting in "dirty water" is considered unhealthy). In southern Italy, the *passeggiatia*, the late-afternoon promenade up and down a favorite thoroughfare, is a delight.

Ask the local people to explain their customs to you. Every country is rich in tradition: marzipan pigs "for luck" appear in confectioners' shop windows at New Year's; a bridal bouquet adorns the hood of the newlyweds' car.

And, yes, there are taboos for women still. Don't go behind the altar of a Greek Orthodox church. Order a half pint of beer in an Irish pub; you probably won't get a whole pint if you ask for it, and you are expected to sit in the lounge instead of at the bar. Some Italian men think it is "unladylike" for a woman to pour the wine, though the same men say it is perfectly acceptable for a woman to attend group functions without a companion. Women who ask a man for directions in Poland are considered flirts—unless the man is a policeman. Women are advised against going into bars or nightclubs alone in Portugal, southern Italy and Turkey, but I have braved them without incident. Obviously, one must use common sense: if the place feels dangerous—leave. In regions where it is customary for women to serve meals, then eat in the kitchen, you as a visitor may be seated and served with the men at mealtime.

Older women may have fewer problems than the young, although European men are adept at "gallantries" toward all women. Age is respected, the more so the farther south you go. Whether you adopt a regal pose or a motherly manner, let it be known that you demand respect and you will receive it.

Once during grape harvest, I went with friends to the property of a small vintner at Nuits-Saint-Georges, near the Burgundy wine capital of Beaune, France. The vintner gave us a tour of his cellar and opened a few bottles of wine for us to sample. Then we wandered up to look at the fermentation vats. The vintner stripped to swim trunks (wine red) and a T-shirt and climbed up to one of the vats. The men followed him up the ladder to have a look, and motioned me to join them.

"No, no," cried the vintner with real distress. "Keep her away!" Superstition says that if a woman looks at the grapes while they are fermenting, the wine will go sour. Sure enough, chalked on the side of the vat was the message, "During the time of viticulture, women please keep your distance." So I sat on the steps in a corner, feeling like a leper as I listened to the cascade of wine pouring through a hose to the next tank. The vintner had crossed himself before going into the vat.

6

YOU ARE HOW YOU EAT

Food and Drink

"I do miss being with other Americans," a woman confided to me during a train ride. "The other day, I saw a woman eating with her right hand, so I started a conversation." The Europeans use both hands when they eat—the fork in the left, the knife in the right—and get down to business. No switching hands after they cut the meat. No putting the hand in the lap. It's okay to prop your arms on the table.

On the Continent, people usually eat with the fork tines turned up and use the knife to push food onto the fork. In Great Britain, they turn the back of the fork up and pile on the food. I've never learned to control peas this way. There are few finger foods: everything from chicken to pizza is eaten with knife and fork, but it's okay to drink your soup if it comes in a cup or a bowl with handles.

Don't be surprised if, in a restaurant, the food for a group is not served all at the same time. It's brought out when it's done, and it is polite to begin before everyone is served—don't sit and let the food get cold. Do wish *bon apetit* to whoever begins to eat, however. People entering a restaurant may wish "good appetite" to those already seated and eating.

Drink is a different matter. Drinks are ordered first and brought at the same time, except sometimes draught beer, which takes time to draw. Wait until the group is served and someone makes a toast before taking a sip. Unless it is a special occasion, the toast will be merely *Cheers,* or *Santé,* or *Prosit.*

If you are unsure whether to click glasses or just raise yours, take your cue from your companions. The woman holds her glass a bit higher than a man's as they toast. Look the others in the eye again after you drink and salute with the glass before you set it back on the table.

You will probably be drinking wine or beer, soft drinks, mineral water or fruit juice with meals. Hot tea and coffee are strictly after-dinner drinks, and iced tea is practically unheard of. Only Americans request ice in their drinks (except in the warmest countries) and tap water.

Sometimes a cube or two of ice is put into long drinks or cola, but Europeans don't fill up the glass with ice unless it's in a bar patronized by many Americans. In Vienna and Budapest, small glasses of plain water are served alongside coffee in the coffee houses, and in France a carafe of plain water usually appears on the table at mealtime. However, most Europeans drink mineral water, which comes with or without the fizz. Taste varies considerably from one mineral water to another; restaurants usually offer a choice of two or three waters. Mineral water costs about the same as beer.

You may wish to dilute your wine with mineral water, a common practice in Europe. You can order it already mixed or get the wine and water separately and do it yourself. If you are having meals at your hotel for several days running, order a large bottle of wine and one of water, drink what you want, and the waiter will set aside what's left for your next meal. As a rule, when you take full- or half-board at your hotel, you keep the same table throughout your stay.

Travelers often take bottles of water along with them. Even though many trains have dining cars or snack carts (check the schedule for services on board), many Europeans bring their own food and drink. They may offer you a bite. One does sometimes hear of people being drugged this way and robbed, though I'm not convinced this actually happens.

Mealtimes vary by country, getting later the farther south you go. In Sweden, dinner is served as early as 5:00 P.M.; in Spain, as late as 10:00 P.M. Lunch rarely begins before noon and goes on until 2:00 or 3:00 P.M. Hotels serve breakfast from about 7:00 to 9:00 or 10:00 A.M.; if you need breakfast earlier, it's sometimes available on request. The larger hotels have the longer serving times. Germans, who are early risers, may have a "second breakfast" at mid-morning, often accompanied by a schnaps or *digestif* containing a high percent of alcohol.

Find out the restaurant hours when you arrive in a new place. Many restaurants close their kitchens for a couple of hours in the afternoon, and in places it is next to impossible to get a meal late at night. Bars sometimes offer late-night snacks and sandwiches, if all else fails.

Mealtimes are for relaxation and enjoyment. Even if you don't sit at table for hours, as the French sometimes do, you will find service relatively slow. The table is yours for as long as you like: only in tourist areas and fast-food shops will you be rushed into moving on. Many restaurants have only one waiter or waitress, and at peak times it may be difficult to get his or her attention. So allow plenty of time for eating, relax and enjoy the meal.

When you are ready to go, ask for the bill. It will seldom be brought until you are ready for it. In most cases, pay the waiter or waitress at the table. Europeans seldom line up at the cash register. To tip, round off the figure when the waiter or waitress is making change instead of leaving the tip on the table. If you are slow making calculations, just drop a few coins back into the change purse. Don't be surprised if, after you have indicated the tip, the waiter or waitress asks you if you have small change to make the transaction easier.

For example, if the bill comes to 15.50 marks and you tell the waiter to keep 16 marks from a 20-mark note, he may ask if you have a 1-mark coin. That way, he can give you a 5-mark coin in return, keeping the small change he needs and keeping your own wallet uncluttered. (See "Practical Matters: Tipping.") In small restaurants, the waiter may add up your bill at your table. He will probably remember what you had, but may ask for prompting. If you need a receipt, ask for one.

Choosing a Restaurant

Selecting a place to eat can be hazardous: if you make a bad choice, you will wonder why everyone was raving about the food.

Contrary to popular belief, you *can* have a bad meal in Paris. I stopped into a horrid little cafe near Les Invalides one hot summer's day for a bottle of water, and at the next table sat a sad American family. "This is supposed to be good," said the grandmother, staring at her leathery omelet and the basket of yesterday's bread.

There are several ways to keep this from happening to you. Use a reliable guidebook. Read the menu card posted in the window or beside the door for selection and price. Take a look inside to see if you like the atmosphere. Plush doesn't necessarily mean the food is good, and some very good meals are served on paper placemats. If the restaurant is full of local people, it is probably good.

Look into the display case for the fresh specials of the day, especially in Italian restaurants. Ask the waiter for recommendations. I have walked out of places when the waiter said, "Everything is good." *Something* must be best. In Hungary or Greece or Yugoslavia, you may be invited into the kitchen to make your choice. This happens particularly when you can't read the menu and no one can translate it for you.

Guidebooks give you basic food terms, and little menu dictionaries are available in a number of languages, but you still run into problems with colloquialisms—the equivalent of Aunt Emma's Blue Plate Special. When all else fails, take your cue from the layout of the menu card (appetizers progress to desserts) and point. If you point to the line that says "Tax and service included," you won't be the first person to have done so.

Be careful when asking for the menu; the word *menu* also means the set meal of the day. You may find yourself being served without having seen what the restaurant offers. Sometimes, there is no printed menu card. Look for a chalkboard, or ask the waiter about the day's specials.

Finding the right sort of restaurant can be a problem at times. You have to choose from restaurants, snack bars, cafeterias—each with different names in different countries. The American fast-food chains are everywhere, but it would be a shame to eat only there and miss the cornucopia of European cooking.

If you are in a hurry, every country has its fast food—its street food. In Germany, an *imbiss* or *schnell imbiss* will serve several kinds of *wurst* (sausage), and at winter festivals you'll find stands selling *kartoffelpuffer* (hot potato pancakes) and *glühwein* (mulled wine—very sweet, but great for keeping the hands warm on a snowy day). The butcher shops almost always have hot prepared meats and a selection of salads, with stand-up counters where you can eat lunch.

In Belgium and the Netherlands, *frites* (fried potato) stands line the highways and sit on every street corner. Belgian and Dutch purists eat their French fries with mayonnaise, while the British prefer vinegar with their *chips*. In the Netherlands, herring is a popular street food. Brussels is famous for its *gaufres* (waffles) and in France you find *crêpes*, plain or filled. Hungary, too, has its *palacsinta*—thin pancakes either sweet or spicy. Spanish bars serve *tapas*, a huge variety of nibblies that stave off hunger while you stand around drinking your beer.

Ice cream is universal and seems to get better the farther north you go. Sweden has exceptionally good ice cream, and in Moscow, even in January, the lines are long at the ice cream stands. Do as the Muscovites do: buy two cones when you finally get there. Italian ices are unique and wonderful and, thanks to the guest workers, *gelateria* can be found all across Europe.

Guides, whether hired or friends, will probably try to take you to the tourist restaurants that serve "international" dishes, a term that usually means food that has had the local spice taken out. Put your foot down; it's best to stick with where and what the locals eat. In Salzburg, I happened into a restaurant celebrating American Week. One of the "specialties" offered was catfish *meunière!* My curiosity got the best of me. Where did they get catfish, and whoever heard of it cooked *meunière?* The dish was *not* a success.

However, a number of American restaurants scattered across Europe are worth trying. The California Restaurant in Zurich is American down to its foil-wrapped baked potatoes served with sour cream and chives, something you seldom find in Europe. Leroy Haynes' is a Paris institution; Papa Maya Tex-Mex Restaurant in the shadow of Les Halles has won a French culinary award.

Vegetarian restaurants can be found in many cities, and the salad bar is popular in Northern Europe. If you can't find a vegetarian restaurant, however, go to an Italian restaurant—they do wonderful things with vegetables: aubergines, stuffed artichokes, mushrooms, even (in season, if you are lucky) fried zucchini blossoms.

Find out what the local specialties are. They can vary by region and even town. Guidebooks tell you a bit, but it never hurts to ask someone—a friend, the waiter, someone at the tourist office. You won't find pork in Muslim areas. In Yugoslavia, whole lambs are roasted outdoors on spits turned by little waterwheels made of paper cups. Do stop and sample it; it is much tastier than the mutton served in some restaurants farther north.

Of course, some specialties will be disappointing. *Yemas,* the egg-yolk sweets of Avila, Spain, are best left untouched, in my opinion.

A friend raved about *heidschnucken,* a kind of sheep found on Germany's Lüneburg Heath, so I took pains to find a restaurant that served it when I was in the region. My disappointment must have shown, because a man at the next table sent me this note: "*Heidschnucken* is a wild sheep that looks like a goat, tastes like a hare and is as tough as an old leather boot." But give everything at least one try, even the *anguilas* in Spain, tiny eels served up sizzling in olive oil and garlic. The most common complaints from Americans are that European food is less salty and less sweet than at home, except for the sticky-sweet desserts in the U.S.S.R., Greece and Turkey.

The Germans serve huge portions, the French small and the Luxembourgers claim French quality in German quantity. The Yugoslavs say their portions will feed one Yugoslav, two foreigners or three French girls. Most restaurants offer two or three children's dishes, but may not allow adults to order these. However, they are likely to have "senior" specialties, as well: smaller portions at lower prices.

The Scandinavian *smörgasboard* can be excellent and it's tempting to overeat. The Dutch give you piles and piles of vegetables, but with their greenhouses they have managed to breed the taste out of every fruit and vegetable known to man. Their tomatoes are as pretty and perfectly formed as their tulips, and about as edible.

The French bake bread twice a day, the Germans once a day but never on Sunday, by law. That means for Sunday breakfast in German restaurants you get sliced bread instead of the usual fresh rolls. In some restaurants, bread is not included in the meal price. In Greece and southern Italy, bread is served without butter, olive oil being the main standby. In Flemish Belgium, bread is not served if potatoes are. The French lay their bread on the table beside their plates, but the Germans insist on a small side plate.

Snacks such as pretzels and little cakes sitting on a table or at the bar must be bought. Just tell the waiter how many you had when you pay the bill. At Paris cafes, you will be served a basket of croissants in the morning; eat and pay for as many as you want. Around Frascati, Italy, many establishments sell only their own wine but provide tables where you can spread out your picnic.

The doggie-bag is not a part of European restaurant culture, and most restaurant personnel will be offended if you ask to have your leftovers wrapped up to take away. Likewise, Europeans seldom drink either beer or soft drinks from bottles or cans—glasses are provided, but not "go-cups."

Breakfast

Continental breakfast is something of a misnomer. In Spain, France, Romania, Portugal and Italy breakfast is limited to bread, butter, marmalade and coffee, tea or hot chocolate. Those oversized coffee cups in France make it easy to dunk croissants.

In Germany, cheese and coldcuts or meat *pâté* will be included; in the Netherlands, expect an array of cheeses. Swedes eat herring at breakfast, as well as yogurt and crisp unleavened breads. If you order an egg anywhere, it will probably arrive soft-boiled, but the Dutch prefer hard-boiled. To the south and east, olives, tomatoes and sheep's cheese will appear on the breakfast table. If you don't get a fork beside your breakfast plate, do as the local residents do—slice your bread and build a meat and cheese sandwich. A knife is always provided. The breakfast buffet is becoming increasingly popular in hotels; selections range from huge to meager.

English breakfasts, with eggs and kippers and kidneys and beans and grilled tomatoes, are justly famous, though they now come in somewhat limited editions. By all means, when in England indulge yourself with early-morning tea brought to you in bed. You can order it with lemon or milk.

Coffee or Tea

It's safest to stick with tea in Britain and Russia; the coffee there can be positively foul. But on most of the Continent, the world of coffee is worth exploring. Almost always it is strong, which creates a problem for those who like to see to the bottom of a full cup. If you prefer your own instant coffee, get one of those little heating coils that goes directly into a cup of water and boils it within seconds. They are available at luggage or electrical appliance stores and in department store travel sections.

Otherwise, try the Dutch coffee served with a few chocolate coffee beans or a cookie, the *café filtre* that drips into your cup as you watch in France or Belgium, the tiny strong espresso and creamy capuccino of Italy and the thick sweet Greek or Turkish coffee that you must strain through your teeth—stop before you get to the mud at the bottom of the cup.

In Denmark, when you order coffee you'll likely get a whole pot. The Portuguese bemoan the fact that Angolan coffee is no longer readily available, but they still brew a tasty cup. At the Aviz Restaurant in Lisbon, I watched fascinated as the waiter brewed coffee in what looked like a sterling silver chemistry set.

Vienna, of course, is the last word in coffee houses. It has one for every mood, from the quietly elegant to the brashly student. One suspects that a few people almost live in them, so don't be surprised if an elderly lady approaches your table with conversation in mind. You may find yourself sitting away the afternoon and trying every coffee on the menu—from the *doppelmocca* (a large cup of strong black coffee) to the *einspänner* (coffee served in a tall glass with lots of whipped cream and powdered sugar). A *brauner* is a simple coffee with cream, *kaffee brulot* contains a shot of brandy, *kaffee verkehrt* has more milk than coffee and a *teeschale* is coffee with milk served in a tea cup. The list goes on.

A few elegant coffee houses remain in Budapest, though most have been replaced by *espressos*. The New York Cafe is all gilt and carving with a decadent ceiling of nymphs and Bacchanalia. Gerbeaud is proud of its Regency fireplaces and its huge selection of cakes and ice creams.

In some East European countries, expensive coffee is "stretched" with malt, and here again it's better to order tea. You'll hardly find coffee in Turkey at all, it's so expensive, but you'll see young boys dashing from shop to shop with tiny glasses of very sweet tea on swinging trays. Tea is a prelude to every business or shopping deal, so take your time and sip as you haggle over that beautiful carpet.

Beer, Wine and Spirits

Wine in Europe is good and, except in the Far North, cheap. Order a bottle of fine French wine for a special occasion, but as a rule, a carafe of the house wine is sufficient. Ask for the local wine—some very good ones are produced in quantities too small for export.

Individuals are welcome at most vintners' estates. Sometimes there is a small charge for a taster's glass of wine, sometimes the vintner simply ushers you into the cellar and starts opening bottles. Either way, a wine tasting is a great European experience and a good way to stock up on a few bottles.

From late spring until late fall, a wine festival is going on in one village or another throughout Europe's vine-growing countryside. Vintners set up booths in the market square and sell tasters' glasses of wine for the equivalent of about 50 cents to $2 each. For a small fee, you can keep the glass, imprinted with the vintner's coat of arms. The festivals include food stands, handicraft demonstrations and live entertainment. Sometimes there are carnival rides for the children.

Get to know the wine regions of each country and what they produce. Champagne is a sparkling wine, but not all sparkling wine is Champagne. The name belongs exclusively to the Champagne region of France—centered around Reims and Epernay—according to the Treaty of Versailles, which ended World War I. In Germany, sparkling wines are called *sekt,* in Italy, *spumonti.*

Likewise, *Port* refers only to the brandy-fortified wine produced in the Duoro Valley of Portugal, and *Tokaji* is a fortified Hungarian wine from Tokaj. *Cognac* and *Armagnac* are two distinctive types of brandy from those southern regions of France; *Calvados* is apple cider from Normandy. A small region around Frankfurt, Germany, produces apple wine, called *ebbelwoi* in the local dialect.

Beer vies in popularity with wine. The Germans may be the most famous beer drinkers in the world, but the Belgians and Czechs are holding their own. In these countries, you don't just order a beer, you order by type, and often by brand name.

In Germany, you'll have a choice of *export* and *pilsner* beers (shortened to *ex* or *pils*). It takes seven minutes to draw a pilsner properly, so that it wears a lovely, thick head. The export is quicker if you are thirsty. Then there are wheat beers—fairly light and served in tall glasses with lemon slices—and heavy *bock* beers.

The Belgians make a huge variety of beer: bottom-fermented, top-fermented, *lambic,* strawberry, raspberry and extra strong *trappiste* beers brewed in the monasteries. Czechoslovakia is where pilsner beer originated, and many beer drinkers swear that's where the best beer in the world is brewed to this day.

If you order a martini in Europe, chances are you'll be served a straight vermouth. American-style drinks are generally limited to large hotels and expensive bars. (At this writing, a shot of Jack Daniels Black Label cost about $12 in Zurich.)

Go easy on your pocketbook while you are in Europe; try the local drinks. The Germans have a variety of schnaps, strong clear brandies, and *digestifs,* syrupy potent drinks that look and taste like rusty nails. They are said to be good for the digestion. The Austrians make a wicked *obstler,* a clear brandy, from whatever fruit happens to be lying around fermenting.

I met the Yugoslav *slijivovica* (plum brandy) at nine o'clock one morning to celebrate signing my apartment lease. An Italian friend keeps me supplied with a very special *sambuca* flavored with fifty

herbs—a secret recipe, of course. Everyone has a secret recipe, including the French monks who make that indescribable liqueur *chartreuse.*
For aperitifs, sparkling wine mixed with orange juice is popular, as is
kir, white wine with a dash of cassis, and Campari with orange.

Bars and restaurants may set aside a special table for their regular
customers. It is reserved with a sign or an ornate ashtray. Don't sit
there unless invited. Some restaurants will not allow you to sit and
drink, either coffee or alcohol, at mealtime—you must also order
food. Others reserve a couple of tables for those who only want a
drink; look for a table that isn't set.

At long last, the drinking hours in Great Britain have been
reformed. For years, the pubs closed in the late afternoon, just when
my feet told me it was time to sit down and have a drink. But as of
August 1988, the pubs were finally allowed to remain open 11:00 A.M.
to 11:00 P.M. without a break. (The afternoon closings were instituted
during World War I to discourage the munitions workers from
drinking so much.) Meanwhile, the Soviets have cracked down on
alcohol, setting 2:00 P.M. as the hour you can order your first drink
and closing the bars at 10:00 P.M. The Scandinavians, too, have tough
liquor laws—and high prices—to try to curb alcoholism. If you are on
a budget, drink sparingly in Scandinavia.

European countries have stiff penalties for driving while intoxi-
cated, and in many places it is against the law for drivers to have any
alcohol whatsoever in the bloodstream. Take a taxi if you plan to
drink. Among friends, Europeans often take turns doing the driving
and the driver doesn't drink during the evening out.

Eating Alone

The time-honored way for a woman to enjoy a meal alone in
peace is to bring along a book. It gives you an excuse not to look
around and perhaps catch someone's eye. It usually works, but not
always.

In Poland, it is not unusual for men to join you uninvited. Even in
conservative Switzerland, the occasional drunk may find his way to
your table and be difficult to dislodge. You may ask the *maître d'* for help,
or simply pay and leave. The experience is unpleasant, but it need not
ruin your trip. Such things are the exception rather than the rule.

You need not eat in restaurants at all, though it would be a shame
to miss the atmosphere and conviviality, as well as the cooking.

Throughout Europe, self-catering rooms and tourist apartments are available, with kitchen utensils provided. You can rent rooms with kitchen privileges and most youth hostels have communal cooking areas.

Cooking requires shopping, and while there are plenty of super-market chains, the farmers' markets and small shops are the most fun. Even tiny villages have markets once or twice a week (go early—they close by noon), and the cities have them daily. Some are open-air, others are in covered halls. They attract farmers bringing local produce, and near the sea fresh fish are plentiful. There may be butchers, cheese vendors and bakers, flower sellers, stands of dried fruit, nuts and spices—even artisans who find this a good place to demonstrate and sell their crafts. You also can buy directly at farm houses. Hand-lettered roadside signs point the way to farms selling vegetables, apples, honey, *foie gras.*

When there is no market, the local butchers, bakers and greengrocers can supply your needs. You may not recognize all the cuts of meat or some of the vegetables. You will find more varieties of bread that you ever imagined—fresh, crusty and free from plastic wrappings. Yes, it is perfectly sanitary to tuck a long loaf of French bread under your arm and go along home. Note that bakeries and pastry shops are often separate establishments.

Even if you don't have a kitchen at your disposal, you can find plenty of ready-to-eat food: bread, cheese, sausage, grilled chickens, *pâté*, yogurt, salads. Avoid the temptation to over-buy. Preservatives may not be used, and the fresh *pâté* that was so good yesterday will likely be spoiled tomorrow. When the shops are closed, go to the train station. Those in the cities have shops catering to travelers that keep late hours.

Don't be surprised at the shops and markets to find chickens, rabbits and game freshly slaughtered and undressed. I always know winter is just around the corner when the first wild boar is displayed at my local butcher's. Take advantage of the seasonal food in Europe. In cold weather, restaurants sometimes have special game menus. In spring and summer, don't miss the fresh cherries, raspberries and little wild strawberries, and in Scandinavia, the cloudberries. Autumn is mushroom season. November is the time for new wines. They may be cloudy and taste not quite like wine. Drink them with caution; they are excellent for flushing out the system.

7

SHAMPOOS, PEDICURES AND TURKISH BATHS

How to Look Good and Feel Fit

You know you have been traveling too long when you begin to see the same faces on every railway platform. The world becomes a blur; you feel as if you can't walk across the room, much less across town—the devil with seeing the *Mona Lisa*.

It is tempting, on the road, to go full speed ahead. After all, you have only a week, or a month, or a summer to see Europe and you want to squeeze in as much as possible. But if you keep your days and nights full to overflowing, you will end up exhausted and will not appreciate any of the things you see.

My rule of thumb is to allow half a day twice a week simply to rest. Sleep late. Soak in the bath. Do your nails. Read a book. Then wander down to a cafe to read, write letters or talk to people. It's worth skipping a museum to break the hectic pace.

Travel can be an excuse for letting your hair frizz, putting on a few extra pounds, becoming a bit crumpled—but it's not a good reason. Beware the attitude "No one knows me and I'll never see these people again anyway." The independent woman keeps fit, mentally and physically, out of pride in herself. It actually takes little extra effort to keep in shape while traveling. A good wardrobe and a good haircut will see you through, and getting enough rest ensures a good attitude.

Hair Care

The best bet for your hair is to get it cut at home. Don't take a chance with a strange salon unless you know by reputation that it really is top-notch. Start out with a freshly cut, "easy" style, one that can be washed and fluffed dry with your hands or needs a blow dryer at most. Some hotels have dryers in the rooms (though they seldom have much drying power), and dryers are also provided in the dressing rooms of some public swimming pools and thermal baths.

If you wish to go to a beauty salon, ask advice from the hotel concierge or from friends. Major hotels and department stores usually have reliable salons. Be especially careful with hair coloring: it varies by country no matter how good the salon. You may wish to bring along your own favorite brand. If you want just a wash and dry, chances are that no damage will be done. I spent a delightful couple of hours in a Budapest salon where the staff was using everything from blow dryers to curling irons heated over an open flame. Some hair salons also give manicures and facials, but you can also find cosmetic practices. Pedicurists are popular. If you want to treat yourself to a real makeover, visit these establishments.

Toiletries

A wide variety of cosmetics and toiletries can be found in Western Europe, including many of the brand names you are familiar with at home. For short trips, take along what you need. On extended journeys, just pick up another travel-size container when you run out. Hypoallergenic cosmetics are widely available in the West. In the East, some familiar brand name cosmetics have always been available in the hard-currency shops and are beginning to appear in the normal stores.

While you can find your favorite brand of tampons or panty liners in Northern and Central Europe, don't count on being able to pick them off the shelf everywhere. A few years ago, there was a shortage of tampons in Yugoslavia. It's best to bring along an ample supply no matter where you plan to travel. That means bringing extras; no matter how regular you are at home, the stress of travel can throw you off schedule. When you are traveling on heavy days, be doubly safe by using both tampons and pads. If you travel in Spain, Ireland and other mostly Catholic countries, you may have problems getting birth control pills. Take an ample supply with you if you use them.

Keeping Clean

Travelers seem to be magnets for grime. You'll find that your face needs to be cleansed twice after a long trip and that your fingernails have attracted plenty of dirt. Because the strain of travel makes you vulnerable to infection, it is especially important to keep clean.

Take along packaged wet tissues to wipe your hands when you can't get to a washroom. Pat them on your wrists and forehead for a quick pick-me-up. Wash your hands often, and use cream to keep them from chapping. In hot weather, stand for a few minutes with your eyes closed and run cold water over your wrists to refresh yourself. In cold weather, running warm water over your wrists will get your blood tingling again.

You may think *eau de cologne* went out of fashion along with palpitations in nineteenth-century novels, but it still works to revive your spirits. Pour a bit into the palms of your hands, inhale it deeply, then pat it on your face and neck. (Köln, Germany, still produces some of the best known colognes.) Try not to overdo soap and water on your face and body, and use cream generously. In places where the water is hard, rub bath oil lightly over your body after a shower or bath.

Even in good hotels, if you shower at peak hours (early morning and late afternoon), you may run out of hot water. In small hotels, the hot water heater may be lit only at certain hours of the day or on request. Sometimes, a small hot water heater is mounted over the tub and comes on only when the water is turned on. Ask about the availability of hot water before you check in, especially in small guest houses.

If you are staying in a room without a private bath, it probably will have a sink. Sometimes these sinks have hot water, sometimes only cold. Note that "C" on a tap does not necessarily mean "cold."

In Italy, "C" is for *caldo*, which is a relative of our word "scalding." In France, rooms almost always have bidets, even if they have no bath. Sit astride the porcelain bowl, turn on the warm water and treat yourself to a thorough wash. Most hotels provide bath towels; in luxury establishments, however, you are expected to bring your own washcloth. It is also a good idea to bring along soap, though more and more hotels are providing it.

If you are traveling long distances by train and sleeping in *couchette* compartments, you may want to take advantage of showers at railway stations and airports. For the equivalent of a couple of dollars, you can have half an hour or more in a private stall that has enough room to allow you to open your luggage and get yourself reorganized to your heart's content. Airport hotels may rent rooms for part of a day if you need just a few hours of rest and privacy. If you are taking a "barefoot cruise," which means cramped quarters on board a small boat with a cold shower, if there is a shower at all, you can probably find a hotel on shore that will allow you the use of a bath for a small fee.

Public baths can still be found in some cities. If you can't find one, go to the swimming pool and scrub yourself down in the shower before taking a swim. Even in winter, you'll find plenty of indoor pools, and outdoor heated pools steam invitingly all winter long in (among other places) Moscow, Seefeld (Austria) and Bad Homburg (Germany). Thermal baths, saunas and Turkish baths abound on the Continent and they should be experienced whether you go to a full-fledged spa or a street-corner sauna. They may be mixed or not, nude or not.

The Finns have about as many saunas as they have cars, maybe 1.5 million for a population of five million. Their saunas are not mixed. You shower, sit in the sauna for as long as it feels good, then repeat the process. You can end with a swim. The Finns switch themselves with birch branches called *vihtas*—usually only in summer, for the branches must be fresh, although they are sold deep-frozen for devotees.

Saunas are *not* for people suffering from asthma, varicose veins, rheumatic disease, overproductive thyroid, heart problems or tumors. Alcohol and saunas definitely do not mix, and you should avoid coffee or tea at sauna time. Drink juice or mineral water to quench your thirst.

In Turkey, the *hamam* (baths) are separate for men and women, and they are as much a social institution as a place to wash. The marble halls can be a bit intimidating when you enter, wondering just what you should do. Don't worry; you will be a curiosity and the attendants will literally lead you by the hand.

Pay the fee for what you want (try the bath and massage) and you will be ushered into a private cabana to change. An attendant will lock the door on your belongings and keep the key; don't forget to tip her. You are expected to be modest, so wrap a towel around you when walking through the baths.

In the steamy bathing area, put the towel aside, dip one of the copper pans into the hot running water and empty it over your head. The attendant will take over the shampoo job, and don't expect gentleness. After several sudsings and rinses, your hair will be squeaky clean. Then comes the massage, starting with a rough glove that peels off dirt and dead skin and ending with a tough kneading that forces your muscles to relax. Now return to the pool and soak as long as you like in the warm waters. Send out for little glasses of strong, sweet tea if you like. You may want to bring your own towel, washcloth, soap and shampoo. Wear either your own shower shoes or those provided at the baths, because the marble floors are slippery.

Variations on these baths exist in almost every country in Europe. "Taking the cure" has a long tradition, and while there are many types of medically supervised treatments for specific illnesses, the spas almost always have baths and steam rooms and massages for the public.

A friend and I stayed at the old spa hotel Gellèrt in Budapest; we had only to throw on a robe and ring for the back elevator, which took us directly to the pools. We wandered from cold pool to warm pool to hot pool; we tried the steam rooms in varying degrees centigrade; we fell into conversation with elderly women taking rheumatism treatments and with young girls fending off future ailments. (See "Practical Matters: Spas.")

Many thermal and curative baths set aside certain areas or certain days when mixed bathing and saunas are nude. However, nudity is hardly shocking on the Continent and you'll soon become accustomed to it. Nudist beaches are as popular as nudist pools, and even in "clothed" areas, toplessness is not uncommon. I remember my surprise my first summer in Germany when I happened upon a group of women sunning in bras or less at a roadside park. But after a few years of living under gray skies, I began to understand the need to undress and soak up the sunshine when it does appear.

Toilets

Europeans are not averse to the sexes sharing toilet facilities or taking to the roadside when nature calls. The quality of European toilets varies immensely, from gilt at the Ritz to two-footprints-and-a-hole in southern France or Turkey. Actually, those porcelain squares with a hole in the middle are often spick-and-span and more sanitary than a sit-down toilet. If you are wearing a jumpsuit, however, you have a problem: you may have to take it off. At any rate, the proper way to use such a toilet is to squat. Try it standing up and you will be thoroughly splattered.

Finding the flush can be a challenge. It may be an old-fashioned pull chain or a button so neatly molded into the tank that you have to search for it. Sometimes the flush is on the floor (step on it), sometimes on the wall (push it). A few years ago, the Germans were experimenting with an automatic-flush toilet, but the idea was dropped when a child was injured. A Swedish manufacturer is producing deluxe public toilets that include piped-in classical music.

Pay toilets are fairly common, especially at roadside restaurants and areas of high tourist concentration. Coins may be required to open the stall door, or the toilet attendant may set a little dish at the entrance, where you leave a tip. (One attendant usually takes care of both men's and women's toilets, and men are expected to tip, too.) At some roadside rest houses, use of the toilet is free but you must buy the toilet paper. In Germany, the paper is dispensed from a machine. In Turkey and southern Yugoslavia, an attendant doles out the paper squares sparingly.

Not only may there not be enough toilet paper, the quality may be less than desirable. The tissue may be very thin or as rough as crepe paper. For reasons I cannot fathom, the British prefer waxed paper. It is a good idea, no matter where you travel, to carry a packet of tissues in your bag.

Sometimes, paper seatcovers are provided, but this is not the general rule. Recently, toilets with plastic covers have appeared: push a button and a plastic strip rolls neatly around the seat. It is almost as astonishing as finding sinks that automatically turn on as you step up to them. The Golden Rule of travel is *go to the toilet at every opportunity.* The next one may be a long way away, and when you do find it, it may not be as good as this one.

Keeping Fresh

Since staying fresh makes travel more pleasant, take along talcum or baby powder for the underarms, feet and groin area. Cotton panties are best, especially in warm weather, because their absorbency and ability to breathe help prevent rashes. If your feet sweat, wear cotton socks or put absorbent insoles into your shoes. Perspiration is necessary to keep the body from overheating; you may want to wear a headband in hot weather.

Use deodorant, though when you step onto a crowded bus you may think that no one else does. At times, the smell of humanity—sweat, garlic, mothballs—can be overpowering. (You will probably also notice that shaving the legs and underarms is not a usual practice among European women.) Whatever you do, don't try to cover up body odor with perfume. The only time to apply perfume is fresh from your bath. A bit on the wrists and behind the knees is enough. An overpowering sweetness is as nauseating as body odor. If you are tempted to buy French perfume in France (like French underwear, it is truly delicious), try several kinds *on your skin* before you buy. Perfume reacts with body chemistry, so "try it on" for a couple of hours to decide which one is right for you.

Exercise

If you are on your feet sightseeing all day, you may think you have had enough exercise. Nevertheless, you should pay attention to the quality of exercise and to whether you also spend long periods sitting. Jogging is popular in Europe; you may want to join the local joggers on the river banks or in the parks and forests, where marked courses are laid out.

Walking is one of the best exercises. It is also the best way to see a city. But when you are trapped on transportation going from place to place, try to exercise there, too. It's easiest in trains, where you can explore the length of the cars or spend time standing at the window doing gentle calisthenics. On planes, make a point of walking around the aisles, swinging your arms as you go.

If you are driving, make rest stops every couple of hours. Walk around the parking lot or roadside park. Drink your coffee standing up. Even do a few bends and stretches. I know a woman who keeps a jump rope in her car and spends five minutes in this childhood pursuit at every stop. Buses present the most difficulties. They are usually cramped, and aisle-wanderers earn nothing better than frowns from their fellow passengers. Take advantage of every rest stop; stay off the bus for as long as you can.

If you have overdone the walking, on the other hand, give your feet a massage. If you have foot cramps, slowly bend the toes inward several times. It's great to soak your feet in hot water at the end of the day.

Pregnancy

There is no reason that a pregnant woman should not travel, provided she is reasonably healthy. Extra care should be taken, certainly, and plenty of rest time allowed.

A pregnant women will be more comfortable traveling during the mid-trimester. The first weeks may be taken up with morning sickness; the last find her feeling cumbersome and needing to urinate frequently. Airlines restrict (or downright prohibit) travel after the eighth month. Always wear loose clothing, low shoes, a support bra and maternity pantyhose.

Be careful of immunizations or medication. It is best to travel in countries where immunizations are not required. Talk to your doctor before you go; discuss medications you might need along the way and take them along. Pay special attention to what you eat. Low-salt diets are recommended; airlines and many hotels offer special meals on request. Doctors advise being very careful to avoid sunburn, which can aggravate fluid retention. Swimming is okay, they say, but avoid hot tubs and whirlpools.

Travel Appliances

In my travels, I have steadily reduced the number of electrical appliances that I carry. The travel iron was the first casualty, then the lighted makeup mirror. At the moment, all I have to plug in is a hair dryer.

Dual-voltage appliances are the most practical. Just don't forget to change the regulator when you change voltages, or you may blow all the fuses in the hotel. But there's more to appliances than a matter of 110 or 220 volts. Electrical plugs come in various shapes and sizes.

The plug poles in Northern Europe are slightly larger than those in Southern Europe (including Switzerland). Some sockets are recessed, others are flush with the wall. Even when the plug poles are the proper size, a round plug won't fit into those diamond-shaped recessed sockets in Switzerland. Square British plugs are totally different from the Continental kind.

If you don't want to carry around a complete collection of plug adapters, buy a universal converter/adapter that changes to five different shapes and sizes. Sometimes, too, the hotel can provide adapters or converters on request.

Don't mix up the two. An adapter simply allows the plug to fit into the socket. A converter changes the voltage and is to be used when you don't have dual-voltage appliances. Don't leave converters plugged in; they can overheat and cause a fire. When choosing a converter, be sure it can handle the appliances you are using. Appliances that heat up need more wattage than a clock or a razor.

Most European current is 220 volts, but quite often hotels have 120-volt plugs beside the bathroom mirrors for electric shavers. If you try to use a hair dryer in this plug, you may blow a fuse.

Some hotels have plenty of sockets, but the lack of conveniently located plug-ins is one of my biggest gripes about hotels. I have been reduced to crawling under tables and beds to unplug a lamp so I could plug in my hair dryer. If that happened to be the only light in the room, I had to wash my hair during the day. If the plug was far from the mirror, I had to make do with a tiny pocket mirror—seldom with optimal results. Also, always test your hair dryer before washing your hair, in case the plug-in is dead.

The other appliances I carry—an alarm clock, a tiny reading light, sometimes a radio—are battery operated. The clock is insurance; very seldom, but usually at the worst time, the hotel will forget the wake-up call. (Telephones with self-dial wake-up calls and built-in radio–alarm clocks are appearing more and more often.) Make sure all batteries are fresh before you start out.

Clothing Care

Once upon a time, all you had to do to have your shoes shined was to place them outside your hotel room door at night. No more. A few luxury hotels carry on this tradition, but the majority have switched to the shoeshine machine in the hall beside the elevator.

In Turkey and some parts of Yugoslavia, shoeshine men line up along the streets with ornately decorated stands. Somehow, they always come up with the right color of polish.

Keeping your shoes shined may be the least of your wardrobe concerns. Washing underwear and stockings in your room is simple enough—bring along a few clips for hanging them up, or dry them on the radiator. In an emergency, dry them with your hair dryer.

But what of the blouses and the suits? Having laundry done at your hotel is convenient, but it can run up the bill quickly. You can save money by finding a laundry or drycleaner on your own, though they are not always satisfactory. I have yet to find a drycleaning shop in Germany that does not run the back creases of slacks all the way to the waistband. In London, plenty of laundromats are available, but self-service laundries are not as common on the Continent as they are in the United States. Ask the tourist office if there are any in town. When you find one, wash everything.

Unpack as soon as possible upon arrival so that the wrinkles can "hang out" of your clothes. Bring a few wire or folding clothes hangers in case the hotel does not provide enough. You can steam wrinkles out of clothes by turning on a hot shower, closing the bathroom door until the steam builds up and then hanging the clothes in the bathroom. Many hotels will lend you an iron on request, though some do so grudgingly and others only provide pressing service.

Keep a supply of plastic bags in your suitcase and purse. They are useful for shopping, packing wet washcloths, carrying gear to the beach or packing lunch for the train. Start out with just a few; they breed like rabbits.

8

Getting Around

Europe operates on the twenty-four-hour clock. If you don't understand how it works, you may be like the woman who assumed that her airline ticket meant evening departure when it said her flight left at 0700. She was wrong; she missed her plane and she didn't get a refund.

Once you get the hang of it, though, it makes more sense to say 0700 hours and 1900 hours than to try to interpret 7:00 A.M. or 7:00 P.M. in a language you hardly understand. The twenty-four-hour clock reduces errors in schedules. It is used not only for transportation timetables, but also when making business appointments and reservations in restaurants. The numbers 0001 to 1200 are one minute after midnight through noon; from 1201 to 2400, one minute after noon through midnight. For example,

0900 is 9:00 A.M., 1500 is 3:00 P.M. and 1900 is 7:00 P.M.

You won't be crossing many time zones within Europe. Great Britain, Ireland, Iceland and Portugal are on Greenwich Mean Time (GMT), which is five hours ahead of Eastern Standard Time. Most of the rest of Europe is on Central European Time, one hour ahead of GMT. However, Bulgaria, Finland, Turkey, Greece and Romania are on East European Time, two hours ahead of GMT. The U.S.S.R. is on GMT plus three hours (the U.S.S.R. extends over eleven time zones, but rail and air timetables are on Moscow time).

Jet-lag is hardly the problem within Europe that it is with transatlantic flights, but north-south travel can be almost as disconcerting as changing time zones. The length of daylight varies considerably between the North Cape and the toe of Italy's boot. At midsummer, only slight dusk settles over Leningrad in the wee hours. It doesn't get really dark in central Germany before 10:00 P.M., but in southern Turkey the sun has set by dinnertime. Conversely, in winter there is hardly any daylight at all in the Far North while in the South the short days are not so pronounced. European Daylight Savings Time, called Summer Time, begins at the end of March and runs to the end of September.

Pay close attention to time differences when you telephone outside Europe—otherwise you will rouse someone out of bed at 4:00 A.M. or wonder why the office phone goes unanswered, although it's midday where you are. Noon in Paris is 6:00 A.M. in New York.

Distances

Distances in Europe can be deceptive. Although the countries are close together and are much smaller than the United States, don't underestimate the time it takes to get from one place to another. It can take as long to go between some major cities by plane as it does by express train. You must get to the airport early, while you can arrive at the train station just in time to hop on board. Then you must add the time it takes to go into the center of town from the airport, while the main railway stations are usually in the center of town. Before deciding which method of transportation to use, check the schedules and find out if where you are going is nearer the airport or the railway station. If you are driving, study the map closely to see if you can use the expressways or whether you'll be taking slow back roads. Of course, using the expressways is not always the fastest. Five-mile-long traffic jams are notorious on Germany's *autobahnen*.

Travel Seasons

At peak vacation periods, allow for the crowds—the Europeans on their vacations, as well as the foreigners flooding in—on the highways and on public transportation. I once had to drive in second gear on the expressway all the way from Salzburg, Austria, to Stuttgart, Germany (more than 200 miles) because I made the trip on the last day of vacation.

European vacation periods are staggered to help alleviate this problem, but July and August are still the most popular times. The Christmas and Easter seasons, as well as summer, mean traffic jams as skiers head to the Alps or guest workers drive south to Turkey, Italy, Greece and Yugoslavia. (See "Practical Matters: Holidays and Summer Vacation Periods.")

Autumn is my favorite time in Europe. The children are back in school, the crowds are gone, the weather is often better than in summer and hotels lower their prices. In winter, ski resorts will be less crowded in the weeks before Christmas and just after the New Year. Their peak is mid-January to mid-March. Many ski resorts have low-priced packages (often called *white weeks*) for the off-peak times.

Americans and Europeans have different styles of traveling. Europeans tend to go to the same spot for one to six weeks. They think the short American vacation is barbaric and can't understand our rush to see all the sights without taking time to comprehend them. Don't be surprised to find it difficult to book a room for just a night or two in ski or beach resorts. Most hotels there work in units of one or two weeks.

Trains

Travelers have a number of alternatives for getting around. You'll probably find it most convenient to combine several methods of transportation. The European rail system is superb. Especially in Central Europe, the trains are fast, frequent, comfortable and clean. Most (but not all) main stations are located in the center of the city, and some major airports have direct train connections to the main stations.

Take time to learn to read a rail schedule. It not only tells you when and from what track the train leaves, it also indicates the kind of train, whether a fast-train supplement is charged, where the major stops are and whether there is a dining car on board. The Germans are even experimenting with "shopettes" on board a few InterCity trains. (See "Practical Matters: Transportation, Sample Train Schedule," pages 148-149.)

Several kinds of trains operate in Europe: express trains, fast trains, local trains and the superb EuroCity (EC) express. Local trains wait if connecting express trains are late, but it doesn't work the other way around. The French are continuing to expand their network of superfast TGVs *(Train Grand Vitesse)*, which started out on the Paris-Lyon run. The Germans have just completed the first high-speed ICE (InterCity Express) line, which runs between Hannover and Würzburg; it begins service June 2, 1991. When the entire route is completed, trains reaching speeds of 250 k.p.h. (about 150 m.p.h.) will run between Hamburg and Munich via Hannover, Kassel, Frankfurt a.M. and Stuttgart. Sweden has just put new high-speed trains on the Stockholm-Gothenburg route.

If you are traveling between major cities, you can use the express trains exclusively; if you are going off the beaten track, you will have to use the not-quite-so-comfortable locals. Many small towns have very limited rail service. If a fast-train surcharge is required for the train you are taking, it is sometimes a bit cheaper to buy the surcharge ticket before you board the train than to get it from the conductor. It may be purchased along with your ticket or bought from a machine in the station.

Rail passes are highly recommended if you plan to do a lot of train travel. You not only save money, you have the convenience of not waiting in line to buy a ticket, being able to make spur-of-the-moment side trips or changing your plans in mid-track, so to speak.

The Eurailpass, which is available only to non-European citizens, will take you through seventeen countries. (More East European countries may be added in the near future.) It is available in several variations; adult passes are for first-class only and youth passes are for second-class. The fast-train supplement is now included. An Interrail pass for young people under age twenty-six is good in twenty-two countries. If you plan to travel in just one country, however, you may prefer to buy a rail pass for that specific country. (See "Practical Matters: Rail and Bus Passes.") For those under age twenty-six or over sixty-five, special rates may be available on single-trip rail tickets. Inquire at the ticket counter or at your travel agency.

Seat reservations, which cost a few dollars, are advisable in peak season and during holidays, but at other times they are hardly worth the trouble and expense. If you travel first-class, you will find a seat more easily than in second-class. Both first- and second-class have no-smoking sections. Trains have two kinds of seating cars: the compartment, made up of a number of small "rooms," each seating six or eight people, and the cars with long rows of seats on each side of a middle aisle. I prefer the compartments, where you face your traveling companions and it's easy to strike up a conversation.

Dining cars are found on InterCity and EuroCity trains. Other long-distance trains usually have snack service from little trolleys. Local trains have no food or drink service. Payment for meals and refreshments can be made in several European currencies, but not in dollars.

If you travel during the day, you can watch the change of scenery. However, night travel saves time and, if you are on a budget, the price of a hotel room. Some night trains are made up only of sleeping cars, while others have both seats and sleepers. It is a good idea to reserve a sleeper, but if you haven't reserved, walk along the train looking for a sign that says beds are available. The car conductor should be at the door and can be paid directly. If all the sleepers are full, you may be lucky enough to find an empty seating compartment. Turn up the arm rests or pull the seats together and stretch out.

There are several types of sleeping cars. Cheapest is the *couchette*, in which four or six persons (sexes sometimes mixed) are stacked like cordwood on either side of the compartment. Normally, a sheet, pillow and blanket are provided. Germany offers a super-cheap *couchette* for the young, in which no bedding is provided: use your sleeping bag. France has introduced the *Cabine 8* on selected trains—eight semi-reclining bed-seats to a compartment for the price of a seat reservation. They are presently on the following runs: Paris-Marseille/Beziers, Metz-Nancy-Nice, Paris-Briancon, Paris-Bourg St. Maurice, Paris-Amsterdam and Paris-Venice. *Cabine 8* cars run only on certain days, with a higher frequency in the summer season. Details are available at railway stations, particularly those listed here.

Second-class sleeping compartments (sexes usually not mixed unless you are traveling and making reservations together) sleep two or three. Private compartments can be booked with first-class tickets, at prices comparable to a very good hotel. These compartments have sinks and mirrors, with a shower at the end of the car.

For *couchette* travel, here are a couple of hints to make life easier. Wear comfortable clothing. In winter, long cotton underwear under slacks is ideal. When you settle into the berth for the night, just take off the top layer and you are ready to sleep. Carry slippers, makeup and reading material in your purse or a small tote; it is impossible to rummage in your suitcase in this cramped space.

The top berth is most comfortable (people won't be climbing past you all night), although it may get a bit stuffy. A net is usually attached to the wall beside the berth for your purse, and there will be a reading light. Stash a small bottle of water in the net in case you get thirsty. Keep your money and valuables where no one can reach them without waking you. First- and second-class compartments give you enough space to change into a nightgown. Sealed cups of drinking water, soap and hand towels are provided.

On sleeping cars in Central Europe, the conductor will provide food and beverages on request, at an extra charge, and often will take your passport for border crossings. Some will also take care of having your tax-refund papers stamped at the border. (Don't forget to tip him.) However, on one sleeper trip I took, I was awakened no less than four times for passport and customs checks.

When traveling by train, make sure you get into the right car. Cars are often switched, so that at some point certain cars are split off the original train and head one direction while the others go a different route. A sign on the car gives its destination, but double-check with the conductor if you are in doubt. He will catch an error if you are traveling with a ticket, but a rail pass doesn't indicate your destination. The seat direction sometimes changes after a switch or when a train pulls away from a dead-end station. If you have been facing forward, suddenly you find yourself riding backward.

Many large cities have several stations; don't get off at the wrong one. When you have to change trains, check to see which station you need. For example, you may arrive at Paris Gare de Lyon and have to cross town to the Gare du Nord for your connecting train.

Before you jump off the train, make sure you are on the platform side. Some older cars don't have automatic locks on the "track side" doors. At a few stations, you'll see platforms on both sides of the train, but only one side leads to the exit. A good way to know you are on the correct side is to notice if there are benches on the platform or if waiting passengers are standing there. More common is one platform between two trains. Double-check to be sure you are getting on the correct train.

Airplanes

Flying within Western Europe is expensive. With the opening of Eastern Europe's borders, the formerly cheap fares available there will probably soon be on a par with those in the West. Charter flights may offer the best bargains if the timing fits your schedule. Also, "last-minute" travel agencies have begun multiplying. They offer sizeable savings just a few days before departure on unfilled plane seats and unbooked package vacations. Ask your travel agent about airline holiday tickets that operate the same way as rail passes. Finnair has a fifteen-day pass for Finland, for example.

Early airport check-in is required for flights within Europe as well as transatlantic flights. The exact amount of time required depends on the security measures of the individual airline, so inquire when you make or confirm your reservation. Confirming reservations is always a good idea, especially for international flights.

If you are on a budget, ask the taxi fare from the airport into town before you climb in. It can be very expensive. You may prefer to take a bus, train or limousine. The Stockholm Airport is 40 kilometers outside the city, and the limousine service offered by SAS is cheaper than the taxi fare. A bus also connects the airport with the city at a fraction of the taxi price.

In Frankfurt a.M., Germany, and Zurich and Geneva, Switzerland, fast InterCity and Eurocity trains stop at the airports on their regular routes. Frankfurt is connected to Cologne/Bonn and to Stuttgart by the Lufthansa Airport Express, a fast train only for persons holding Lufthansa airline tickets. Baggage can be checked at the train station straight through to your final destination. Iceland Air tickets to and from Luxembourg include bus or train transportation between several European cities and the airport.

City buses and subways offer regular connections with airports. Don't forget, you need the local currency in small change to buy a ticket, though a few cities are introducing ticket automats that accept small bills. If you are taking a package tour, the transfers to and from the airport are usually included. Some luxury hotels offer free limousine service. And once again, if you are making airplane connections, check to see if you are landing and departing at the same airport. Otherwise, you could be faced with getting from London Heathrow to London Gatwick, or from Paris Charles de Gaulle to Paris Orly. ("See Practical Matters: Airports.")

Bus Tours

The best bus tours, in my opinion, are the half-day city orientation variety. Anything more can lead to hemorrhoids. However, there are some advantages to bus tours—not the least of which is price. Group-tour operators get the best hotel rates; it is not unusual for tours to offer an entire trip for the price you would pay for the hotel alone. You may feel safer with a group than on your own. You may wish to go with a group to learn your way around for a later trip alone. Group tours are still the easiest way to get to the Soviet Union, even though it has become more open to individual travel in the past few years.

On a group tour, you are spared the trouble of making your own arrangements, but you give up your freedom of choice to some extent. If you dislike being herded into a museum when you want to linger in the coffee shop or are tantalized by glimpses out of the bus window, group tours are not for you.

However, some tour operators are taking pains to provide the best of both worlds. If you want to take a tour that lets you do your own thing, look for one that provides centrally located hotels. That way, you can go along on the group excursions if you like, but if you prefer, you can walk or use public transportation to do your own exploring. Read the tour itinerary carefully to see how much free time is allowed and how much time will be spent on the road. Many cheap trips include night travel; it saves time and money, but you may be so groggy the next day that you don't really see the sights.

Choose a tour that conforms to your interests: a study tour is the wrong place for the inveterate shopper. Many good special-interest tours do exist: art history tours, cooking school tours, folk dance tours. Some travel agents offer tours geared to women's interests for women only. (See "Practical Matters: Women's Hotels, Cafes, Centers, Groups and Travel Agencies.")

When you take a group tour, remember that the guide and bus driver are service professionals just as waiters and waitresses are. Tips should be given at the end of the trip, based of course on the quality of service, as well as on the length of the trip. Generally acceptable tips are the equivalent of $1 to $2.50 per person per day each to the guide and driver. Tip in the currency of the country, unless the guide accompanies you from America. If you must use dollars, don't give coins—they cannot be exchanged and are therefore worthless.

Public Buses

Tours aside, sometimes when you are using public transportation the only way to get where you are going is by bus. The yellow Swiss Postal Buses are an excellent supplement to the railway system. Countries that have limited railway service often have superb bus connections. In major cities, the bus station is almost always near the railway station. Some rail passes are also good on buses.

National Express and Caledonian Express of Britain have two travel passes for tourists who wish to travel by bus—though they prefer the term *coach*. The Britexpress Card, purchased for just a few dollars, allows adults one-third discount on fares and is good for thirty consecutive days. Persons over sixty and young people aged five to fifteen automatically travel at this discount without the card. The second pass is the Tourist Trail Pass, which provides unlimited travel in England, Scotland and Wales for five, eight, fifteen, twenty-two or thirty days. The passes are available through travel agencies before you leave home or at bus stations in major British cities.

The North Norway Bus traverses one of Europe's longest scheduled bus routes. It takes four days to travel the 1,320 kilometers between Fauske and Kirkenes, and there are pit stops along the way. Turkish buses are plentiful and cheap—so cheap that you can buy two seats and stretch out on long journeys. Many of them offer complimentary tea, and even meals, to entice customers. Shop around carefully among the many operators before choosing which bus to take. In addition to national bus services, the Europe-wide Europabus operates scheduled runs all the way from Helsinki to Istanbul. It is cheaper than train fare, but unfortunately there is no Europabus pass.

If you plan to travel long distances on a bus, take along a small pillow. Whoever designs bus and airplane seats is evidently a direct descendant of the inventor of the torture rack. Inflatable neck pillows are the most comfortable and most practical to carry. You may also want to bring along folding slippers or heavy socks to wear when you kick your shoes off.

Boats

Whether you take a first-class cruise, a barge trip through the canals of France or hop across a river by ferry, boats can be a pleasant and easy way to travel in Europe. Sea voyages may be organized cruises or overnight jaunts by ferry. Good sea connections exist all along coastal Europe, whether they be the large Scandinavian ships capable of ferrying whole trains or island-hopping Greek boats for foot-passengers only.

In high season, make ferry reservations, especially if you are putting a car on board or want a cabin. The large ships have good cabins, but it pays to check closely just what kind of ferry you are taking and what services are offered. Otherwise, you may end up sleeping on deck with the locals and their livestock.

A student recounted his misadventures in crossing from France to Ireland with a Eurailpass in August, when a gale on the English Channel forced him to change ports:

"About this boat ... I have never seen so many students in my life. All on deck passage—on the cafeteria floor, in the life-jacket rooms. I had a cabin which I never saw. To ride this boat, one must be on guard. Take minimal (i.e., purse-size) luggage, as even cabin-holders must stow large stuff in one of the unguarded open baggage rooms.

"Reserve and pay for (my error) a cabin six weeks in advance. Bring Irish pounds, because the exchange line is four hours long and closes even if you've been waiting. Bring food, because the cafeteria and restaurant run the same way and are extremely expensive. Call before committing yourself to either the Cherbourg or Le Havre train, as the boat might be at the other port.

"It really isn't a system for the regular traveler. Either have the luxury and organization to get a cabin, food and money in advance, or the vitality to do without. This is the only Eurail/Interrail line straight to Ireland, too. But many odd passengers like geriatric Canadians and profs from Paris also inhabit the ship, and their company is interesting."

When you travel between the Continent and Great Britain, you may want to take the boat train. Boat trains connect specifically with ferry services, so the train waits for the boat, and vice versa, if one or the other is late. If you want to take a hydrofoil across the English Channel, remember that it doesn't run in rough weather—and the Channel seems to have a disproportionate number of gales. Work has begun on the railway section of the "Chunnel," the tunnel under the Channel, but completion is still a long way away (scheduled for 1993).

Barge trips are popular, not only on the canals of France and the Netherlands, but also in England and Sweden. The barges hold only small groups, and bicycles may be provided for exploring the countryside when the barges dock.

Cruises of the day-trip and longer variety are possible on the larger rivers of Europe, especially the Rhine and the Danube. Without a doubt, the boat ride between Mainz and Koblenz, Germany, is one of the most beautiful and most popular of all. The Cologne-Dusseldorf German Rhine Line (K-D) has an agreement with the German Federal Railway (DB) whereby you can travel one way by boat and the other by train on the same ticket: just have it validated before boarding the alternate method of transportation. K-D and other shipping companies have Rhine cruises of up to a week, taking in as many as five countries between Basel, Switzerland, and Rotterdam, the Netherlands. Local boats all along this stretch offer day and half-day trips.

It is possible to cruise the Danube River from Passau, Germany, all the way to the Black Sea, passing through seven countries. A popular stretch is Vienna-Budapest, which can be done by boat or hydrofoil. No trip to Paris would be complete without a ride on the Seine, but fewer people take the delightful trip through the locks of the St. Martin Canal.

Boats go to the Bosporus Islands at Istanbul. In Venice, *vaporetti* are the city "buses," but don't pass up at least one gondola ride (agree on the price before you embark). The coastal steamers of Norway and the lake steamers of Switzerland are first class, pass by remarkable scenery and often have very good kitchens. With a rail pass, you may be able to get reduced rates on some ferry and steamer services.

Automobiles

If tailgating at 100 miles per hour is not your fancy, don't drive on Germany's *autobahnen*. However, if you learn the rules of the road for the country you are in, you should have no major problems. Going by car is the best way to explore out-of-the-way places and to find the charming, inexpensive guest houses off the main route. If you plan to visit only the cities, a car is just a headache.

Rental cars are available everywhere. Most cars are straight shift, especially the small models. Air-conditioning is not common and is seldom necessary except in the far South in summer. Gasoline is expensive in Europe. France, Italy and Denmark have the highest prices as of this writing, Andorra and Luxembourg the lowest. However, prices may even out somewhat once the European Economic Community becomes more closely united after 1992.

Coupons giving tourists a price break in Italy and Yugoslavia are available from automobile clubs and at border crossings. In some East European countries, foreigners are required to have vouchers to buy gasoline—though in many instances gas stations will ignore this rule. The vouchers are issued at border crossings, large hotels and roadside facilities. However, this system is changing in some countries, so inquire at your travel agency or at the border. Gasoline stations are few and far between on many roads. Fill up before your tank level gets critical. Diesel is generally available, but lead-free gas is not found everywhere.

You should have an international driver's license, which can be obtained through your national automobile association. You must have an international auto insurance card to cross borders; otherwise, you will be required to buy expensive insurance for the country you are entering. Make sure this "green card" is included in your rental papers if you plan to cross borders. Few companies sell insurance to include the U.S.S.R., so you may have to purchase extra insurance at the border if you bring in a car.

In Europe, only Germany has no speed limit on its expressways. While neighboring countries have been lowering speed limits, the auto lobby in Germany has succeeded in defeating several such attempts. However, sections of the *autobahnen,* especially around large interchanges, are speed controlled. Speed limits and road laws vary by country. (See "Practical Matters: Speed Limits.") Almost everywhere, seatbelts are required, children must ride in the back seat and drunk-driving penalties are stiff. Radio stations in many countries have periodic traffic reports to give road conditions and warn of traffic jams, accidents and heavy traffic. Some car radios have the capability to switch to the traffic report, which is coded with a sound signal, even when you are listening to the tape player.

Whether you are buying a car in Europe to ship home or just renting one, drive around a bit to familiarize yourself with it and to make sure it has no obvious "bugs" before you start on a long trip. The manufacturer should include a list of service centers in Europe; the rental agency can give you addresses of its European offices. Use a reputable car-rental firm, one that won't "disappear" when you need help. If you are buying a second-hand car to resell at the end of your trip, have it checked at a garage or an automobile club service center. There are many pitfalls in buying a used car, and the money you think you will save could go down the drain if the car breaks down.

Can you imagine how a foreigner in the United States feels when she sees a street sign that says "Ped Xing"? International road signs are a boon when you don't speak the language, so familiarize yourself with them before you start out. (See "Practical Matters: International Road Signs.") Color codes are helpful, too; red is universal for "Stop." Switzerland and Germany have installed blue lights beside some traffic signals to remind motorists to switch off their engines when the light is red—an energy-saving method to cut down pollution. Colors also can be confusing, however. Blue direction signs in Germany indicate expressways, while in neighboring Switzerland, blue is used for secondary roads and green indicates expressways.

Expressways are very often of superior quality (Belgium's are even lighted), but many villages have cobblestone streets; they are treacherous when wet or icy. In Greece, many roads are made of tar and marble. In Iceland, few roads in the interior are paved and mud flaps are compulsory. Bridges there are mostly one-lane, and some rivers are unbridged. But there are free car washes at the gasoline stations!

In an effort to alleviate congestion in summer, trucks are not allowed on some countries' expressways from Friday night until Monday morning. Austria has forbidden night travel year-round by heavy trucks in an effort to curb noise in residential areas. And although expressways get you there in a hurry (except when you are caught in a traffic jam), the side roads are the scenic routes, from the wide-open spaces in Sweden to the village-every-mile in the Netherlands.

Driving laws—and manners—vary considerably. Ask the local automobile club or tourist office for the basic rules of the road. (See "Practical Matters: Automobile Clubs.") In Germany, traffic is highly disciplined; in Italy and France, it seems on the surface to be mass confusion, but it's not so bad once you get into the middle of it. Drive defensively everywhere. Use turn signals, be alert to what is going on around you and use your mirrors.

On the Continent, drive to the right. The left lanes are for passing, and if you cruise sedately along a German *autobahn* in the left lane, you will suddenly find an angry Porsche—lights flashing—on your rear bumper. European cars are capable of doing more than 120 m.p.h., and they do. It takes literally just the blink of an eye for one of those cars to appear out of nowhere, so look behind you (again) before pulling out. Whereas speed is the rule in Germany, slow is the byword in Scandinavia. Norway has a top speed of 90 k.p.h. (about 55 m.p.h.).

Driving in the British Isles is a unique experience. The British do not drive on the wrong side of the road, they drive on the other side. It takes awhile to become accustomed to driving on the left, but it is easier if you have a right-hand-drive car. Pedestrians crossing the street also have to get used to looking in the opposite direction for oncoming cars! For safety's sake, get into the habit of looking both ways before crossing.

While the cars in Germany are models of maintenance, the opposite is true in Turkey. In the cities, decrepit American automobiles vie for space with horse-drawn carts, overloaded trucks and buses—and the drivers are just as aggressive as their German counterparts. In the Netherlands, bicycles are everywhere. Some bike lanes are so large that a driver will pull onto one by mistake. When the bike lanes end in the cities, cyclists mix with the auto traffic—but they always have the right-of-way.

Belgian drivers may be the most unpredictable in Europe. The Dutch, outside their own country, often have travel trailers attached to their cars and travel in slow convoys of three to five vehicles. In the Netherlands, expressways suddenly end in traffic circles, controlled by traffic lights. The British are especially fond of traffic circles—or "roundabouts"—as a means of avoiding traffic lights and turns at intersections.

In Scandinavia, headlights must be turned on, day or night, no matter what the weather. Yellow fog lights are required in France but are illegal in Germany. Fog is a problem all over Europe and is often blamed for those spectacular seventy-car pile-ups in southern Germany. The weather is a major factor in winter driving. Snow tires or chains are required then in Scandinavia and in the Alps. A phenomenon called "black ice" is especially hazardous in Central Europe. You can't see it, you just suddenly start to slide. Farm vehicles, whether tractors or donkey carts, crawl over everything but the expressways. In Germany, military convoys often tie up even *autobahn* traffic.

Right-of-way can be a problem for anyone unused to driving in Europe. In some countries, the car entering a traffic circle has right-of-way; in others, the entering car must yield. At many intersections, there is no stop or yield sign at all; the car on the right has right-of-way. There are many pedestrian-only traffic lights: it can be disconcerting when a car pulls out in front of you, although you have a green light. Notice that the traffic light faces only the main street and has a push-button control for pedestrians wishing to cross.

Parking on the sidewalk is common practice and is permitted in the absence of no-parking signs. Be polite: leave enough space for a baby carriage or wheelchair to pass between your car and the adjacent building. Be careful when parking beside canals in Amsterdam; don't forget to put on your hand brake. The city has a special rescue team for pulling cars out of the canals.

Feeding parking meters is illegal. If the meter is limited to one hour, that's as long as you can park there. Often there is no meter, but at intervals pay-ticket machines. Buy a ticket for whatever length of time you intend to stay and put it on the dashboard. Sometimes parking is free, but time-limited. In such a case, you should have a little blue time disc to be set at the time you arrived and placed on the dash.

The *autobahnen* in Germany are free and extremely congested; in France, heavy tolls are charged for the expressways, so they are relatively clear. Italy, too, charges expressway tolls, except in the far south. Auto clubs sell packets of toll coupons for Italian and Yugoslav expressways and for some Alpine tunnels. Expressway restaurants in Germany are open twenty-four hours a day; in Austria, many close between midnight and 4:00 A.M. In Belgium, you'll be hard put to find one open before 6:00 A.M.—on weekends, 7:00 A.M.

If you drive in Austria, Switzerland, northern Italy, parts of Spain, Yugoslavia or southern France, you will be in the mountains. The main mountain roads are quite good, having lay-bys where you can pull off to enjoy the scenery. But the narrow side roads—often one-lane only—are another story. You need a small car with plenty of power to drive here. The basic rule of mountain driving is that the car coming up the mountain has right-of-way.

Keep your headlights on low beam in tunnels. The tunnels are spotless and bright in Switzerland, but in some other countries they are like driving inside jack-o-lanterns—blindingly dark with a few blobs of orange light. You must pay a toll for some of the major tunnels. (See "Practical Matters: Major Alpine Tunnels.") If crossing mountain passes is more than you want to cope with, don't turn back. At many passes, trains will ferry your car across the scariest stretches (usually through tunnels) while you sit in comfort.

Europe's automobile clubs offer on-the-road assistance. Like driving habits, the breakdown services vary by country. In Germany, the *autobahnen* are equipped with emergency phones every 2 kilometers. Arrows on black-and-white roadside poles point toward the nearest phone. These phones are monitored twenty-four hours a day, seven days a week, to coordinate radio-call cars from the country's two main auto clubs, ADAC and AvD. Other countries have roadside emergency phones at similar intervals. Major auto clubs have agreements whereby members of a club in one country are entitled to the services of a club in another country. If you are an auto club member, you may be entitled to some free emergency assistance, though you must pay for parts. Off the expressways you must find a public phone, seek help at the nearest garage or rely on a passerby to stop and help.

Most of Britain's major highways are in the industrial Midlands and most run north-south, so traveling on the secondary east-west roads can be time consuming. Roadside facilities are scarce at night and in rural areas. Emergency telephones are situated at 1-mile intervals on the motorways, with markers every 110 yards to indicate the direction of the nearest phone.

Customs vary considerably in police procedures against traffic violations. In Spain and Yugoslavia, for example, the police can collect speeding fines on the spot. In Germany, such violations as speeding and running red lights are recorded by automatic cameras— the notice of a fine reaches you as much as three months later.

When driving in Britain and Ireland, Greece, Turkey and Yugo- slavia, watch out for animals. Dogs, cows and sheep wander onto the road here almost as much as wild animals do in other countries. Near grazing lands everywhere, don't be surprised to find a herd of cows being driven down the road. If you kill a domestic animal in Britain, you must stop and notify the owner or report it to the police. This does not apply to cats or poultry, but it is an offense under the Protection of Animals Act to leave a domestic animal injured and suffering on the roadside. If your car is damaged or if anyone is injured as a result of hitting an animal, you may have a claim against the animal's owner in Britain and in some Continental countries. However, in Greece or Turkey, you will probably end up paying for the sheep if you crash into a herd crossing the road.

Equip yourself with good maps, study them carefully before starting out and refer to them often. It is difficult to drive and navigate at the same time; I like to plot my route, write down the turns and tape the directions to the dash. However, a detour or an unexpected one-way street can upset the best laid plans. In European cities, it is seldom a matter of going around the block if you miss your turn. Streets are not laid out on a grid pattern, and in some places you find yourself across town or lost in a maze of narrow, winding streets before there is a chance to turn around. Before starting out on the highways, make a mental note of the major cities in the direction you are going. You may not see a sign naming your destination until you are nearly there.

If you wish to have an automobile at your disposal but don't wish to drive, chauffeur services are available in most cities. You may be able to hire a taxi with an English-speaking driver to show you around for a few hours. In Frankfurt a.M., Germany, certain taxi drivers have been designated by the tourist office as taxi-guides. In other places the system is less formal—ask the driver if he or she speaks English and can give you a short tour.

Hitchhiking

The time-honored way for students on low budgets to get around Europe is to hitchhike. In the Soviet Union, hitchhikers pay the driver for a lift. In Poland, hitchhiking is highly organized. The hitchhiker can buy an inexpensive book of coupons to give to drivers during the season, from May 1 to September 30. Each year, the driver with the most coupons receives an award. For information, along with maps, write at least three months before your visit to Spoleczny Komitet Autostop, ul Narbutta 27a, PL-02536 Warsaw. Tel. 22-49 62 08.

If you are planning to hitchhike, invest in a guidebook especially for hitchhikers. In most countries, it is illegal to hitchhike on expressways—you must stand near the exits or try your luck at rest stops. It helps to hold up a sign indicating where you are headed. Even in Northern Europe, a woman alone hitchhiking runs a risk. In southern Italy, even two women hitchhiking together most likely will be expected to "pay" for a lift—and not with money.

Lift Centers

An alternative to hitchhiking is to pay a small fee to a lift center—an organization that gets people with cars together with people who need rides. They are popular in Central Europe, where drivers wish to have someone share the expense of a trip or just someone to talk to.

Germany has well-developed lift centers, called *Mitfahrzentrale,* with about forty offices in major cities. France has about twenty centers, most using the name *Allostop:* they are part of a nonprofit organization that collaborates with youth centers and tourist information offices. In Belgium, the centers are called *Taxistop* and in Switzerland, *Téléstop.* Centers can also be found in Austria, the Netherlands, Greece and Spain. A handbook of lift centers coded in German, French and English is available from Georg Beckmann, Belfortstrasse 55, 7800 Freiburg, West Germany.

Here's the way a lift center works. In Germany, the driver gives the center the destination, the date and time of departure, plate number and kind of car, name, address and phone number. There is no charge. The passenger pays a fee according to distance traveled. The center fixes prices, which come to about 40 percent of train fare. The passenger must fill out a form, primarily for insurance. It is also important to be precise about the amount of luggage, as there may not be much space in a small car. Centers outside Germany require the passenger to either pay a set fee for a single trip or buy a year's membership card, in addition to paying a share of the gas.

Germany also has a service called *MitFlugzentrale* allowing you to fly in private or corporate planes at a bit more than half the cost of a commercial air ticket.

Taxis and City Transport

Getting around a city is just as easy as getting around the countryside. Walking is the best way to explore, but there are times when you'll want to hop into a taxi or bus. Taxi fares vary greatly, by country and by city. In an increasing number of cities, at least some taxis accept credit cards. In Western Europe, taxis are metered; in the East, even when a taxi has a meter the driver may not turn it on. Insist the meter be used, or agree on a price before starting out. In Prague, three groups of people going from the same hotel to the same restaurant at the same time paid three different taxi fares. The group with the Czech-speaker on board paid considerably less than those relying on English and sign language.

In some East European countries, both state- and privately owned taxis operate. While prices do vary, an informal survey I conducted showed that neither was consistently the more expensive. In some of these countries, the state-owned taxis may very well be phased out in coming years. Extra charges for luggage as well as night supplements may be added to taxi fares. Finding a taxi can be a problem, too, late at night. It's best to let a hotel or restaurant call one for you. In Paris, among other places, the number of passengers per taxi is limited to three.

In Llanelli, Wales, a woman runs a women-only taxi service. At least three small towns in Germany have introduced subsidized night-taxi service for women. All over Western Europe, you'll find many women taxi drivers. I have never heard of a woman being attacked by a taxi driver in Europe, though taxi drivers of both sexes are themselves often victims of crime.

European cities and towns also have excellent public transportation systems. The Paris Métro is justly famous, but the city also has good bus service, and the same ticket can be used for both. Buy the green *Le Guide Paris Bus* at tourist offices or bookshops and see the sights as you travel across town.

From the three-line Metro in Budapest to the huge networks in London and Paris, the system for riding is the same. Find the place you are and the place you want to go on the color-coded map. Follow the route with your finger to see where you need to change. To be sure you are heading in the right direction, check the name of the line's end station as well as the line number. If you have trouble reading the station names (they're in Cyrillic in Moscow), count the number of stops to the place you change or get off.

Even small cities have buses, trolley buses or streetcars. If you are unsure which line to use, ask for advice at your hotel. If you plan to be out late at night, find out when the public transport system shuts down. Most city public transport doesn't run, or has very limited service, between about midnight and 5:00 A.M.

Tourist tickets for public transport take a variety of forms. Paris has the *Paris Sesame pass,* which gives unlimited travel on the Métro and buses for two, four or seven days. It is rather expensive, so if you aren't planning much travel you may find the *carnet* of ten tickets a better buy. In Munich, as in many other cities, you can buy a *24-Hour Ticket* from the ticket automats. Scandinavian cities often sell "city passes," which include public transport, museum entry and various shopping perks.

Penalties are stiff for riding without a ticket, whether the system operates on the honor system or not. In Paris, you must put your ticket into the turnstile before it will turn. In London, a gate guard often checks your ticket as you exit the station. In Germany, you ride on your honor, but spot checks are made on all city and suburban transport and you pay a large fine if you don't have a valid ticket. Certainly, you see many people boarding the underground without stopping to buy a ticket from the automat, but in most cases they have month-long commuter passes.

A confusing situation for tourists exists in places where city and suburban trains run along the same routes as long-distance trains. A friend told me this story: "The guidebook said I could buy my ticket on board the train, but when the man I thought was the conductor came along, he fined me for not having a ticket—60 German marks— and the ticket should have cost less than 10 marks." She had simply boarded the first available train heading where she wanted to go and hadn't been able to read the signs (in German only) posted on the train windows that said, "Board only with valid ticket." She had boarded a suburban train instead of a long-distance one. If you are uncertain what kind of train you are boarding, either get your ticket first or ask someone what kind of train it is.

In Turkey, the *dolmus,* a shared taxi, is a good method of transportation and cheaper than a normal taxi—if you can figure out the routing scheme. Many places have nostalgic horse-drawn carriages—the *fiaker* in Vienna, for example—not so much for getting around as for sightseeing.

Bicycles

Bicycle touring is popular in Europe; one even sees a surprising number of bicyclists working their way up the mountains of Switzerland

and Austria. Mountain bikes are for rent at a number of Alpine resorts. Organized bicycle tours are available through travel agencies. If you want to go on your own, bikes can be carried aboard buses and subways and shipped in the luggage cars of trains. Bicycles are for rent at many railway stations, with preferential rates for persons holding railway tickets. Bike rental shops abound. The Netherlands, without a doubt, is the number one bicycle country, but many other countries also have marked cycle paths. Local tourist offices can provide information about bicycle trails in the area.

Walking

Like bicycle trails, wandering and hiking trails are well marked in the European countryside. Tourist information offices and shops can supply large-scale maps of their regions. "Wandering without a pack" vacation packages are popular; you walk from hotel to hotel, and the tourist office or other organizer transports your luggage. Accommodations for such holidays range from farm houses to hostels to castle hotels.

Dedicated mountain hikers will take to the Alps, where accommodation in Alpine huts costs just a few dollars a night. Many areas are so wild, however, that it is advisable to hike only with a professional mountain guide. Information is available from tourist offices and Alpine clubs. Many Alpine resorts sponsor short "wanderings" in which you receive souvenir pins for the treks.

The *volksmarsch* is a popular pastime in Germany and has spilled over to other countries. The sponsored "marches" are announced in the press; just show up, complete the 10-, 20- or 30-kilometer route, checking in at the "stations" along the way, and collect your souvenir pin or plate at the end.

Crossing Borders

The borders separating countries of the European Economic Community will be "erased" at the end of 1992, as far as tourist crossings are concerned. Crossing into East European countries is also becoming easier. Already, it is possible to go from Belgium into the Netherlands without realizing you have changed countries. Border stations are still manned at the French-German border, for example, but the officers seldom do more than wave you through when you are driving. Even so, during peak vacation times there can be waits of several hours at highway border crossings, and the occasional truckers' blockade (most often at the Italian border) makes crossing well-nigh impossible.

On trains, guards come through checking passports, and customs officials take random looks at the luggage; at airports you must at least walk through the checkpoints. It is a good idea to know what you are permitted to take duty-free across borders. Most common limits are a liter of liquor, two liters of wine, a carton of cigarettes and a few ounces of perfume. It is illegal to take antiques and artworks out of some countries without a certificate.

While customs officials aren't too concerned about rooting out that extra bottle of wine, they do check closely for drugs. They are adept at spotting hiding places, and they have trained dogs to help. I was once on a train that was delayed for more than an hour while the drug team took the cars apart, from the couplings to the light fixtures. If you are arrested on drug charges, don't expect help from your embassy.

Take care of your passport and be sure it is up-to-date. Should it expire while you are abroad, go to your nearest consulate for renewal. Some countries require that your passport be valid for at least six months after your entry. In most of Western Europe, visas are not required for Americans, even though the United States still requires visas for most Europeans. You will probably have to ask for a stamp in your passport if you want one as a souvenir. Liechtenstein charges for the stamp, which you get at the tourist office.

In 1990, Czechoslovakia and Yugoslavia dropped their visa requirements for both U.S. and Canadian citizens. Hungary and Bulgaria dropped their visa requirement for U.S. citizens but not for Canadians. Americans can get visas at the Romanian border, and Canadians can get visas at all Bulgarian borders and at the Hungarian borders except on board trains. Bulgaria, Poland and the U.S.S.R. still require Americans to get visas in advance, but changes may take place here too. It's a good idea, nevertheless, to bring along a few extra passport photos. If you don't need them for visas, you might need them for ski lift passes. Instant photo machines can be found in many railway stations.

Crossing into some of the East European countries, once a time-consuming process, soon should be little different from crossing Western borders. The guards manning the passport stations in the U.S.S.R. still proceed with deliberation, but most people go through without a hitch. Be patient, be polite and you won't have any trouble.

Tourist Offices

Throughout this book, I have advised using tourist offices for information and help. They are wonderful sources of information, most of which is free. Almost every country has at least one tourist office in every other county. In addition, there are many regional and local tourist offices.

The tourist office is a good first stop to make in every town you visit. Local tourist offices are usually found in or near main railway stations, in airports and at strategic highway stops. They may be open every day of the year in the big cities or only in high season or for abbreviated hours in small towns. They offer a variety of services: brochures, guide-hire, sightseeing tours, money-changing and hotel booking, though not every tourist office offers every service. Most have employees who speak a bit of English, and in many places they speak it very well.

Before you leave home, get in touch with the national tourist offices of the countries you plan to visit. (See "Practical Matters: Tourist Offices.") Ask for hotel and restaurant listings, museum listings, maps, off-season specials, calendars of events or information about your favorite sport. Be specific about what you want, or you will receive just a few brochures that speak in glittering generalities.

Travel Agents

A wealth of information is available at travel agencies. Whether you want to book your entire tour or simply buy a rail pass or reserve your plane seat, a travel agent can help you. Shop around for the agency that suits you; in these days of specialization, many different kinds of agencies are available. Some specialize in adventure trips and others in cultural programs, for example. Most agencies are computerized and should be able to answer your basic questions. But if you find an agent you really like, one who is full of good advice and seems concerned to help, you can develop a rapport that will be invaluable.

9

SPECIALTY VACATIONS

Meeting People Who Share Your Interests

You can come to Europe just to wander around and see the sights, but if you have a particular interest or hobby, there are plenty of activities for you to pursue. Tell your travel agent or the tourist office what you would like to do, and most likely you will be inundated with possibilities. Here is a small selection of specialty vacations that may suit your fancy.

Schools

Choose from language courses, cooking schools, folk-dance classes or handicraft classes. They may be taught in real schools or may be informal instruction with more or less serious intent. I spent three weeks "learning" German in Salzburg and emerged with little to show for my time. The "school" seemed more interested in selling its weekend excursions than in teaching the language. However, there are good schools. Among the old reliables are the Goethe Institute for German (Postfach 20 01 009, W-8000 Munich 2) and L'Alliance Française for French (101 Boulevard Raspail, F-75270 Paris). Many travel agencies offer holiday language-study tours. Before selecting a language course, send away for a selection of brochures and study them critically. American students are eligible for Junior Year Abroad and similar programs through many European universities.

In almost every country there are cooking schools for the national cuisine, from weekend look-and-learn classes to serious hands-on courses running several months. Wine appreciation seminars are popular in wine-producing regions. In Paris, you can make guided early-morning visits to markets or go behind-the-scenes at bakeries, cheese shops and restaurant kitchens.

Handicraft courses run the gamut from weaving in Denmark, to spinning in Hungary, to pottery-making in England, to woodcarving in Germany. Often the tourist office of a small town will set up a couple of classes a year with a local craftsperson. In other cases, craftsmen's associations organize learning vacations. For example, the Association of British Craftsmen has learning weeks for ceramics, glass-blowing, batik, blacksmithing, furniture restoration, etc. Lodging is offered in thatched cottages or converted pubs and such in picturesque corners of the country. The Swiss National Tourist Office has a brochure listing a variety of handicraft courses available. Most national tourist offices can provide such information.

Almost every ski resort has a ski school, and many have ski kindergartens for the very young. Coastal and lake resorts offer windsurfing and sailing lessons; mountain regions have hang-gliding and mountain-climbing courses. In both Yugoslavia and Hungary, you can learn to ride the famous Lipizzaner horses. Tennis and riding lessons are almost universal.

Sports Vacations

If you don't need lessons but wish to practice a sport, there is no problem finding places to ski or sail, canoe or go white-water rafting, dive and snorkel, make photo safaris or hunt. Golf is especially good in

Scotland and Portugal. Sunningdale Golf Course in England has a women-only course (it's called the Ladies' Course) in addition to its regular course, which is also open to women. The tourist office of Upper Austria has vacation packages for singles, called "Go Solo," which include horseback riding, dance weeks, tennis, hiking, golf and bicycling.

Resorts usually offer sports-week packages to include hotel, meals, equipment rental, guides in the case of hiking or climbing and use of tennis courts and golf courses, swimming pool, etc. Dedicated skiers can ski on glaciers in summer at certain resorts, mostly in Austria and Switzerland. Sweden has "Midnight Sun" skiing in summer.

Holiday Clubs

If you like the enclosed atmosphere of a club, several organizations operate within Europe. Club Med and Robinson Club are two well known ones. The travel agent Transalpino, which specializes in trips for the under-twenty-six crowd, has clubs for this age group. Clubs are strong on organized sports, beaches and discos, weak on sightseeing and meeting local people.

Nostalgia Trips

Traveling across Europe on the revitalized Orient Express is just one example (and an expensive one) of the train nostalgia sweeping Europe. Actually, two different Orient Expresses are running. The Nostalgic Orient Express, operated by a Swiss firm, makes the Paris-Istanbul run. The Venice-Simplon Orient Express, operated from London, travels London-Paris-Venice in summer and does day-trips from London into the English countryside.

Spain has its own nostalgia train, the Transcantabrio, which travels June through September some 625 miles along the northern coast between Léon and El Ferrol. It is a narrow-gauge train with veteran rolling stock, fitted out with air-conditioning, showers and a lounge. Breakfast is served on the train; other meals are taken at inns and restaurants along the way. A bus tags along to take passengers on excursions and on to Santiago de Compostela at the end of the trip. The luxurious Al-Andalus Expreso operates a circular tour in the deep south of Spain: Málaga-Granada-Córdoba-Sevilla-Jarez de la Frontera.

Austria has a summertime Danube Nostalgia Express that combines a paddle-wheel steamboat and historic train on the route Passau-Linz-Vienna.

Steam train clubs throughout Europe organize hundreds of short trips, usually in summer and on weekends. The Great Little Trains of Wales are lovingly preserved narrow-gauge steam trains traveling on ten lines. Volunteers keep the trains' brass fittings and lamps polished and the pretty stations spotless. They serve wine, beer and snacks in the buffet cars. Five of the ten lines are linked by the regular British Rail service that follows the spectacular Cambrian Coast route. A Great Little Train Wanderer Ticket is good for travel on eight of the lines on eight consecutive days.

Several spectacular scenic routes are available on the Continent as part of the regular rail service. The Glacier Express travels across the bottom of Switzerland between two leading ski resorts, Zermatt and St. Moritz. It is billed as the slowest express train in the world. The trip lasts all day; make reservations for the dining car. The train now runs year-round, thanks to the Furka Pass Tunnel that bypasses the Rhone Glacier. If you want to see the glacier, you can break the trip at Gletsch in summer and make an excursion by postal bus. The Bernina Express (you can connect from the Glacier Express), which runs between Chur, Switzerland, and Tirano, Italy, covers some of the most spectacular mountain scenery in Europe.

Switzerland again offers superb mountain views between Montreux and Lenk aboard the Super-Panorama-Express. Glass-domed cars cover the stretch in summer only. The William Tell Express is a combination paddle-wheel lake steamer and parlor-car train trip that runs between Lucerne and Lugano. It travels both directions daily from mid-May to mid-October. The Trans-Siberian Railway links Moscow and Khabarovsk in Soviet East Asia. It is a very long journey, so the Soviet travel agency Intourist organizes piece-meal rail trips along selected stretches combined with air transport, adding tours and excursions along the way. Visits in China and Japan can also be combined with a Trans-Siberian trip.

Nostalgia trips need not be only by train. If you wish to slow your pace, covered wagon/gypsy wagon/horse-drawn carriage trips are available in Germany, the Netherlands, Ireland, France, Greece, Hungary, Poland and Yugoslavia. A Swiss firm specializes in mule safaris. Ballooning is especially popular in France, Switzerland, Austria, Sweden, England and Germany's Black Forest. You can choose a package to include hotel, meals and sightseeing, or book just a single flight.

Staying on Farms and in Castles

Almost every country offers farm house vacations, and they are becoming more popular every year, especially for families with children. However, they also attract many singles who enjoy the outdoors. The advantages are the price (usually low), the peace and quiet (no, you don't have to help with the chores) and the personal contact (it's easy to become friends with the farm family). If you have a car, there is no problem making a farm house your base and exploring the countryside. Most farms are within easy reach of public transportation, but when selecting a farm house be sure to ask how far you must walk to the nearest bus stop.

Also, pay close attention to the facilities offered: rooms range from bare bed and cold running water to positively luxurious apartments outfitted with kitchen, bath and toilet. If you demand absolute peace and quiet, choose a family without children. If you are traveling with your child, choose a family with children in the same age group.

At the other end of the spectrum are vacations in castles. Germany, France, England and Ireland are especially strong on castle packages, and Hungary recently began promoting castle hotels. Denmark has a number of manor house hotels. In Spain and Portugal, many *paradors* and *pousadas* are castles or mansions.

The German organization *Gast im Schloss* (Guest in a Castle) has more than fifty member-hotels, including one each in Austria, the Netherlands, Sweden and Switzerland. It offers single nights or packages such as "walking without a pack" from castle to castle in either the Neckar River Valley or the land of the Brothers Grimm. Other packages include stays in moated castles and stays in castles on the Fairy Tale Road.

The French group *Relais & Chateaux* has castle and coach house hotels in fifteen European countries. You can also camp at nearly fifty castles in France. They are listed in the brochure "Castles & Camping-Caravaning," available from the French National Tourist Office or from the CCC Secretariat, B.P. 301, F-56007 Vannes, France.

Meet the People

It is easy to organize groups—study tours, seminars—for discussions of shared interests, but it is more difficult for the single traveler to make such contacts. However, a number of organizations and tourist offices provide such services. For example, the Danish Tourist Office can tell you which towns have *Meet-the-Danes* programs. Once in town, you can arrange to have dinner or coffee with a Dane who shares your interest, whether it be profession or hobby.

Zurich sponsors a *Meet-the-Swiss* program; the tourist office keeps a list of English-speaking people who will show you around. Frankfurt a.M., Germany, also has a *Friends' Circle:* telephone 069-47 93 61 or 069-58 39 22 and make an appointment with someone who will show you the city. The U.S.S.R. has *The Land and the People* programs available through Intourist that offer a chance to visit in local homes.

Women traveling on their own in England can get in touch with *Women Welcome Women,* a service begun by Frances Alexander in 1984 to put women with similar interests in touch. In Germany, *We Travel Together* operates for single travelers. It publishes a monthly newsletter filled with advertisements of singles looking for traveling companions (see pages 12, 124). Two Turkish women operate a travel agency in Istanbul that specializes in getting Turkish and foreign women together. Programs are geared to cultural, political or religious interests, as well as handicrafts courses and sports.

Women's bookstores, cafes and activity centers are popular, not only in big cities but in some smaller communities as well. (See "Practical Matters: Women's Hotels, Cafes, Centers, Groups and Travel Agencies.") Bookstores at railway stations and airports most likely will have local publications that list such addresses: several cities now have their own women's handbooks.

Sections of interest to women are included in the German-published *Anders Reisen* guidebook series (in German only), designed for alternative travel—whether political, religious or sexual. *Contacts,* published in France, contains 3,000 useful French addresses under such topics as women, health, culture and senior citizens. Listings of interest to women can be found in the local press, alternative press and telephone-book yellow pages. Services for women are varied, being best in the North and dwindling away as you move South and East.

Working Holidays

If your budget is strained or if you just want to lend a helping hand, working vacations can be good experiences. Most vacation jobs are low-paid or volunteer, but may provide room and board. They range from *au pair* and domestic help to work in vineyards, assisting the handicapped, joining conservation camps or going on archaeological digs. A plethora of guidebooks is available. One of the most comprehensive to finding vacation work worldwide is *Working Holidays,* a book nearing its fifth decade of yearly editions, sold by the Central Bureau for Educational Visits and Exchanges, Seymour Mews, London W1H 9PE, England.

Traveling with Children

Seeing Europe with children is such a large subject that it deserves—and has—guidebooks of its own. All sorts of activities are available, both parent-child and for children to enjoy by themselves. Possibilities range from ski kindergartens to youth camps to pony farms. There are even children's hotels that provide special facilities and programs for children. Austria is especially strong in this area; a booklet from the tourist office lists more than fifty *kinderhotels.*

Tourist offices can advise you about which hotels welcome children. For example, the Swiss publish a leaflet listing hotels suitable for families. Some of these have supervised playrooms, children's menus and organized family activities. Most hotels in Europe offer reduced rates for children staying in the parents' room and a few have off-season reductions on separate rooms for the children. Children under age three or four usually stay in hotels free, but there is a charge for putting a crib in the room.

Some trains in France have nurseries on board and children's menus in the restaurant cars, and you can arrange for children from four months to fourteen years to travel in the care of a hostess. A few German trains now include playrooms. The railways of many countries have family tickets. Inquire at the ticket office or at your travel agency, since offers change continually. Most public transport has space to accommodate strollers and baby carriages, and almost always people will help you put them aboard. If you are driving, children should sit in the back seat (that's the law in many countries), with safety seats for tots.

In Germany, it sometimes seems that dogs are more welcome than children in restaurants. The Germans look on eating out as an adult privilege and quite a number of restaurants do not provide highchairs. If you are traveling in Germany with a young child, it might repay you to bring along a collapsible seat that snaps onto the table. In France and Italy, on the other hand, children are not only welcomed, they are fussed over. They are integrated into adult mealtime very early; don't be shocked to see a child given a glass of wine—well watered down. Water is pure in most places, but if you have your doubts, stick to bottled or boiled water. Off the beaten track, it's a good idea to use canned rather than fresh milk.

Every country has its parks and playgrounds; small ones may be found at hotels and roadside rest stops. There are hundreds of amusement parks. *Legoland* in Billund, Denmark, is a world built of Lego plastic blocks. Miniature towns include *Maudurodam* in the Netherlands and *Catalonia in Miniature* near Barcelona, Spain. *Brupark*, just completed in Brussels, features an entire *Mini-Europe*. In addition, there are plenty of open-air museums where full-size houses or whole villages from the past have been preserved and handicrafts are demonstrated by people wearing traditional costume.

The Salzburg (Austria) Marionette Theater is just one of many marionette and puppet shows in Europe; it produces primarily operas with a strong repertoire of Mozart. The Guignol Shows of France are earthier; Lyon has a permanent Guignol Theater. Many cities have children's and young people's theaters—don't worry that the language is strange; the action says enough. For the young shopper, an Austrian toy factory invites children on a tour of the premises. And don't forget the circuses and zoos and animal parks everywhere.

Traveling with Pets

Chances are, you will find a pet-sitter or leave your pet in a boarding kennel, but just in case you want to bring Fido along, you should be aware of some regulations. Quarantine laws are toughest in Great Britain, where every animal is held for six months. Rabies has been wiped out there, and the British want to keep it that way.

In all cases, you need proof of inoculations for your pet, and you should be aware that, while animals are allowed on most public transportation, you must pay for their rides as well as yours. Many hotels and restaurants allow pets inside, but not all do, so inquire before making reservations. Shops that require animals to remain outside usually provide hooks where you can attach the leash. A few also set out bowls of water. If you plan to travel with a pet, get specific information from the tourist office or your travel agent.

Travel for the Elderly

Not only students get breaks for travel in Europe: senior citizens and retired persons also qualify for reduced prices. The minimum age is usually sixty or sixty-five, but can be as young as fifty-six. Show proof of age to get reductions on public transportation and entry to museums. Sometimes hotels and resorts offer low-rate packages for seniors, but, like the specials for singles, they are usually in the off-season.

Nudist Vacations

Nudism, called *FKK* (for *Frei Korper Kulture,* that is, Free Body Culture) is accepted—and popular—in Europe. Tourist offices publish guides to nudist resorts and travel agents offer nudist vacation packages. Nudist beaches are found as far north as Finland (that beach, near the port city Turku, was established by Swedes) and as far south as you can go. Yugoslavia is the leader in nudist resorts; in fact, it has been called one great nudist beach. Actually, the nudist beaches are set apart, but few people complain about toplessness on regular beaches. Topless is also accepted at beaches in southern France and northern Germany. Greece, however, suppressed nudism for years. Recently, the tourist industry succeeded in establishing a few nudist bathing centers, but some local police officers and judges remain dedicated anti-nudists. Check out the local practice before you doff your swimsuit—the places where nudism can be practiced tend to shift from season to season.

10

THE
TRAVELING
BUSINESSWOMAN

Although the number of women business travelers has sharply increased in recent years, men still far outnumber women as business travelers in Europe. Most of Europe has accepted the traveling businesswoman, but she is still a rarity in such places as eastern Turkey. How well she is accepted may be more a matter of the attitude of the company or profession than the country. Often there are obstacles to overcome; the best approach is a positive, self-assured demeanor.

In the past few years, businesswomen have begun to get together to compare experiences and share insights into their particular problems and achievements as business travelers. One such group is the Businesswoman's Travel Club, Ltd., in London, coordinated by Trisha Cochrane. Members receive a monthly newsletter and may participate in networking by providing information about cities or areas they are familiar with and by requesting information about new places they are planning to visit. (See "Practical Matters: Women's Hotels, Cafes, Centers, Groups and Travel Agencies.")

Understanding the customs of the country where you are working will smooth your way in the business world as well as in social situations. Rule number one is to know your subject well and know how it is treated in the country you are visiting. Develop a thorough understanding of the political situation of the country to avoid making remarks that could threaten your business success. Do your homework before you go. You can often get good information from the chambers of commerce of the country or city you will be visiting and from the commercial services of your own consulate.

Women have made some headway in business in Germany; about three-quarters of all new businesses are started by women, and a number of high government posts are held by women. Switzerland is still rather grim; women there haven't even had the vote for very long. On the other hand, Finland was the first country to grant women suffrage, and it is still at the forefront of equality. Scandinavia in general accepts the businesswoman as the norm. The situation is also good in France, where women head numerous corporations; even though male executives are gallant to the point of flirting, they are seldom condescending. However, men are much more chauvinistic in Italy, Greece and the Iberian Peninsula. Women are making more headway in parts of Turkey.

Businesswomen are accepted very well in Eastern Europe, except for Romania. The style of doing business here is still a bit waterlogged in red tape and tedious negotiations. You may find it better to telephone or telex your business contacts, rather than to write letters. Also, don't be surprised if your business partner asks rather personal questions about your income and life style (modesty is advisable).

Be professional in your dress. Clothes do make the first impression. Choose clothing suitable for the country—darker colors and skirts instead of slacks in the South and East. It is not necessary to try to dress like a man: that tailored "dress-for-success" suit will look terribly provincial in Paris. Some women prefer to carry briefcases instead of handbags, while others carry both. It's a matter of personal taste—and how much you have to carry. I often use a large, expandable briefcase and keep a small handbag inside it. That way, when I am in a hurry for a dinner appointment after a long day of meetings, I simply fling the briefcase into my hotel room, grab my bag and go.

Courtesy demands that you make appointments to conduct business; don't just drop in. Even if you are "passing through" and wish to make a quick call on a business partner, telephone first. Punctuality is important. If you are delayed or must cancel an appointment, telephone as soon as possible.

Observe office hours, which vary by country. Work may begin as early as 7:00 A.M., but the usual day starts at 8:30 or 9:00 A.M. Don't make appointments at lunchtime unless it's for lunch: for example, avoid the period 2:00 to 4:00 P.M. in Spain. Lunch breaks last from thirty minutes (Scandinavia) to three hours (Spain and France). Government offices, especially, may close early in the afternoon, and in many countries offices of all kinds may close early on Friday. Check the local holidays when you plan your trip; local or regional holiday closings can throw off your entire schedule. Almost everywhere, it is advisable not to plan a business trip at the Christmas/New Year's season, during Easter week (it's later in Greece, remember) or during the summer vacation season, generally July and August.

Letters of introduction are often a help, but are seldom absolutely necessary. Business cards, however, are especially useful in foreign countries where you and your business partners may have trouble with pronunciation and spelling of names and addresses. In Europe, the common practice is to print both your business and private addresses and telephone numbers on the card. You may prefer to use only your business address. If you wish to give someone your private address, you can write it on the card or carry personal cards, as well. It is a good idea to have your academic degrees printed on your cards, a common practice in Germanic countries. You may also wish to have cards printed in the language of the country you are visiting, a special courtesy that may well promote your business interests. In a few countries—Portugal, for example—only executives on the higher levels have cards.

Shake hands when you say hello and again when you leave. It is courteous to address your business partners by name (although in France, simply *madame* or *monsieur* is enough), but avoid first-name basis unless you are also close friends. Europeans are much more formal in this respect than Americans. An exception is Iceland, where the first name is the usual form of address.

Expect to exchange courtesies and small-talk before getting down to business. The length of such an exchange varies by country. Familiarize yourself with the local habits, and take a hint from the conversation of your business partner. In many countries, you'll be offered coffee or a drink before the business discussions begin. It is courteous to accept; if you don't want to drink alcohol, there is seldom an objection when you ask for coffee, juice or water. If the host insists, you may use the excuse that you are driving.

You probably will be invited to business lunches or dinners, though the Italians say there's no such thing as a business lunch: "You don't get any work done and you don't enjoy the meal either." These meals often start with an aperitif, when a toast is drunk. Don't take a sip before the toast is made, and return the toast when appropriate. The mealtime conversation may be of a general nature until coffee is served, a signal for the "business" to begin.

If you plan to host a business meal, remember that some businessmen have problems allowing women to pay for their meals. You can avoid an embarrassing situation either by making it clear that this is a business lunch and the company is paying for it or by discreetly arranging with the waiter to give the bill to you. In some restaurants, the waiter automatically gives the bill to the man, so make it clear that you are paying. Occasionally, when no signal is given, the waiter puts the bill in the middle of the table. If a man insists upon paying for your meal when you feel Dutch-treat is more appropriate, you may try the approach, "You may offer me a drink, but I always pay for my own meals." However, an invitation to a meal usually means that the person who invites pays. Waiters are learning to ask who will take the wine list and who will taste the wine, rather than assuming that the man will. If your dinner partner is more familiar with the regional wines than you are, let him or her make the choice, or ask for advice, but don't hesitate to choose yourself if you prefer.

Presenting flowers or a small gift to business partners is commonly done in European business circles. Each situation must be judged on its own merits, but refusing a gift can be extremely discourteous, so accept small gifts graciously. You should be prepared to reciprocate with a token from your company or a typical souvenir from your town or region. If you are invited to a colleague's home, always take a gift of flowers, wine or candy.

There are times when a man will take advantage of a business situation to make advances. More than once, I have found myself confronted by an amorous man in a car or private office—and this happens no more often in the South and East than in Central Europe. Be firm, be cool, be icy. Make it plain that you are there for business and business only. If the situation threatens to get out of control, let the man know that you will not hesitate to call for help. A scene will be worse for him than for you, so stand your ground.

A more common problem, however, is the "macho" man who condescends to businesswomen. Even unintentionally, his words and actions betray an attitude of superiority. When possible, correct him—tact goes a long way. In interviewing for this book, I corrected one man at least six times for talking about "girls." We parted friends, and he later wrote to me, "I will forever remember the difference between your girls, ladies and women." If you have no opportunity to make a comment, simply doing your job well may help correct his attitude. Once, on the third day of a group business trip, a man looked at me in surprise and said, "You really are serious about your work, aren't you!"

In most countries, you can find facilities to help you get your work done. If you do not wish to carry a portable typewriter or laptop computer, many hotels catering to business people provide them. If you do bring yours along, you may have a problem with the electrical current (the difference in electrical cycles may cause a glitch even if you have a converter). Battery-operated models are the most practical for travel. Secretarial, translation and interpreting services are also available, either through hotels or offices in town. Telex and telefax services are offered by many hotels and post offices.

When you travel on an expense account, you need to know how to ask for a receipt. This normal request can produce some surprising reactions. I was taken aback when a taxi driver once flatly refused to give me a receipt; then I realized he had no receipt forms. Since that time, I carry a few blank receipts with me. As a businesswoman, you may find it more convenient and appropriate to use a chain hotel catering to business people than a quaint pension. Many such hotels have begun to realize that businesswomen are an important force and are providing rooms decorated and outfitted for women. However, as one traveling woman put it, "They don't have to paint the rooms pink. A security chain on the door is more important."

A few hotels have introduced women-only floors; others give women rooms near the elevator so they don't have to walk down a long hall past many doors. A few have set aside a "travelers' table" for single business people who would like to share conversation without looking for a pick-up. And bravo to the bartenders who tactfully assist women in guarding their rights to have a drink without being pestered.

11

WHAT IF THE WORST HAPPENS?

Coping with Sickness, Accidents and Crime

The most common travel-health complaints that I hear about are diarrhea and constipation, which seem to result from a combination of stress and fatigue. With the idea that prevention is preferable to cure, I once asked a doctor for pills to prevent diarrhea. He told me I should wait to see if I got sick, and then worry about it. I didn't get sick.

Taking care of yourself is the first step to healthy travel. Pay close attention to sanitation. Realize that you don't have to eat a huge meal every day just because the food is delicious. A sudden change in eating habits will probably affect your system. If you are not used to highly seasoned food, the spice of Hungary may cause stomach rumbles. The opposite can also happen. I moved to Germany, where the food is bland, from hot-and-spicy New

Orleans and my intestinal tract rebelled.

Don't be afraid of the local cooking, but do make a special effort to eat well-balanced meals while on the road. Wash and peel fruit; salads are usually safe to eat, especially in Central and Northern Europe. Water, too, is usually safe, though I have known ecology-conscious waitresses in Germany to refuse to serve tap water because "it isn't healthy." However, don't even brush your teeth with Leningrad water or you will likely get the Czar's Revenge.

Medical Kit

Anticipate what you may need and pack a small medical kit accordingly. Aspirin, nose drops, cough drops and cold medication can be included, along with hydrogen peroxide and a few bandages for cuts and scrapes. Bring insect repellent in summer (Denmark is plagued by tiny black flies) and sunscreen for summer in the South and winter on the ski slopes.

If you feel ill but haven't brought what you need, go to a pharmacy and explain your symptoms. The pharmacist may be able to give you an over-the-counter preparation. European pharmacies are not like American drugstores. They do not sell beer, beach balls, cosmetics and paperback books; they sell medicine. Almost everywhere, pharmacies take turns providing twenty-four-hour emergency service. The shops post the name and address of the on-duty pharmacy in their windows, or the on-duty pharmacies may be listed in the local newspaper. The concierge at the hotel can help you, too. If you are so ill that a visit to the pharmacy will not suffice, turn to the hotel for help. If there is no house doctor, the hotel can reach one or at least recommend one for you.

Medical Information

A reliable network of English-speaking physicians in more than 140 countries is International Association of Medical Assistance for Travelers (IAMAT), Dept. TH, 736 Center Street, Lewiston, NY 14092; tel. (716) 754-4883. Contact the organization for listings before you leave home. Other travel-health organizations include:

Worldcare Travel Assistance Association, 5249 Duke Street, Suite 105, Alexandria, VA 22304; tel. (703) 823-4800.

International SOS Assistance, P.O. Box 11568, Philadelphia, PA 19116; tel. (215) 244-1500. This company is also responsible for the Safe Travel Network operated by Bank of America for purchasers of its traveler's checks.

Travel Assistance International, 1133 15th Street, N.W., Suite 400, Washington, DC 20005; tel. (202) 347-2025 or 2027. This American subsidiary of the Paris-based Europe Assistance is tied in with Carefree Insurance.

World Access Inc., 1825 I Street, N.W., Suite 200, Washington, DC 20006; tel. (202) 822-3978.

American Express Company offers a medical and legal referral service, called Global Assist, to its Gold and Platinum Card members without additional charge.

Access America Hotline, operated by American Travel Insurance, offers a brochure through travel agencies on health conditions overseas. For information, telephone toll-free (800) 284-8300 or send a postcard to Access America, 600 Third Avenue, Box 807, New York, NY 10163.

Should you become ill after you return home, or if symptoms of illness persist, tell your doctor where and when you traveled, even if considerable time has elapsed. Be especially wary of lingering symptoms such as persistent diarrhea, swollen glands, skin rashes and fever. A pioneer program of travel health care has been introduced by International Health-Care Service of the New York City Hospital-Cornell Medical Center. Specific tests are given, or you can participate in the complete pre- and post-travel illness-prevention program. For information about services and fees, contact the center at 440 East 69th Street, New York, NY 10021; tel. (212) 746-5454. In the same area, services are available from the Travel and Immunization Center of Long Island Jewish Hillside Medical Center in New Hyde Park, Queens, NY 11042; tel. (718) 470-7290. Elsewhere, get in touch with your local hospital or public health department.

Contagious Diseases

Travelers no longer need to get a battery of vaccinations before boarding the plane to Europe. However, it is important to remember that some serious contagious diseases do exist and to take reasonable precautions. For travel in developed countries, simply make sure that your tetanus/diphtheria booster vaccination is up-to-date. You may also want to be immunized against influenza. If you plan to travel in areas where purity of food and of water are questionable, take precautions against hepatitis. There may be a risk of malaria March through October in some parts of Turkey, particularly in southeast Anatolia.

Disease-bearing ticks cause occasional problems in Austria and southern Germany. Rabies has not been wiped out on Continental Europe, so use caution if you go hiking or walking, and avoid playing with strange animals running loose on the streets. The most frightening contagious disease today is AIDS. While it hasn't reached the proportions in Europe that it has in America, the number of victims is increasing. And while the main focus today is on AIDS, remember that venereal diseases such as gonorrhea, syphilis and herpes are still a very real threat. Travel romances are especially risky. If you decide to take a chance, insist on condoms. Provide them yourself if need be. They are for sale in automats in some women's toilets now, as well as at pharmacies.

Chronic Illness

Having a chronic illness—heart disease, diabetes or respiratory illness—need not keep you at home. You will have to plan your trip thoroughly, but you can still enjoy travel. Get the name and address of an English-speaking doctor where you are going. Take along a brief medical history and a description of your illness in the language of the country you are visiting. Take along more than enough medication as well as both its brand name and its generic name. Carry the medicine in your hand luggage in case your checked luggage is lost. If you are dependent on eyeglasses, carry a spare pair and a copy of your prescription.

If you have heart disease, avoid high altitudes and strenuous activities. If you wear a pacemaker, inform security guards at airports, since the metal can trigger the alarms. Respiratory illness may be aggravated by changes in location (the air pollutants also change) and by the pressure in airplane cabins. If you have diabetes, ask your doctor to help you plan your insulin schedule, taking into consideration the time zones you must cross. In every case, discuss your trip plans with your doctor.

More and more attention is being paid by the travel industry to the needs of physically handicapped persons. Wheelchair ramps have been built. Elevators, toilets and phone booths can accommodate wheelchairs. A few trains have lifts for wheelchairs. Many gentle walking trails are suitable for wheelchairs. Hotels may provide dietary meals and will give you rooms on lower floors on request. Of course, not all these facilities are available everywhere. Tourist offices can provide pamphlets with special information for the handicapped. A good contact is the Society for the Advancement of Travel for the Handicapped, 26 Court Street, Brooklyn, NY 11242.

Insurance

Medical care in most of Europe is subsidized—for Europeans. Without European insurance, you are expected to pay cash. A colleague, taken ill in Switzerland, went to the local hospital. Almost immediately, he was ushered into a room for a pretreatment interview.

"What do you have?" asked the attendant.
"I don't know," he said. "My throat is so swollen that I can't eat and I can hardly talk."
"No, no," the attendant replied. "Do you have Eurochecks, traveler's checks or cash?"

A couple of ski resorts in Austria have automatic accident insurance for their hotel guests, but this hasn't caught on everywhere. Mountain resorts employ highly competent search-and-rescue teams, but airlifting you to a hospital involves heavy expense—which you have to pay. Before you leave home, find out if your medical insurance covers medical care abroad. If it does, it probably works on a reimbursement basis: you must pay the doctor or hospital, then apply for a refund. If it does not, you would be well advised to buy a traveler's policy.

Emergencies

Health care in many West European countries is of a very high standard, but if you are in such places as southern Italy, eastern Turkey or Romania, avoid hospitalization if at all possible. Lack of modern equipment and drug supplies, as well as personnel shortages, may slow down your recovery. Ambulance service in Europe can be superb. In Germany, for example, some ambulances are actually operating rooms on wheels. In Spain, the Red Cross is alert and highly visible.

Emergency telephone numbers for ambulance, fire and police should be (but not always are) posted in public telephone booths and beside hotel phones. If you can't find such a list in your room, ask for one—*before* you need it. The numbers may be printed in large type just inside the phone book, sometimes even on the cover. If you can't find the numbers, dial the operator. If you are trying to communicate in a foreign language you don't know, remain calm, speak slowly and use as few words as possible. Fire! Police! Auto crash! Most tourist offices and many hotels provide leaflets of practical information that include emergency telephone numbers. For example, in Britain you can dial 999 anywhere in the country for the fire department, police or ambulance.

If you need emergency cash, you can have money wired to you, but the process can consume several days and is expensive. If you need to send an emergency telegram, the hotel can help. Most large cities have one or more all-night post offices with telegram services.

Crime and Terrorism

Crime in Europe has increased but has not yet reached the proportion that it has in the United States. Given the statistics, I am surprised by Americans who say they are afraid to travel in Europe. Terrorist attacks have become a fact of life, but according to figures compiled by experts in international terrorism, your chances of being involved in such an attack are much slimmer than your chances of being murdered at home.

Most crime against tourists in Europe involves purse snatching and robbery. In the East Bloc countries, the rate for even petty crime was once extremely low; however, crime is increasing as these countries adopt Western ways. The U.S.S.R. has a high rate of violent crime, but it is usually domestic—seldom directed at tourists. Drug use is an increasing problem, though again not of the magnitude that it is in the United States. Various methods of fighting it include methodone programs and opening certain areas (usually parks) to drug users. High drug-use areas are high crime areas; find out where they are and avoid them.

Pickpockets are a problem almost everywhere. A common ploy is for a group of children to surround you chattering and scuffling while one of them takes your wallet. This can vary when a woman with several children starts a squabble—while you are distracted, one of the children takes your wallet. Sometimes, thieves on motor bikes grab a woman's purse as they ride by—let go or be dragged along. Be on your guard, especially in crowded public transport and at tourist attractions. Carry your purse on the side away from the street; don't hang it on the back of your chair in a restaurant. Keep it closed; a zip is better than a snap. Don't keep all your money in one wallet. Tuck your cash into several compartments of your purse, or even use a bra pouch or money belt. Keep cash separate from credit cards, airline tickets and your passport. Above all, do not use one of those hold-all wallets. If it is lost or stolen, you have lost everything.

Don't leave valuables in your room. If you must go out of the room to the toilet or bath, put your rings and money into your robe pocket or cosmetic bag and take them along; or use the hotel safe deposit box. Safes are usually available at no charge, though small guest houses do not have them. If you are on a bus tour, never leave money, passports or cameras on board. If you go to the dining car on a train, take money, passports and cameras with you. Don't flash large amounts of money or expensive jewelry and camera equipment. Don't use showcase luggage. Choose bags with combination locks; the keys for standard brands of luggage open many cases easily. Keep your luggage next to you at all times and use luggage tags that conceal your name and address.

Small hotels and bed-and-breakfast establishments are generally safer from theft than are large luxury hotels. Small towns are safer than big cities. If you wish, take along a travel lock that can be attached as extra protection to hotel room doors. As of now, few hotels provide safety chains or peepholes on the room doors. If someone knocks, ask who's there before opening the door. Be aware that maids and room-service personnel have master keys and will probably give only a cursory tap on the door before opening it and coming in.

Many hotels are switching to plastic card-keys so the lock combinations can be changed after each guest checks out. Checks reveal, however, that the keys aren't always reprogrammed and that these locks, too, can be "fiddled." If your room has a connecting door to the next room, make sure it is locked. If you feel nervous, slide a heavy piece of furniture in front of it.

Happily, bottom-pinching is not the problem it once was in Italy. However, when you walk alone, especially after dark, men in almost every country will speak to you, although the frequency does tend to increase the farther south and east you go. In Italy or Yugoslavia, men may tell you that you are beautiful and they love you as you walk past. Most of them don't expect an answer. Those who do usually will not persist if ignored. Don't make eye contact and walk briskly. If the man follows you, shouting a few choice swear words (in English, if you don't know any local curses) is much more effective than threatening to call the police. In such instances, going into a shop or restaurant is also a good way out. Watch to see if the man leaves; if he doesn't, ask for help. People will usually help if you ask, but they will not interfere if they think you welcome his attentions or that perhaps you are lovers having a quarrel.

Once in Turkey, a taxi driver invited me to go to a disco. When I declined, he shrugged, grinned and said, "Okay, let's go to bed." He took my refusal good-naturedly and made no further passes, though I was pragmatically inventing a very large, very jealous husband with which to threaten him. I think he would have understood that better than a philosophical argument about a woman's right to say no.

Such episodes are the exception rather than the rule. Usually, a "street-wise" bearing is protection enough. Be confident; timid-acting people are broadcasting that they are easy to attack. I went for a stroll one night along Hamburg's Reeperbahn, one of the most scarlet of Europe's red-light districts. No one approached me. It may be that the woman tourist in such places is bothered less than on a normal street. In general, red-light districts are well policed. The biggest problems will come from the prostitutes, who view any woman as competition.

In Hamburg, the street called the Grosse Freiheit has been closed to women because of a series of unpleasant incidents. In one case, a group of tourists was strolling along looking into the "shop windows" where the prostitutes sit. Some women in the group were making condescending comments—loudly. To retaliate, one of the prostitutes emptied a chamber pot from a window onto the group. Be sensible.

Think before you speak. Don't go to such places if they bother you. When riding at night on public transportation, take a seat near the driver or in the first carriage near the driver's compartment; chances are, you can alert the driver if you need help.

Women driving alone should observe basic safety rules. Avoid lonely areas; there has been a series of attacks against women at some roadside parks in France. Try to make all your stops at gasoline stations or rest houses or at *busy* roadside parks. Make sure your car is in good condition to avoid breakdowns. Don't run out of gas. Learn to change a tire quickly in case you have to, and make sure the spare is in good condition.

A few parking garages have begun reserving parking spaces near the exits for women after 7:00 P.M., the result of increasing attacks in garages. Other parking garages have attendants who will park and retrieve your car. Wherever you park, look around carefully before you get out of the car. If you feel suspicious of anyone loitering nearby, drive away. Look in the back seat before you get into a car to make sure no one is hiding there. Keep the car locked at all times, and don't leave luggage, clothes or cameras in it to tempt thieves. Never leave money or your passport in the car.

In Yugoslavia, Poland and some other areas where there is a shortage of car parts, removables such as windshield wipers often disappear. It's a good idea to take them off yourself when you park your car, and push in the radio antenna, or lower it as much as possible. I was very worried about my new car when I drove all the way to the toe of Italy's boot because I had heard so many car-theft stories. But I parked on the street every night and nothing happened. Every morning, I found an admiring group of youths clustered around it, but they never so much as touched it.

Opinions differ as to whether it is best to drive with the car doors locked or unlocked. Some people always leave the passenger side unlocked out of fear of being trapped in the car in case of an accident. Others lock all doors so they can't be opened by a would-be attacker. I compromise by locking the passenger door and leaving the driver's side unlocked—unless I am driving through a lonely spot late at night.

If you have a traffic accident, don't move the car until the police arrive unless traffic is totally blocked. First, assist anyone who is injured (you are required to have a first-aid kit in your car) and put out the warning triangle (also required for driving). If you have a camera, take photographs of the scene from several angles. It is best not to sign anything; if the police insist that you sign a form in a foreign language, write down that you do not understand what the form says above your signature. Get a copy of the police report.

If you are robbed, report the crime to the police at once. Get a copy of the report they file. You will need it for your insurance claim, and it can be almost impossible to obtain once you leave the country. If you are raped, go to the police or a rape crisis or women's center (if there is one). Even though women's educational and support groups are making progress, rape is still fraught with local prejudices in much of Europe. Rape crisis centers have been established in many cities, but don't count on sympathetic police action everywhere. It is worth repeating: stay out of dives, avoid lonely streets and dark alleys. If you find yourself in a threatening situation, try to stay calm and look for a way out. Training in self-protection by a professional is a good idea, whether you travel or stay at home. Greece and Turkey have networks of "tourist police"; their first job is to patrol for such things as unauthorized camping, but they can help in emergencies.

Be careful of local customs: you may find that you have unwittingly committed a crime. Do not speak disrespectfully of Ataturk in Turkey. You know the old saw about not photographing bridges and military installations in the East Bloc, but the same applies in Western countries, too. If you photograph a U.S. military installation in Germany, for example, the M.P. who arrests you probably won't take kindly to your reminding him that your tax money is paying for the place. And don't show too much interest in Swiss bridges and tunnels—they're all mined, just in case.

If you cross against a traffic light in Germany (even if there is no traffic), don't be surprised if a solid citizen rebukes you. In Italy, it is a good idea to get a receipt for everything and hold onto it. In an effort to crack down on tax dodging, the Finance Police sometimes make spot checks for receipts as people leave shops or restaurants. The effect this can have on you is delay and frustration (you have not committed a crime) if you cannot produce a receipt—the police may decide to check the shopkeeper's cash register receipts and may hold you as "evidence" until the job is done.

If you do get into trouble, don't expect your embassy to rush to bail you out. In some cases it may intervene, but if you break a local law, you probably will have to pay the penalty. When you travel, keep in touch with someone. Carry the name, address and telephone number of a person to be notified in case you are injured. Search announcements are aired after news broadcasts on American Forces Network radio stations and as part of traffic reports in some countries. The *International Herald Tribune* has a coded-message section in its classified advertising pages.

12

MEMORIES ARE THE BEST SOUVENIRS

Souvenirs, in French, are fond remembrances. In these days of mass-produced kitsch, the word has been vulgarized to become synonymous with those horrid plastic Eiffel towers and Manneken Pis corkscrews. But even those who cringe at garish displays of commercialism collect souvenirs.

Souvenirs need not be objects, though it is rare indeed for anyone to return from Europe empty-handed. My best souvenirs are in my head: a spontaneous tour of a French restaurant kitchen when I sent my compliments to the chef, an hour in a tiny wine cellar with the vintner's entire family. The first time I saw Trogir, a lovely little town on Yugoslavia's Adriatic coast, was on a moonlit night after a warming bottle of red wine. It was late, and the floodlighting on the church cast heavy shadows. Nearby in the still darkness a group of young men was singing old Dalmatian fishermen's songs. It is a memory I cherish.

Festivals

Celebrations and festivals have all the makings of good memories. Every year in Europe there are many anniversaries—Switzerland's seven-hundredth birthday, the two-hundredth anniversary of the death of Mozart—all going on at the same time. These anniversaries involve festivities, exhibitions, concerts and seminars organized under one theme. Tourist offices can provide calendars of events and brochures about them.

Europe celebrates far more annual festivals and holidays than anyone can list. One of my favorites is Carnival, the pre-Lenten bash that most Americans will recognize under the name Mardi Gras. Super Carnival celebrations are held in Lucerne, Switzerland; Maastricht, the Netherlands; Rottweil, Germany; Nice, France; and Venice, Italy. Perhaps the best of all is in Basel, Switzerland—held one week later than the others because it stems from military rather than religious tradition.

Easter is a big event in Spain (especially Holy Week in Seville) and Greece (the Greek Orthodox Easter is later than the Roman). "Winter" is burned in Zurich on the third Monday of April in an old guild celebration called *Sechseläuten*. The French celebrate their Independence Day on July 14. Christmas is lavish almost everywhere, even in atheist U.S.S.R., where the festivities are officially for the New Year, although the Orthodox Christmas on January 7 may now be observed. May Day is Labor Day in Europe.

Each autumn, the Lower Saxony Stud Farm sponsors a Parade of Stallions in Celle, Germany (tickets sell out two to three years in advance). There are horse races on the frozen lake at St. Moritz, Switzerland, every January, and in summer the *Palio* in Siena, Italy, recalls medieval riding splendors. Not every celebration is annual. *Unspunnen*, a nationwide folk festival, takes place every ten years in Switzerland. Passion plays, such as the famous one at Oberammergau, Germany, are performed every six, seven, ten or even twenty years.

There are hundreds of jazz festivals, rock festivals, folk music and dance festivals, art festivals, flower festivals and saints' days. In Bregenz, Austria, opera and ballet are performed on a stage floating on Lake Constance. During the Dubrovnik (Yugoslavia) Festival, the entire city becomes a stage: Shakespeare is superbly performed in the shadow of those mighty city walls. During the summer, towns along the Rhine River in Germany have Rhine Aflame nights. The largest of these is held on the second Saturday in August, when thousands of people cruise down the river in a flotilla of seventy ships while spectacular fireworks light up the towns and castles on shore.

Midsummer in Sweden is a big event; Maypoles are raised (even though the celebration takes place in June) and dancing goes on all night. The best celebrations are in Dalarna Province. In Echternach, Luxembourg, a unique dancing procession honors Saint Willibrord on the Tuesday after Whit Sunday. Tourist offices publish calendars of festivals and travel agents offer package arrangements for the most popular events.

Look Around

Read your guidebooks before you go so that you don't keep your nose buried in them instead of seeing what they describe. Look up, look around. Notice the chimney pots in England, the ornate drainpipes on buildings, the variety of shapes of haystacks. History and legend are recorded on many a carved church door and glowing fresco—events leaping out of the dry pages of a textbook. Almost every village has its local museum, and the small ones can be quite good. Give them more than a cursory look. The exhibits usually are not labeled in English, but you can glean some information.

I wandered into the museum of Burda, Turkey, one noontime, thinking at first that it was closed. But the museum guard approached, and when he had ascertained that I was American he pulled out a bruised scrap of paper that said, in English, "Museum open, no money." Together we made the rounds of pot shards and ancient coins and headless statues—he explaining everything in Turkish while I nodded and tried to look wise.

For special interests, a museum can be found somewhere on almost any subject. There is a wallpaper museum in Kassel, Germany; a museum of funerary rites and customs in Vienna; a music box and street organ museum in Utrecht, the Netherlands; and museums of mechanical musical instruments in Rüdesheim, Germany, and Paris. Cameras are prohibited in some museums and churches; in others, you can photograph without a flash. Sometimes you must pay a small fee to use your camera.

With so much to see and do, how can you remember it all? You can keep a diary, of course, but I prefer to write letters. When I travel, I write to a friend who gives the letters back to me. Not only does this save time, but I find it easier to write to someone than to record facts on pages that no one else will see.

Shopping

Tourists are notorious shoppers, akin to swarms of locusts, and Europe offers a cornucopia of things to buy. Getting your priorities and your budget to harmonize can be difficult, but you may find it more rewarding to share a bottle of fine wine with a newly made friend than to take the bottle home for your cellar. But you do want to shop! What are the best things to take home? That, of course, is a personal choice and a matter of taste and pocketbook.

Explore the department stores, the boutiques, the street markets. If you thought America invented the shopping mall, think again. Europe has elegant covered *galeries* or *passages* (use the French pronunciation) of shops. Hamburg, Germany, boasts the largest covered shopping area in Europe, including the *Galleria,* the *Hanseviertel* and the *Gänsemarkt-Passage.* The *Galeries Royales St. Hubertus* in Brussels, built in 1847, and the *Corridor* in Bath, England, built in 1825, are among the oldest and most luxurious.

Passages are found in many major cities. Some of the loveliest are the *Von-Werdt-Passage* in Bern, Switzerland; *Passage* in Den Haag, the Netherlands; *Passage des Lions* in Geneva; *Galleria Mazzini* in Genoa, Italy; *Galleria Vittorio Emanuele II* in Milan; *Barton Arcade* in Manchester, England; *Passage Pommeraye* in Nantes, France; *Calwer Passage* in Stuttgart, Germany; *Freyung-Passage* in Vienna and *Rathausdurchgang* in Winterthur, Switzerland. Even the famous *GUM* department store in Moscow is more a *galerie* than a store; it resembles a huge greenhouse filled with stalls selling everything from shoes to toys. The cities with the most beautiful *passages* to explore are Paris, Brussels, London and Leeds, England.

Museum shops have lovely posters and reproductions of some of their most interesting treasures—jewelry, glassware, pottery. A number of countries have national handicraft shops, run by organizations dedicated to preserving handiwork. (See "Practical Matters: National Handicrafts Shops.") Some regions or even villages are production centers for particular items: Betschdorf, France, is known for its salt-glazed stoneware, for example, and Germany's Black Forest is the land of cuckoo clocks.

Haggle in bazaars and flea markets, but not in the shops. Before you buy something, think of how to get it home. Is it small enough to carry? Some shops will take care of shipping, or you can mail things to yourself. Post offices in many countries sell packing kits in various sizes—they include the box, tape, string and address label.

The price marked on items usually includes tax, and most West European countries charge a hefty value-added tax (VAT). In 1988, Hungary became the first East Bloc country to introduce VAT; other East European lands will likely follow suit as they move toward market economies. In many countries, tourists can get VAT rebates on expensive items by taking time to fill out a form. (See "Practical Matters: Tax Rebate Plans.")

When you go shopping, be aware of what you cannot bring back home with you. The U.S. Customs Office publishes a pamphlet listing restrictions and limitations. Among items that cannot be brought into the United States are products made from the fur or hide of endangered animals, fresh foods, liqueur-filled chocolates and live plants (Dutch flower growers, however, sell bulbs given an import certificate by the U.S. Department of Agriculture).

Memories Shared

Traveling independently has many advantages, but sometimes traveling alone becomes lonely and we need someone to share the good times. Loneliness is a natural reaction when one is surrounded by couples and families—often the case in travel situations. When faced with lovers over a candlelight dinner, friends chattering away about that wonderful new art gallery or families romping on a mountainside, even the most dedicated loner must feel a twinge of dissatisfaction now and again.

In your travels, you will probably make friends. You may even meet someone who offers more than friendship. What then? First, tread carefully! A vacation romance is seldom more than a fleeting affair. Before you begin, find out if the man has a wife and family (adultery is a crime in Greece). Many European men do not wear wedding rings. Conducting an affair need not be particularly clandestine. Europeans are more tolerant than Americans of unmarried couples, and it is a rare hotel that will turn away two people who do not share a name.

If things progress to the point where he swears he wants to marry you, he may actually be thinking of a way to get a "green card," which lets him live and work in the United States. If you do consider marriage, the big question is "your place or mine?" Do you want to live in his country; can you adapt to its culture? Spend some time there first. Being a resident is quite a bit different from being a tourist. Can you take him home? What will your mother say to a man who knows only "Hello" and "I love you" in English?

Marriage laws vary from country to country. It is a lengthy process to get married in many countries—lots of paperwork and you still have to post the bans. Denmark has made it easier. In fact, the German Federal Railway and the tourist offices of a couple of Danish towns work together to promote a "Darling Denmark" marriage tour. The travel agent helps cut through the red tape and the couple spends just enough time in Denmark to make it legal.

Before you take that final step, visit your embassy and find out if you stand to lose your citizenship and what citizenship your children will have. And finally—before you marry take a look at the country's divorce laws. It isn't easy to get a divorce in places like Ireland and Spain.

But enough of warnings! European men can be delightful, and that extra spice of the exotic really does make an affair more exciting—who hasn't fantasized about a romantic Frenchman now and then! The French aren't the only men in Europe who know how to make life lovely. The British seldom live up to their reputation of being reserved; Poles are considered (and consider themselves) the Romeos of the East. German men love cars first, dogs second and women third. Austrians and Czechs are fun; the Portuguese, sad and serious; the Italians, very macho. Swiss men, are extraordinarily beautiful and extraordinarily cold, but the Yugoslavs are beautiful and spicy, too.

PRACTICAL MATTERS

Accommodation

Youth Hostels

Youth hostels offer low-cost accommodations throughout Europe. They may be in modern buildings, as in Vaduz, Liechtenstein, or in renovated fortresses, as in Koblenz, Germany. One Stockholm, Sweden, youth hostel is a tall-ship anchored permanently near the center of town. Persons traveling alone must be at least fourteen years old to use hostels. There is no maximum age limit, except in Bavaria (southern Germany), where the limit is twenty-seven. Everywhere else, priority is give to those under thirty. Children accompanied by adults may stay in hostels if they are at least ten years old when accompanied by an adult of the opposite sex or five years old when accompanied by an adult of the same sex. Many hostels accept families; the age limit does not then apply.

To use a hostel, a traveler must have the International Youth Hostel Guest Card, which is issued by any of the 5,000 Youth Hostel Associations worldwide. Senior, junior and family cards can be purchased. Handbooks are published each year, listing hostels and the services and facilities each offers. Some hostels require or accept International Advance Booking Vouchers for reservations. A number of Youth Hostel Associations have travel sections that offer inexpensive hostel vacations all over the world.

More information is available from:

American Youth Hostels Inc., 1332 I Street, N.W., 8th Floor, Washington, DC 20005, U.S.A.; tel. (202) 783-6161.

Canadian Hostelling Association, 333 River Road, Vanier City, Ottawa K1L 8H9, Ontario, Canada; tel. (613) 746-0060.

Women's Hotels, Cafes, Centers, Groups and Travel Agencies

Few European countries have hotels for women only, but women's cafes, bookshops and other centers can be found in major cities. Several women's travel groups have been formed to help women network, and some travel agents cater to singles or women. The following is a selection of such groups and places. Look for others in the alternative press of the place you are visiting. When requesting information, send a self-addressed envelope and an international reply coupon to cover the postage.

A number of convents have rooms for women and girls who wish to spend a few days in meditation or to participate in spiritual programs. Arrangements should be made in advance, since some convents accept guests only in summer or only during certain weeks. The age limit varies greatly. Length of stay may be limited.

Austria

Ursulinenkloster, Reimmichlgasse 2, A-6020 Innsbruck.

Barmherzige Schwestern, Rennweg 40, A-6020 Innsbruck.

Franziskanerinnen Missionärinnen Mariens, Leystrasse 25-27, A-1200 Vienna.

Barmherzige Schwestern, Gumpendorferstrasse 108, A-1062 Vienna.

Missionsschwestern "Königin der Apostel," Kreuzwiesengasse 9, A-1170 Vienna.

Arme Schulschwestern, Clementinengasse 25, A-1150 Vienna.

Salvatorianerinnen, Auhofstrasse 189, A-1130 Vienna.

Schwester v. Armen Kinde Jesu, Döblinger Hauptstrasse 8, A-1190 Vienna.

Sta. Christina, Willergasse 55, A-1238 Vienna-Rodaun.

Marienschwestern v. Karmel, Seilerstätte 9, A-4020 Linz.

Benediktinerinnen, A-4652 Steinerkirchen.

Abtei St. Gabriel, A-8350 Fehring, Steyer.

Barmherzige Schwestern v. Hl. Kreuz, A-2361 Laxenburg.

Barmherzige Schwestern, Meriengasse 12, A-8020 Graz.

Zisteraienserinnen "Marienfeld," Maria Roggendorf, A-2041 Wullersdorf.

Kloster vom Guten Hirten, A-4342 Baumgartenberg 1, Upper Austria, or Harbacherstrasse 70, A-9020 Klagenfurt.

Ursulinen, Ursulinenweg 1, A-9020 Klagenfurt.

Englische Fräulein, Linterstrasse 11, A-3100 St. Pölten.

BELGIUM

Abbey of Male, Pelderijnstraat 38, B-8310 Brugge 3. Advance arrangements required.

DENMARK

Women's Museum, Domkirkeplads 5, DK-8000 Aarhus C. Seven women working at the local university founded the museum on a voluntary basis. It has grown and moved into larger premises and now receives a subsidy from the city. Tel. 086-13 61 44.

GERMANY

Haus am Dom (hotel), Tolpferstrasse 9, W-2380 Schleswig. Tel. 04621-21388.

Frauenhotel Artemisia (hotel), Brandenburgischen Strasse 18, W-1000 Berlin. Tel. 030-87 89 05.

Frauen Infothek, Leibnizstrasse 57, W-1000 Berlin 12 (4th floor). The group can provide guided tours, recommend "women-friendly" hotels and restaurants, suggest museum visits, etc. Tel. 030-324 50 78.

Frauenbuchladen Labrys (bookshop), Hohenstaufenstrasse 64, W-1000 Berlin 30. Tel. 030-215 25 00.

Lilith (bookshop), Knesebeckstrasse 86/87, W-1000 Berlin 30. Tel. 030-312 31 02.

Frauen Café and Buchladen (bookshop), Kiesstrasse 27, W-6000 Frankfurt a.M. Tel. 069-70 52 95. Selection of books in English.

Frauenmuseum (women's museum), Nerostrasse 16, W-6200 Wiesbaden. Tel. 06121-52 84 00.

Lillemors Frauenbuchladen (bookshop), Arcisstrasse 57, W-8000 Munich 40. Tel. 089-272 12 05.

Frauenferienhaus Dornhan (guest house), Aistaigerstrasse 10, W-7242 Dornhan 6. The house, run by sculptor Ilse Teipelke and dancer Gabi Gross, can accommodate ten women. Kitchen privileges. Bring own bed linen for short stays. Tel. 07423-1461.

Frauenhof Oberpfaffing (lesbian camp), Oberpfaffing 72, W-8381 Münchsdorf. Tel. 08564-1434.

Frauenferienhaus Stemmen (guest house), Hammer 22, W-8491 Tiefenbach. Tel. 09673-499.

Friends' Circle of Single Travelers–"We Travel Together," P.O. Box 52 05 51, W-2000 Hamburg 52. Tel. 040-880 74 21. For women who are interested in sharing trips with others who have similar interests.

konnex gudrun klein, Am Botanischegarten 3, W-6600 Saarbrücken 11. Tel. 0681-39 96 34. Fax 0681-34733. Accommodation service for guest houses/apartments/small hotels suitable for women alone or for those who would like to participate in art groups, meditative sessions, etc. Information available in English and French.

Frauen Reisebörse (travel exchange), Lutticher Strasse 25, W-5000 Cologne. Tel. 0221-51 52 54. The exchange compiles lists of women seeking travel partners; yearly membership fee for frequent travelers or single-trip fee.

Hoffmann Reisen (travel agency), Hess Strasse 27, W-8000 Munich 40. Tel. 089-52 18 88. Travel section for women, especially to exotic destinations where a woman alone might encounter problems.

Single Travel (travel agency), Heidelberger Strasse 1, W-6054 Rodgau 3. Tel. 06106-72400. Caters to single travelers of both sexes; provides single rooms for everyone. Tours concentrated on the southern coasts.

Frauen Unterwegs (Women Traveling), Potsdamerstrasse 139, W-1000 Berlin 30. Tel. 030-215 10 22. Plans study and adventure tours such as wandering in Wales, painting in Tuscany, through France by motorcycle.

Frauen auf Reisen, Geschwister-Scholl-Strasse 11, W-2000 Hamburg. Tel. 040-480 77 02. Plans work-training vacations and cultural programs, usually lasting at least two weeks.

GREAT BRITAIN

Reeves Private Hotel for Women, 48 Shepherd's Bush Green, London W12 8PJ. Tel. 081-740 11 58.

Sisterwrite (bookshop), 190 Upper Street, London. Tel. 071-22 69 782. In addition to books, the shop sells crafts made by women.

Women Welcome Women, Granta, 8a Chestnut Avenue, High Wycombe, Buckinghamshire. Tel. 0494-43 94 81. The service is free but depends on donations.

Businesswoman's Travel Club, 520 Fulham Road, London SW6 5NJ. Tel. 071-384 11 21.

TURKEY

Odin Tourism and Travel, Barbaros Bulvan Marmara Ap. No. 38/4, Balmumcu-Istanbul, Turkey. Tel. 1-167 28 00. Run as a hobby by two women who arrange for women travelers to meet Turkish women. Activities include religious, political, sociological and cultural tours, Turkish language and handicrafts courses, trekking and cruises.

"First-Stop" Hotels

When you arrive in a brand new place, it sometimes helps to know of a good hotel near the railway station. Usually several price categories are available in the vicinity of the main stations. Of course, price is relative: you will have to pay more in London, for example, than in Lisbon for similar accommodations. Hotels in East European countries are disproportionately expensive and likely will remain so until more hotels are built as tourism develops under the new market economy; however, the number of private bed-and-breakfast rooms is blossoming. Here is a selection of hotels located near railway stations in some of the major cities of Europe. Where stars are given, they are local standard, indicating the type of facilities offered as given by local hotel and tourist associations.

AUSTRIA

Vienna: Near the South Railway Station—**Prinz Eugen** (four-star), Wiedener Gürtel 14, tel. 0222-505 17 41. **Hotel Congress** (three-star), Wiedener Gürtel 34-36, tel. 0222-505 91 65. Near the West Railway Station—**Austrotel** (four-star), Löhrgasse 3, tel. 0222-96 36 26. **Hotel Westbahn** (four-star), Pelzgasse 1, tel. 0222-92 14 80.

BELGIUM

Brussels: **Ibis Brussels Center**, rue Marché aux Herbes 100, B-1000 Brussels, tel. 02-514 50 67. **Novotel Brussels Grand Place**, rue Marché aux Herbes 120, B-1000 Brussels, tel. 02-511 77 23.

BULGARIA

Sofia: **Grand Hotel Sofia** (three-star), Narodno Săbraenie Square, tel. 02-87 88 71.

CZECHOSLOVAKIA

Prague: **Hotel Paříž** (four-star), U obecního domu 1, tel. 02-23 22 051. **Hotel Europa**, Václavské Nam (Wenceslas Square), tel. 02-26 27 48. Both are charming art nouveau buildings, but the Europa lacks private baths and toilets.

DENMARK

Copenhagen: **Hotel Triton**, Helgolandsgade 7-11, tel. 045-31 23 09 10.

FINLAND

Helsinki: **Rivoli Jardin**, Kasarmikatu 40, tel. 090-17 78 80 (owned by women). **Seurahuone Socis**, Kaivokatu 12, tel. 090-17 04 41.

FRANCE

Paris: Near the St. Lazare Railway Station—**Ouest H.**, 3 rue Rocher, tel. 14-387 57 49. Near the North Railway Station—**Gare du Nord**, 33 rue St.-Quentin, tel. 14-878 02 92. Near the Lyon Railway Station—**Viator**, 1 rue Parrot, tel. 14-343 11 00.

GERMANY

Berlin: **Hotel am Zoo**, Kurfürstendam 25, tel. 030-88 30 91. **Ibis**, Messedamm 10, tel. 030-30 20 11.

Frankfurt a.M.: **Park Hotel** (five-star), Wiesenhüttenplatz 36, tel. 069-26970. **Hotel Rhein-Main**, Heidelberger Strasse 3, tel. 069-25 00 35. **Hotel Arcade**, Speicherstrasse 3-5, tel. 069-27 30 30.
Hamburg: **Bellevue**, An der Alster 14, tel. 040-24 80 11. **Europäischer Hof**, Kirchenallee 45, tel. 040-24 82 48. **Baseler Hof**, Esplanade 11, tel. 040-35 90 60.
Munich: **Hotel Westend**, Landsberger Strasse 20, tel. 089-50 40 04. **Hotel Amba**, Arnulfstrasse 20, tel. 089-59 29 21. **Hotel Maria**, Schwanthalerstrasse 112-114, tel. 089-50 30 23.
Cologne: **Intercity Hotel Ibis**, Bahnhofsvorplatz, tel. 0221-13 20 51. **An der Philharmonie**, Grosse Neugasse 36, tel. 0221-21 05 32. **Kunibert der Fiese**, Am Bollwerk 1-5, tel. 0221-23 58 08.

GREAT BRITAIN

London: Near Euston Station—**Hotel Ibis**, Cardigan Street 3, tel. 071-724 10 00. Near Charing Cross Station—**The Strand Hotel**, 143 The Strand, London WC2 R1GE, tel. 071-836 48 80. Near Victoria Station—**Hotel La Place**, 17 Nottingham Place, London W1, tel. 071-486 23 23. Near Kings Cross Station—**The Crescent Hotel**, 49-50 Cartwright Gardens, tel. 071-387 15 15.
Edinburgh: **North British**, 1 Princes Street, Edinburgh EH2, tel. 031-554 71 73.
Glasgow: **The Capthorn**, George Square, Glasgow G1, tel. 041-332 67 11.
Cardiff: **Angel Hotel**, Castle Street, Cardiff CF1 2QZ, tel. 0222-232 633.

GREECE

Athens: Near Omonia Square—**King Minos** (Category A), 1 Pireos, tel. 01-523 11 11. **Acadimos** (Category B), 58 Akadimias, tel. 01-362 92 20. **Athens Center** (Category B), 26 Sofokleous & Klisthenous, tel. 01-524 85 11.

HUNGARY

Budapest: Near the East Railway Station—**Hungaria** (four-star), Rákóczi út 90, tel. 01-22 90 50. **Hotel Astoria** (three-star), Kossuth Lajos út 19, tel. 01-17 34 11. **Hotel Erzsébet** (three-star), Károlyi Mihály út 11-15, tel. 01-38 21 11.

IRELAND

Dublin (in the city center): **Park View House**, 491 North Circular

Road, Dublin 1, tel. 01-74 36 97 or 74 22 08. **Clifton Court Hotel**, 11 Eden Quay, O'Connell Bridge, Dublin 1, tel. 01-74 35 35. **Ashling Hotel**, Parkgate Street, Dublin 1, tel. 01-77 23 24.

ITALY

Rome: **Britannia**, via Nappoli 64, tel. 06-46 31 53. **Diana**, via Principe Amedeo 4, tel. 06-475 15 41. **Milani**, via Magenta 12, tel. 06-494 00 51.

LUXEMBOURG

Luxembourg City: Near the railway station—**Alfa**, 16 place de la Gare, tel. 49 00 11. **Arcotel**, 43 avenue de la Gare, tel. 49 40 01. **International** (four-star), 20-22 place de la Gare, tel. 48 59 11. Near the airport—**Ibis** (three-star), Route de Trèves, tel. 43 88 01.

NETHERLANDS

Amsterdam: Near the railway station—**Hotel Avenue**, N.Z. Voorburgwal 27, tel. 020-23 83 07. **Delta Hotel**, Damrak 42, tel. 020-20 26 26. Near the Rijksmuseum—**American**, Leidsekade 97, tel. 020-24 53 22.

NORWAY

Oslo: Near the railway station—**Hotel Christiania**, Biskop Gunnerusgt. 3, tel. 02-42 94 10. **Oslo Plaza Tower**, Sonja Henies Plass, tel. 02-17 10 00.

POLAND

Warsaw: Near the Central Railway Station—**Marriott** (deluxe), Aleje Jerotolimskie 65-79, tel. 022-30 63 06. **Hotel Forum** (four-star), Nowogrodska 24/26, tel. 022-21 019. **Holiday Inn** (four-star), 2 Zlota Street, tel. 022-20 65 34.

PORTUGAL

Lisbon: Near the Rossio Railway Station—**Hotel Lisboa Plaza** (four-star), Travessa do Salitre 7, tel. 01-34 63 922. **Hotel Mundial** (four-star), Rua D. Duarte 4, tel. 01-86 31 01. **Hotel Botanico** (three-star), Rua da Mae d'Agua 16-20, tel. 01-32 03 92. **Hotel Metropole** (two-star), Rossio 30, tel. 01-36 91 64. **Hotel Suico-Atlantico** (two-star), Rua da Gloria 13-19, tel. 01-36 17 13.

ROMANIA
Bucharest: **Nord Hotel**, Calea Griviţei 143, tel. 0-50 60 81.

SPAIN
Madrid: **Chamartin**, estación de Chamartin, tel. 091-733 90 11. **Foxá 25**, Agustin de Foxá 25, tel. 091-733 70 64. **Aristos y Restaurant El Chaflán**, avenue Pio XII-34, tel. 091-457 04 50. Barcelona (in the city center): **Terminal**, Provenca 1-piso 7, tel. 093-321 53 50.

SWEDEN
Stockholm: **Adlon**, Vasagatan 42, tel. 08-24 54 00. **Prize Hotel**, Kungsbron 1, tel. 08-14 94 50.

SWITZERLAND
Zurich: **Arc Royal Confort Inn** (three-star), Leonhardstrasse 6, tel. 01-261 67 10. **Franziskaner** (three-star), Niederdorfstrasse 1, tel. 01-252 01 20. **Limmathof** (two-star), Limmatquai 142, tel. 01-47 42 20. **Leonhard** (two-star), Limmatquai 136, tel. 01-251 30 80.
Basel: Near the Swiss Rail Station—**Gotthard-Terminus** (three-star), Centralbahnstrasse 13, tel. 061-22 52 50. **Steinengraben** (three-star), Steinengraben 51, tel. 061-23 59 43. **Bristol** (two-star), Centralbahnstrasse 15, tel. 061-22 38 22.
Geneva: **Astoria** (three-star), 6 place Cornavin, tel. 022-732 10 25. **International et Terminus** (three-star), 20 rue des Alpes, tel. 022-732 80 95. **Savoy** (three-star), 8 place Cornavin, tel. 022-731 12 55. **Eden** (two-star), 135 rue de Lausanne, tel. 022-732 65 40.
Bern: **Alfa** (three-star), Laupenstrasse 15, tel. 031-25 38 66. **Astor-Touring** (three-star), Zieglerstrasse 66, tel. 031-45 86 66. **Kreuz** (three-star), Zeughausgasse 15, tel. 031-22 11 62. **Goldener Schlüssel** (two-star), Rathausgasse 72, tel. 031-22 02 16.

TURKEY
Ankara: **Etap Altinel Oteli**, Gazi Mustafa Bul. Tandogan Mey, tel. 04-231 77 60. **Stad Oteli**, Istiklai Cad. No. 20 Ulus, tel. 04-310 48 48.
Istanbul: **Sahinler Oteli**, Koska Cad. No. 10, Laleli, tel. 01-520 75 56. **Washington Oteli**, Genctürk Cad. No. 12, Laleli, tel. 01-

520 59 90. **Zürth Oteli**, Harikzadeler Sok. No. 37, Laleli, tel. 01-512 23 50.

U.S.S.R.

Moscow: **National**, 14/1 Prospekt Marksa, tel. 095-203 65 39. **Metropol**, 1 Prospekt Marksa, tel. 095-225 66 77. **Berlin**, 3 Ulitsa Zhdanova, tel. 095-925 85 27.

Leningrad: Near Moscow Station—**Hotel Moskva**, 2 Ploshchad Alexandra Nevskovo, tel. 812-274 95 05. Near Finland Station—**Hotel Leningrad**, 5/2 Vyborgskaya Nabeleznaya, tel. 812-542 94 11. In the city center—**Hotel Astoria** (deluxe), 39 Ulitsa Gartsena, tel. 812-219 11 00.

Yugoslavia

Belgrade: **Inter-Continental**, Vladimira Popovica 10, tel. 011-222 33 33.

Zagreb: **Esplanade**, Mihanovič Ivi 1, tel. 041-43 56 66.

Dubrovnik: Most hotels are located in parks or along the beach. Near the walled Old Town—**Hotel Excelsior** (Category A), Frana Supila 20, tel. 050-23566. **Grand Hotel Imperial**, M. Simoni 2, tel. 050-23688.

Hotel and Restaurant Voucher Plans

Most voucher plans are for double occupancy; a single supplement is charged where single rooms are available under the voucher plan.

Denmark

The **Kro Check** is a voucher good at some fifty inns in small towns and in the countryside; information available from the tourist office. Several hotel voucher plans operate all week in summer and at weekends the rest of the year throughout Scandinavia. With the **Passepartout**, guests get one stamp for each night's stay. Four stamps entitle you to a free night in a participating hotel. The second plan, a **Bonus Pass**, is good for discounts of 15 to 50 percent on bed and breakfast. First- and last-night stays can be booked in advance, with other reservations made from hotel to hotel. Persons holding a **Nordtourist** railway pass get the same benefits without having to buy the **Bonus Pass**. The **Passepartout** is accepted in Denmark at Grand

Hotels Denmark, and the **Bonus Pass** at Danway Hotels.

Pro Scandinavia Vouchers are accepted at participating hotels, on ferries and at car rental firms. **Best Western Hotelcheques** offer discounts at Best Western Hotels. **Scandic Hotel Checks** are accepted in summer and on weekends all year at Scandic Hotels. The **Scandinavian Hotel Express** is a travel club that offers members up to 50 percent discount at participating hotels.

FINLAND

The **Finncheque**, good from the beginning of June to the end of August, comes in three price categories. Category I is for the better room at a higher price. Category II is for a standard room with breakfast. Category III is the same room as II, but also includes lunch in a self-service restaurant or a packed lunch. **Finncamping Check** is good mid-May to mid-September at national campgrounds. The **Passepartout** (see Denmark) is good at SOKOS Hotels; the **Bonus Pass**, at Arctia Hotel Partners hotels. **Scandic Hotel Checks** are accepted at Cumulus Hotels.

FRANCE

The **French Youth Card** can be bought by anyone under the age of twenty-six. It is good for reductions on lodging, travel, cultural and sports events. It is for sale at 6,000 outlets in France, including tourist offices, town halls, youth centers and some banks. With the card, you get a listing of 4,000 addresses where benefits are available.

GREAT BRITAIN

A **Mid-Wales Country Club Card** is good for discounts on lodging as well as in shops and on entrance fees to tourist attractions. It is sold by the tourist association. An **AA Country Wanderer** voucher is available through the Automobile Association for hotels in two price categories. Rooms on **university campuses** in summer are available from University Accommodation Consortium Ltd., University Park, Nottingham NG7 2RD, England.

GREECE

Hotel bookings throughout the country can be made by the central agency **Xenodochiako Epimelitirio** (Greek Hotel Rooms), 6 Aristidou St., GR-10559 Athens. In Athens, book at Syntagma Square/ 6 Karageorgi-Serivas Street. It is open 1:00–4:00 P.M. in winter, 8:30 A.M.–8:00 P.M. in summer, closed Sundays and holidays.

NETHERLANDS

Restaurants participating in the **Tourist-Menu** plan post signs on their doors or windows. About 400 establishments serve a three-course, fixed-price set menu. The Dutch hotel trade has set up a **Netherlands Reservations Center** offering rooms all over the country in all price categories. Contact NCR, Post Box 404, NL-2260 AK Leidschendam, tel. 70-20 25 00.

NORWAY

The **Passepartout** (see Denmark) is good at Rica, Müller and RESO Hotels; the **Bonus Pass**, at Inter Nor Hotels; the **Pro Scandinavia Voucher** at Euro Hotels; the **Scandic Hotel Check** at Scandic Hotels; the **Best Western Hotelcheque** at Best Western Hotels; the **Scandinavian Hotel Express** card at participating hotels. A **Fjord Pass** is good at 243 hotels for at least a 20 percent discount from May 1 to September 30.

POLAND

Student Tourist Vouchers are available to full-time students and **Youth Tourist Vouchers** are available to those under thirty-five. The vouchers entitle the holder to stay at university dormitories that are converted to student hotels (two to four beds per room) in July and August. Student shelters can be found in the mountains of southern Poland. Information from Almatur-Travel Shop, ul. Kopernika 15, PL-00359 Warsaw, tel. 22-26 43 72 or 22-26 53 81.

SWEDEN

The **Quality Check** is good for rooms with bath and toilet and the **Budget Check** for rooms without private facilities at more than 200 hotels. Vouchers are good mid-June to the end of August. **Camping Checks** are accepted at 350 campgrounds. The **Passepartout** (see Denmark) is accepted at RESO Hotels; the **Bonus Pass** at Sara Hotels; also accepted are **Pro Scandinavian Voucher** and **Best Western Hotelcheques**. Some 200 hotels offer **Bilturlogi** (inexpensive lodging) in budget, good value and comfort categories. **CountrySide Sweden Hotelcheque** is valid at thirty-six hotels during the summer; **Sweden Hotels Pass** is good for a 50 percent discount at hotels belonging to the Sweden Hotels (SH) group. The **Scandic Hotel Check** is accepted at Scandic Hotels.

U.S.S.R.

The **Passepartout** (see Denmark) is accepted at the RESO Hotel
Olympia in Leningrad.

Spas: A Selection

"Taking the waters" has a long tradition in Europe. Spas and baths
have attracted the ill and the hypochondriacs, royalty and philanderers
for centuries. Everywhere the Romans went, they built bath houses
with advanced heating systems. Many of the ruins have been uncov-
ered and are open to view: Trier, Germany, has a first-rate Roman
bath. The eighteenth and nineteenth centuries saw the rise of resorts
where the leisure class could sip or soak up mineral waters and
promenade in the well-groomed parks. Mineral springs, often thermal as well, have all the makings of a spa. Just add hotels, medical
staff, entertainment and perhaps a casino.

Almost every country in Europe has spas. In Germany alone,
more than 200 towns are named *Bad*—that means bath. There is a
Baden in both Austria and Switzerland and a Bath in England. Here
are just a few of Europe's spas. Complete listings are available from
national tourist offices.

AUSTRIA

Baden bei Wien, within easy reach of Vienna and in the middle
of some of the best vineyards in Austria, has had Beethoven and
Mozart among its guests. **Badgastein,** an elegant spa near Salzburg,
has some 100 hotels and pensions connected with the hot springs. A
fashionable cure takes guests by a little train into the Heilstollen
abandoned mine galleries, where the air is considered therapeutic.

BELGIUM

Spa, in the Ardennes Mountains, became so fashionable in the
last century that its name is now synonymous with "health resort."

BULGARIA

The most important of the 130 spas are **Hisarya** in the Gora
Mountains, **Velingrad** in the Rhodope Mountains and **Sandanski**
(the largest) in the foothills of the Pirin Mountains. Several spas are
found along the Black Sea coast. Within the capital city Sofia, mineral

springs are found in the **Ovcha Koupel**, **Gorna Banya** and **Knyazhevo** districts, and in outlying **Pancharevo**.

CZECHOSLOVAKIA

Karlovy Vary (Karlsbad) and **Mariánkè Láznè** (Marienbad) are two of the best known of the fifty-six health resorts in the country. Beware the water at Karlovy Vary—it is laxative. Sip it from the specially shaped cups whose handles serve as straws. The town's specialties are a crisp, thin wafer called *oplatky* and rather ugly roses petrified by the strong minerals in the water.

DENMARK

Many hotels and vacation cottages have saunas. Public baths and pools can be found in most cities and towns.

FINLAND

The best sauna is a smoke sauna heated by a wood fire, in the country beside a lake where one can take a swim after the sauna. Finns often switch themselves with birch branches to stimulate the circulation. Saunas also can be found in hotels.

FRANCE

Like *Bad* in German, *les-Bains* in French indicates a spa town. There are **Vals-les-Bains** in the Rhône Valley, **Charbonnières-les-Bains** near Lyon, **Bains-les-Bains** in the Vosges. **Évian**, looking across Lake Geneva at Switzerland, is known for its tasteless bottled water. Next door **Thonon** is not as famous and, therefore, less expensive. **Vichy** in the Auvergne is one of the world's most famous watering places, which also bottles its water, especially recommended for digestive ailments. In Paris, a luxury thermal bath, **Les Thermes du Royal Monceau**, is open daily as a private club.

GERMANY

Baden-Baden is the superlative, with a wonderfully renovated Roman-Irish bath; its casino and the horse races held in August/September attract the jet set. **Wiesbaden**, a beautiful city on the Rhine, was a favorite spot for *emigré* Russians early in this century. **Bad Nauheim** has a delightful *Jugendstil* (art nouveau) treatment complex that probably escaped bombing in World War II (the town was a Nazi radio relay headquarters) because President Franklin

Roosevelt had spent time there as a child. **St. Peter-Ording** on the North Sea coast is a *luftkurort* (fresh air resort); sand-yachting is a popular sport on its wide beaches. **Bad Mergentheim**, the only spa on the Romantic Road, is one of the country's busiest cure resorts.

GREAT BRITAIN

Spas are enjoying new popularity in Britain. Once there were 100, now there are only ten, but these ten have benefitted from the fact that Princess Diana's father and stepmother are Britain's leading spa promoters. **Bath** is foremost, with fine Roman remains and elegant architecture. Then come **Buxton, Cheltenham, Droitwich, Harrogate, Leamington Spa, Llandrindod Wells** in Wales, **Malvern** and **Strathpeffer** in the Scottish Highlands, and **Tunbridge Wells.** Droitwich boasts water ten times saltier than the Dead Sea; Harrogate has Turkish baths and Tunbridge Wells has the country's oldest covered shopping area, dating from the 1630s.

GREECE

The country has twenty spas, mostly along the seacoast.

HUNGARY

Budapest has a long tradition as a spa town and retains several elegant, green-roofed Turkish baths. The *belle epoque* **Hotel Gellért** has its own bathing and medical facilities, as do two modern hotels on traffic-free **Margit Island** in the Danube. The large **Széchenyi Baths** in the City Park include open-air pools; the **Rudas Baths** are more than 400 years old and have just been renovated. Of the spas scattered around the country, the most interesting is **Hévíz**, whose bath houses are built directly over Lake Balaton, Central Europe's largest lake.

ICELAND

There are no organized spas here, but plenty of hot springs. It's just you and nature. Use care around the hot springs—they can be scalding. Around the springs, mud and hot water can splash into the air unexpectedly. The edges of springs can collapse; walk only on the brown earth—avoid the light patches. Public swimming pools may also have hot-water pools.

ITALY

Montecatini Terme, 25 miles from Florence, is one of the favorite watering places of Europe's wealthy. It has been known for its mineral waters since Roman times, but its ten spa buildings date from the eighteenth and nineteenth centuries. **San Pellegrino Terme** lies in a beautiful Alpine valley; its bottled water is among the best in Italy. The Automobile Club d'Italia publishes a spa map, locating and describing 160 health resorts in the country.

LUXEMBOURG

Mondorf-les-Bains, in the extreme south, boasts a casino and celebrates the national holidays of France, Belgium, Britain and the United States—as well as its own—with fireworks.

NETHERLANDS

Scheveningen, a seaside resort with a renovated "cure house" (it has been declared a protected national monument) got a new start with the opening of its casino in 1979. The resort is a suburb of The Hague. The only true spa in the country is **Bad Nieuwe-Schans**, Groningen, which opened in 1985.

NORWAY

No spas. Some hotels have saunas, but the sauna does not enjoy the same popularity here that it does in Finland and Sweden.

POLAND

Ciechocinek is the largest of several dozen spas in the country.

PORTUGAL

Most of the forty-four *caldas or termas* are showing their age, but doing so elegantly. They are concentrated in the northern half of the country, and three are found in the Azores. **Caldas da Rainha** (the Queen's Baths) is also famous for ceramics. The springs of **Caldas de Monchique** rise from volcanic rock in a verdant mountain region wooded with pine, cork and eucalyptus trees.

ROMANIA

The 160 health resorts particularly promote their "anti-aging" compounds and mudpacks. Along the Black Sea are **Mangalia, Neptun** and **Eforie Nord**. Inland, one finds **Călimăneşti-Căciulata, Sovata, Covasna** and **Tuşnad**.

SPAIN

The country has ninety-one registered *estaciones termales*. **Caldes de Montbui** near Barcelona has hot-water springs reaching 70 degrees C, which it claims are the best in Europe. The springs of **Caldes d'Estrac-Caldetes** are located almost on the beach.

SWEDEN

The *bastu* (sauna) can be found in almost every hotel and public swimming pool. Saunas are never mixed. Birch branches are sometimes used, as in Finland.

SWITZERLAND

Baden, not far from Zurich, boasts nineteen hot sulphur springs and was one of the most important European spas in the Middle Ages. **Bad Ragaz** is set in the Alpine Rhine Valley. Its mineral waters rise in the Tamina Gorge from a fissure where guests were once lowered on ropes to take the waters. Nowadays, the water is piped to the cure hotels, but the gorge can be visited.

TURKEY

The *hamam* (baths) can be found throughout the country, which has about 1,000 mineral springs. A natural phenomenon worth visiting is **Pamukkale**, whose minerals have formed a sort of frozen Niagara. Stay at one of the five hotels built around the pools; it is decidedly more pleasant to sit quietly in the pools after the tour buses have gone for the day.

U.S.S.R.

Livadia, near Yalta, is the largest health resort of the Crimea and the former summer residence of the czar. The Yalta Conference of 1945 was held in the White Livadian Palace. **Alupka** claims the most beautiful park on the Black Sea; it boasts giant cedars, 100-year-old magnolias, stone pines and blue spruces. **Sochi** is the largest health resort in the Soviet Union, extending nearly 20 miles along the Black Sea coast in the region often called the Soviet Riviera. Swimming in the sea is possible June to October, and some of the curative establishments have warm sea-water pools. Public bath houses are still very much a part of Soviet life. Try the **Sandunovsky Baths** on Petrovka Street in Moscow, which are divided into men's and women's sections. The decor is czarist: marble and mosaics. Be prepared to spend a long time over the ritual steamings, rubdowns with white pine shavings and cool-offs either in an ice-cold pool or with buckets of water.

Yugoslavia

Of the sixty-two spas in the country, **Opatija** is the best known. It retains the charm of the old Austrian Empire, with its camellia blossoms, its seaside paths and the fading yellow houses peculiar to that ornamental period of history. **Igalo**, on the South Adriatic not far from Dubrovnik, is another important resort. **Portorož** and **Crikvenica** on the coast are popular.

TRANSPORTATION

Airports

City	Airport	Distance in km to City Center	Connections to City
AUSTRIA			
Vienna	Schwechat	18	bus
Salzburg	Maxglan	3	bus
Graz	Thalerhof	6	bus
Innsbruck	Innsbruck	2	bus
Linz	Hörsching	15	bus

City	Airport	Distance in km to City Center	Connections to City
BELGIUM			
Brussels	Zaventem	15	train
Antwerp	Deurne	6	bus
NOTE: No domestic flights.			
BULGARIA			
Sofia	Vrajdebna	11	bus
CZECHOSLOVAKIA			
Prague	Ruzyně	17	bus
Bratislava	Ivanka	11	bus
DENMARK			
Copenhagen	Kastrup	10	bus
Aalborg	Aalborg	3	bus
Aarhus	Tirstrup	40	bus
Odense	Beldringe	15	bus
FINLAND			
Helsinki	Vantaa	12	bus
Turku	Turku	8	bus
Vaasa	Vaasa	10	bus
Maarianhamina	Maarianhamina	8	bus
FRANCE			
Paris	Ch. de Gaulle-Roissy	25	bus, train
	Orly	16	bus, Métro
Marseille	Marignan	28	bus
Lyon	Satolas	27	bus
Nice	Nice/Côte d'Azur	7	bus
Toulouse	Blagnac	21	bus
Strasbourg	Entzheim	12	bus
Bordeaux	Mérignac	11	bus
Lille	Lesquin	8	bus
GERMANY			
Frankfurt a.M.	Frankfurt	10	bus, train subway
Bonn/Cologne	Köln-Wahn	28/18	bus

City	Airport	Distance in km to City Center	Connections to City
Berlin	Tegel	8	bus
Berlin	Schönefeld	19	bus, train
Hamburg	Fuhlsbüttel	12	bus
Munich	Riem	10	bus
Düsseldorf	Lohausen	8	bus, train
Stuttgart	Echterdingen	14	bus
Bremen	Neuenland	3	bus
Nürnberg	Nürnberg	8	bus
Hannover	Langenhagen	11	bus
Leipzig	Schkeuditz	23	bus

GREAT BRITAIN
ENGLAND
London	Heathrow	30	bus, subway
	Gatwick	40	bus, train
Birmingham	Birmingham	13	bus
Manchester	Ringway	20	bus
Bristol	Lulsgate	11	bus

SCOTLAND
Glasgow	Abbotsinch	13	bus, train
Edinburgh	Turnhouse	11	bus
Aberdeen	Dyce	10	bus

WALES
Cardiff	Rhoose	19	bus

NORTHERN IRELAND
Belfast	Aldergrove	22	bus

GREECE
Athens	Hellinikón	12	bus
Thessaloniki	Thessaloníki	14	bus

HUNGARY
Budapest	Ferihegy	16	bus

ICELAND
Reykjavík	Keflavík	50	bus

City	Airport	Distance in km to City Center	Connections to City
IRELAND			
Dublin	Dublin	20	bus
Shannon	Shannon	9	bus
ITALY			
Rome	Fumicino (Leonardo da Vinci)	28	bus
	Ciampino	17	bus
Milan	Forlanini-Linate	8	bus
Naples	Capodichino	7	bus
Turin	Cittá di Torino	17	bus
Genoa	Cristofor Colombo	7	bus
Florence	Pisa-San Giusto	83	bus
Venice	Marco Polo	13	bus, boat

NOTE: Ciampino (Rome) mainly for charters; Pisa-San Giusto (Florence) for domestic flights.

LIECHTENSTEIN

No commercial airport. Nearest international airport is Zurich, Switzerland, which can be reached by bus or car.

LUXEMBOURG

Luxembourg	Findel	7	bus

MONACO

Served by Nice/Côte d'Azur in Nice, 22 km away. Minibus and helicopter connections.

NETHERLANDS

Amsterdam	Schiphol	15	bus, train
Rotterdam	Zestienhoven	6	bus
Groningen	Eelde	15	bus
Eindhoven	Welschap	10	bus
Enschede	Twente	8	bus
Maastricht	Beek	10	bus

NORWAY

Oslo	Fornebu	12	bus
	Gardermoen	50	bus

City	Airport	Distance in km to City Center	Connections to City
Bergen	Flesland	20	bus

NOTE: Gardermoen (Oslo) for charters.

POLAND

City	Airport	Distance in km to City Center	Connections to City
Warsaw	Okecie	10	bus
Gdansk	Rebechowo	10	bus
Krakow	Balice	10	bus

PORTUGAL

City	Airport	Distance in km to City Center	Connections to City
Lisbon	Portela	8	bus
Oporto	Pedras Rubras	18	bus
Faro	Faro	5	taxi only
Funchal (Madeira)	Santa Catarina	12	bus
Ponta Delgada (Azores)	Ponta Delgada	3	bus

ROMANIA

City	Airport	Distance in km to City Center	Connections to City
Bucharest	Otopeni	17	bus
	Băneasa	7	bus

SPAIN

City	Airport	Distance in km to City Center	Connections to City
Madrid	Barajas	12	bus
Barcelona	Muntadas	11	train
Bilboa	Sondica	15	bus

SWEDEN

City	Airport	Distance in km to City Center	Connections to City
Stockholm	Arlanda	40	bus
	Bromma	8	bus
Gothenburg	Landvetter	24	bus
Malmö	Sturup	31	bus

NOTE: Bromma (Stockholm) for domestic flights; Landvetter (Gothenburg) ferry to Copenhagen airport (Kastrup).

SWITZERLAND

City	Airport	Distance in km to City Center	Connections to City
Zurich	Kloten	12	train
Bern	Belpmoos	10	bus
Basel	Basel/Mulhouse, France	12	bus
Geneva	Cointrin	5	bus, train

City	Airport	Distance in km to City Center	Connections to City
Turkey			
Ankara	Esenboğa	35	bus
Istanbul	Yeşilköy	24	bus
Izmir	Çiğli	25	bus
U.S.S.R.			
Moscow	Sheremetyevo	30	bus
	Vnukovo	30	bus
	Domodedovo	40	bus
Leningrad	Pulkova	17	bus
	Smolny	5	bus
Kiev	Borispol	38	bus
	Zhulyany	3	bus

NOTE: Vnukovo (Moscow), Smolny (Leningrad) and Zhulyany (Kiev) for domestic flights. Bus service erratic.

City	Airport	Distance in km to City Center	Connections to City
Yugoslavia			
Belgrade	Surcin (Beograd)	20	bus
Ljubljana	Brniki	35	bus
Split	Split	25	bus
Skopje	Petrovac	18	bus
Sarajevo	Butmir	9	bus
Dubrovnik	Čilipe (Dubrovnik)	18	bus

Rail and Bus Passes

Europe-wide

Eurailpass is a ticket for unlimited travel on railways (plus some boats and buses) in seventeen European countries, excluding Great Britain. It is available in several variations to persons whose permanent residence is outside Europe (with a few exceptions) and now includes the fast-train supplement. The standard Eurailpass is for fifteen days, twenty-one days, one, two or three months for first-class travel. A **Eurail Saver Pass** for fifteen days or one month is for two (in off-season, October 1–March 31) or three (in high-season, April 1–September 30) persons traveling together. A **Eurail Flexi Pass** is good for a certain number of days' travel within a fixed period of time (i.e., nine days of travel within a twenty-one-day period). The **Eurail Youth Pass**, available for one or two months, is for second-class travel and is limited to those under age twenty-seven. A **Youth Flexi Pass** is also available. Eurailpass can be used in Austria, Belgium, Denmark, Finland, France, West Germany (former East German routes are expected to be added in the near future), Greece, Hungary, Ireland, Italy, Luxembourg, the Netherlands, Norway, Portugal, Spain, Sweden and Switzerland.

The **Interrail Pass** is a one-month rail pass for young people under age twenty-six. It is good for unlimited travel in twenty-two countries, but pass holders must pay half-fare for travel in the country where it is purchased. Therefore, many people buy the pass in Luxembourg because of its small size and convenient location. Countries where the **Interrail Pass** can be used are Belgium, Denmark, Finland, France, West Germany, Greece, Great Britain, Hungary, Ireland, Italy, Yugoslavia, Luxembourg, Morocco, Netherlands, Northern Ireland, Norway, Portugal, Romania, Sweden, Switzerland, Spain and Turkey. Several countries also have rail passes good for travel on their own railways.

AUSTRIA

Among many savings plans, the best for tourists is the **Rabbit Card** or **Junior Rabbit Card**, good for four days of travel within a ten-day period or ten days within one month. It includes boat passage on the Wolfgang Lake.

BELGIUM

The **Benelux Tourrail** ticket is a combined pass for Belgium, Luxembourg and the Netherlands for any five days within a seventeen-day period.

DENMARK

Nordturist Rail Pass for Danish, Finnish, Norwegian and Swedish railways is valid for twenty-one days of unlimited travel. The **Copenhagen Card** is valid for one, two or three days' city transportation plus entry to fifty museums and reductions on long-distance buses, trains and ferries.

FINLAND

Finnrail Pass is for eight, fifteen or twenty-two days. Finland accepts the **Nordturist Rail Pass** (see Denmark). Travelers over sixty-five get a 50 percent reduction on rail and air tickets, 30 percent on bus fares. The **Helsinki Card** gives unlimited travel on the city's public transportation, a guided sightseeing tour and admission to forty museums. It can be purchased for one, two or three days. The **Finnair Holiday Ticket** is available for eight or fifteen days; a cheaper **Youth Holiday Ticket** is available for those aged twelve to twenty-three.

FRANCE

The **France Vacances** pass is available for four days of travel within a fifteen-day period or for nine days of travel within one month. **Paris Sesame** tickets are good on the Métro and city buses for two, four or seven days.

GERMANY

The **DB Tourist Card** is for four, nine or sixteen days and **Tramper Tickets**, for those to age twenty-three (students to twenty-seven), are for one month. Major cities have public-transport day tickets available from ticket automats. On city transportation, single fares are usually cheaper between about 9:30 A.M. and 3:30 P.M.

GREAT BRITAIN

Britrail Pass, sold outside Britain only, is available in Gold (first-class) and Silver (second-class), with extra reductions for those aged sixteen to twenty-five or over sixty. Both passes are valid for four of eight days, eight of fifteen days or fifteen days of one month. Seven-day **Rail Rover** cards are for regional travel in Wales, Scotland (also for fourteen days), southwest England and northeast England. A **Southeast Pass** is available for four or seven days. For National Express and Caledonian Express buses, the **Britexpress Card** gives a one-third reduction for thirty days. The **Tourist Trail Pass** gives unlimited travel in England, Scotland and Wales for five, eight, fifteen, twenty-two or thirty days. The **Visitor Travelcard** is available for one, three, four or seven days unlimited travel on the London Underground.

GREECE

Greece has a limited rail network, but **Touring Card** passes are available for ten, twenty or thirty days. Ferries are more common here than trains, but no ferry pass is available.

IRELAND

Rambler tickets are good for one week of travel on trains or combination trains and buses; two-week tickets are available for the train-bus combination only. **Overlander** Ticket includes Northern Ireland rail and bus.

ITALY

Passes for railways are available for eight, fifteen, twenty-one or thirty days. A **Flexi-Railcard** is good for four days within nine, eight days within twelve and twelve days within twenty.

LUXEMBOURG

Passes are good on rail and bus lines for one day, one month or any five days within a month. A 50 percent reduction is available for those over sixty-five. **Benelux Tourrail** is accepted (see Belgium).

NETHERLANDS

A **Rover Ticket** is available for three or seven days of unlimited travel, first- or second-class. A **Dutch Railpass** is good for three days of travel with fifteen. **Benelux Tourrail** is accepted (see Belgium).

NORWAY

Nordturist Rail Pass is accepted (see Denmark).

POLAND

The **Polrailpass**, sold for Western currency, is good for unlimited travel for eight, fifteen or twenty-one days or one month. Warsaw offers a seven-day **Tourist Ticket** for unlimited travel on the bus, trolley bus and streetcar.

PORTUGAL

Rail passes are available for seven, fourteen or twenty-one days, first-class only.

SPAIN

RENFE Tourist Pass is for unlimited travel for eight, fifteen or twenty-two days.

SWEDEN

Nordturist Rail Pass is accepted (see Denmark). The **Stockholm Card** gives unlimited rides on public transportation for one, two, three or four days, including sightseeing tours and admission to all museums; similar is the **Gothenberg Card**.

Sample of German Federal Railway Schedule – Departures

Abfahrt ⑱ Frankfurt (M) Hbf

Zeit	Zug	Richtung	Gleis

15.00

15.15 D 720 ⚍ ▪ 🛆	Mainz 15.42–Bingerbrück 16.02–Boppard 16.31–Koblenz 16.43–Neuwied 17.01–Bonn-Beuel 17.32–Köln 17.56–Neuss 18.25–Düsseldorf 18.39–Duisburg 18.57–Oberhausen 19.09–Essen-Altenessen 19.20–Gelsenkirchen 19.26–Wanne-Eickel 19.34–Herne 19.42–**Dortmund 19.58** ◯	**9**

15.17 Ⓢ	Ⓢ Hofheim 15.35–**Niedernhausen** nur ④, † 15.50	Ⓢ

15.20 ⎓ 523 ✕	*Heinrich der Löwe* Würzburg 16.38–Augsburg 18.30–**München 19.04** ◯	**6**

✕ **15.20** 8437 außer ④	Ⓢ Goddelau-Erfelden 16.00–Biblis 16.30–**Mannheim 17.01**	**20**

✕ **15.22** Ⓢ außer ④	Ⓢ ✈ Ffm Flughafen 15.32–Mainz 16.00–**Wiesbaden 16.18** → Hält nicht in Wiesbaden Ost ← → bis Rüsselsheim Opelwerk auch an verkaufsoffenen Samstagen ←	Ⓢ

15.23 ⎓ 694 ✕	*Kieler Förde* Fulda 16.20–Göttingen 17.38–Hannover 18.38–Hamburg Hbf 19.56–Hamburg Dammtor 20.02–Hamburg-Altona 20.10–Neumünster 21.04–**Kiel 21.26** ◯	**7**

15.24 D 2074	Friedberg 15.43–Bad Nauheim 15.48–Gießen 16.08–Marburg 16.27–Treysa 16.50–Wabern 17.06–Kassel-Wilhelmshöhe 17.28–**Kassel 17.34** ◯ → bis Gießen vereinigt mit D 812; D 2074 vorderer Zugteil ←	**13**

15.24 D 812 ⚍ 🛆	Ⓢ Friedberg 15.43–Bad Nauheim 15.48–Gießen 16.08–Wetzlar 16.27–Herborn 16.41–Dillenburg 16.47–Haiger 16.53–Siegen-Weidenau 17.10 ◯ Altenhundem 17.35–Finnentrop 17.46–Altena 18.12–Letmathe 18.22–Hagen 18.38–Schwerte 19.04–Unna 19.14–	**13**

EC	**EuroCity,** 1st and 2nd class high-speed special comfort cross-frontier trains require payment of surcharges which include seat reservation. Seat reservation required for groups.
IC	**Intercity train,** 1st and 2nd class, hourly (with supplementary IC charge, seat reservation free; for groups, the reservation of seats is necessary).
FD	**Long Distance Express,** special Express train (with supplementary charge for distances up to 50 km and for sealson-ticket-holders if special marks show this on the schedule).
D	**Express train** (with supplementary charge for distances up to 50 km and for season-ticket-holders).

Trains on which no supplements are payable

E	**Semi fast train**
Ⓢ	**Rapid-transit suburban train**
†	runs on Sundays and Public Holidays only; **official holidays** in the Federal Republik are: **New Year, Good Friday, Easter Monday, May 1st; Ascension Day, Monday after Pentecost, June 17th, Repentance Day, Christmas Day and Boxing Day.**

Sample of German Federal Railway Schedule – Departures

Departures   Départs

Zeit	Zug	Richtung	Gleis

16.00

Zeit	Zug	Richtung	Gleis
16.16	E 3392 ⊡	🔲 Ff-Höchst 16.24–Niedernhausen 16.44 ⊙ Limburg 17.17 (⑥, † 17.20)–Westerburg ✗ 18.08– Altenkirchen ✗ 19.11–Au ✗ 19.32– Troisdorf ✗ 20.22–**Köln ✗ 20.43**	**23**
→ an ④ und † als E 3396 ←			
✗ **16.16** außer ④	E 3580	🔲 Ffm West 16.20–Friedberg 16.42 ⊙ **Nidda 17.30**	**14**
	→ ab Friedberg als Nahverkehrszug ←		
✗ **16.16** außer ④	E 3458	🔲 Ffm Süd 16.20–Offenbach 16.25– Hanau 16.34–Langenselbold 16.47 ⊙ Wächters- bach 17.02–Schlüchtern 17.19–**Fulda 17.48**	**9**
16.17	E 3370 ⊡ ²)	🔲 Rüsselsheim 16.35– Rüsselsheim Opelwerk nur ✗ außer ④ 16.37– Mainz Süd 16.46–Mainz 16.49– Heidesheim 17.00–Ingelheim 17.06 ⊙ Bad Kreuznach 17.27–Idar-Oberstein 18.24– Neunkirchen (Saar) 19.14–**Saarbrücken 19.32**	**2**
16.17 ⑤		🔲 Hofheim 16.38–**Niedernhausen 16.52**	Ⓢ
✗ **16.19** außer ⑥	⑤	🔲 Niederhöchstadt 16.35–**Kronberg 16.40**	Ⓢ
16.20 ✗	🚃 27	*Frans Hals* Würzburg 17.38–Nürnberg 18.38– Augsburg 19.50–**München 20.24** ⊙	**6**
✗ **16.20** außer ⑥	6184 2. Kl	🔲 *ohne Halt bis* Frankfurt-Höchst 16.29– Kelkheim 16.43–**Königstein 16.55**	**22**
✗ **16.22** außer ⑥	⑤	🔲 ✈ Ffm Flughafen 16.32–Mainz 16.59– **Wiesbaden 17.14**	Ⓢ
	→ verkehrt auch an verkaufsoffenen Samstagen ←		
16.23 ✗	🚃 70	*Rätia* Fulda 17.20–Göttingen 18.38– Hannover 19.38–Hamburg Hbf 20.56–	**7**

✗	runs on weekdays only
①	Monday
②	Tuesday
③	Wednesday
④	Thursday
⑤	Friday
⑥	Saturday
⑦	Sunday
⊡	conveys luggage and bicycles
🚃	Train with through coaches: these are listed in the list of coaches on the Timetable
🛏	Sleeping Car
⊢	Couchettes
✗	Restaurant Car
⑪	Quick-Pick-Restaurant Car
⚲	Light snacks available on the train
{	Runs only on certain days, or during certain periods,
†	runs on Sundays and Public Holidays

SWITZERLAND

The **Swiss Pass** gives unlimited travel on 9,000 kilometers (about 5,400 miles) of railroad, boat and post-bus routes, as well as on streetcars in twenty-four Swiss cities and a 25 percent discount on some mountain lifts. It is available for four, eight or fifteen days, first- or second-class. A cheaper **Flexi-Pass** is good for three days within a fifteen-day period. The **Swiss Card**, available in first- or second-class, is good for 50 percent reductions on rail, boat and bus. Pass holders can get a 10 percent reduction on ski rental from participating shops.

HOW TO READ A TRAIN SCHEDULE

The illustration shows (see pages 148-149) a sample departure schedule from the German Federal Railway (DB). Not every country's schedule is the same, but this one gives a general idea of the symbols and how they are used. Departure and arrival schedules are usually printed on different-colored paper: i.e., in Germany, departures are on deep yellow and arrivals are on white.

Notice that departures are listed in time sequence using the twenty-four-hour clock. Symbols indicate that some trains run only on work days, and notations show that some don't run on certain dates (usually holidays). The type of train, its name (express trains only), number and dining or sleeping facilities on board are shown. Major stops and their times are indicated.

Automobile Clubs

INTERNATIONAL ASSOCIATIONS

Fédération International de l'Automobile (FIA), Place de la Concorde, F-75008 Paris, France.

Alliance International de Tourisme (AIT), Quai Gustave Ador 2, CH-1207 Geneva, Switzerland.

AUSTRIA

ÖAMTC (Österreichischer Automobil-Motorrad-und-Touring Club), Schubertring 3, A-1015 Vienna.

BELGIUM

Royal Automobile Club de Belgique (RACB), 53 rue d'Arlon, B-1040 Brussels.

Vlaamse Automobilistendbond (VAB), St.-Jakobsmarkt 45, B-2000 Antwerp.

BULGARIA
Schipka, Organization of Bulgarian Drivers, Sveta Sofia 6, BG-1000 Sofia. Road service: tel. 146.

CANADA
Canadian Automobile Association (CAA), 1775 Courtwood Crescent, Ottawa K2C 3J2, Ontario, tel. (613) 226-7631.

CZECHOSLOVAKIA
AMK ČSFR, Opletalova 21, CS-11001 Prague 1. Road service: tel. 22 49 06.

DENMARK
Forenede Danske Motorejere (FDM), Blegdamsvej 124, DK-2100 Copenhagen.

FINLAND
Autoliitto, Kasankoulukatu 10, SF-00100 Helsinki 10.

FRANCE
Automobile Club de France (ACF), 6-8 Place de la Concorde, F-75008 Paris.

GERMANY
ADAC (Allgemeiner Deutscher Automobil-Club), Baumgartnerstrasse 53, W-8000 Munich 70.

AvD (Automobil Club von Deutschland), Lyoner Strasse 16, W-6000 Frankfurt a.M. 71.

GREAT BRITAIN
The Royal Automobile Club (RAC), Motoring Services, Pall Mall, London SW1 5JG.

The Automobile Association (AA), P.O. Box 50, Basingstoke, Hampshire RG21 2EA.

Royal Scottish Automobile Club (RSAC), Blythswood Square 11, Glasgow G2 4AG.

GREECE
ELPA (Automobile and Touring Club of Greece), Messogion 2-4, Athens 610.

The yellow cars marked *Assistance Routiere* can be reached by phoning 104 in an area 60 km around Athens, 80 km around Thessaloníki and 40 km around Agrinio, Volos, Heraklión, Ioannina, Kavala, Kalamata, Lamia, Larissa, Pátras and Chania. For road information in English, tel. 174 in Athens 7:30 A.M.-10:00 P.M.

HUNGARY
Automobile Club, Bp.II Rómer Flóri útca 4/2, H-1364 Budapest.

ICELAND
Félag Íslenskra Bifreidaeigenda (FIB), Borgar Tun, IS-105 Reykjavík.

IRELAND
Automobile Association, 23 Suffolk Street, Dublin 2.
Irish Visiting Motorists Bureau, 5-9 South Frederik Street, Dublin 2.

ITALY
Automobile Club d'Italia, Via Marsala 8, I-00185 Rome. Road service: tel. 116.

LUXEMBOURG
Automobile Club du Grand-Duché de Luxembourg, 13 Route de Longway, Helfenterbruck/Bertrange. Road service: tel. 31 10 31.

MONACO
Automobile Club de Monaco, 23 Boulevard Albert 1er, MC-98030 Monte Carlo.

NETHERLANDS
Koninklijke Netherlands Automobile Club (KNAC), Westvlietweg 118, NL-2267 AK Leidschendam.

NORWAY
Norges Automobil-Forbund, Storgata 2, N-0105 Oslo 1.

POLAND
Polski Zwiazek Motorowy, Al. Jerotolimskie 44, PL-00028 Warsaw. Road service: tel. 981.

PORTUGAL
Automóvel Club de Portugal (ACP), Rua Rosa Arújo 24, P-1200 Lisbon.

ROMANIA
Automobil Club Român (ARC), Str. Mikos Beloiahis 7, Bucharest.

SPAIN
Real Automóvil Club d'España, José Abascal 10, E-28003 Madrid.

SWEDEN
Kungl Automobil Klubben (KAK), Box 5855, S-10248 Stockholm.
"M" Motormännens Riksförbund, Box 5855, S-10248 Stockholm.

SWITZERLAND
Touring-Club der Suisse (TCS), Maulbeerstrasse 10, CH-3001 Bern. Road service: tel. 140.

TURKEY
Türk Turing ve Otomobil Kurumu (TTOK), Halaskargazí Cad. 364, Şişli-Istanbul.

UNITED STATES
American Automobile Association (AAA), 8111 Gatehouse Road, Falls Church, VA 22047, tel. (703) 222-6000.

YUGOSLAVIA
Auto-Moto Savez (AMSJ), Ruzveltora 18, YU-11000 Belgrade. Road service 8:00 A.M.–8:00 P.M.: tel. 987.
Each republic also has an automobile club.

Speed Limits
in kilometers per hour (approximate m.p.h. in parentheses)

Country	Expressways	Other Roads	In Town	Seatbelts Obligatory
Austria	130 (80)	100 (60)	50 (30)	yes
Belgium	120 (75)	90 (55)	60 (35)	yes
Bulgaria	120 (75)	80 (50)	60 (35)	no
Czechoslovakia	110 (65)	90 (55)	60 (35)	yes
Denmark	100 (60)	90 (55)	60 (35)	yes
Finland	120 (75)	80 (50)	50 (30)	yes[a]
France	130 (80)	90 (55)	60 (35)	yes
Germany, E.	100 (60)[b]	80 (50)	50 (30)	yes
Germany, W.	no limit	80 (50)	50 (30)	yes
Great Britain	110 (65)	100 (60)	50 (30)	yes
Greece	100 (60)	80 (50)	50 (30)	yes
Hungary	120 (75)	100 (60)	50 (30)	yes
Iceland	——	70 (40)	50 (30)	yes
Ireland	110 (65)	90 (55)	50 (30)	yes
Italy	130 (80)[c]	90 (55)	50 (30)	no
Luxembourg	120 (75)	90 (55)	60 (35)	yes
Netherlands	120 (75)	80 (50)	50 (30)	yes
Norway	90 (55)	80 (50)	50 (30)	yes[a]
Poland	110 (65)	90 (55)	50 (30)	no
Portugal	120 (75)	90 (55)	60 (35)	yes
Romania	——	90 (55)	60 (35)	no
Spain	100 (60)	90 (55)	60 (35)	yes
Sweden	110 (65)	90 (55)	50 (30)	yes[a]
Switzerland	120 (75)	80 (50)	50 (30)	yes
Turkey	110 (65)	80 (50)	50 (30)	yes
Yugoslavia	120 (75)	80 (50)	60 (35)	yes

[a] Headlights must be on at all times.

[b] Until the *autobahnen* in former East Germany are brought up to West German standards, the speed limit applies.

[c] The speed limit on Italy's *autostrada* is restricted to 110 k.p.h. (about 65 m.p.h.) on weekends (Friday midnight to Sunday midnight), on holidays, from December 20 to January 7, Easter week from Maundy Thursday to Ash Wednesday, and during summer vacation from the second Sunday in July to the first Sunday in September.

Major Alpine Tunnels

The name of the tunnel and towns at each end of the tunnel are indicated; countries are in parentheses. Tolls are charged unless *no toll* is noted. Cars can piggyback on trains through railway tunnels.

Mont Blanc: Chamonix-Courmayeur (France-Italy), 7.2-mile car tunnel.

Grand St. Bernard: Bourg St. Pierre–St. Rhemy (Switzerland-Italy), 3.2-mile car tunnel.

Lotschberg: Kandersteg-Brig (Switzerland), 10-mile railway tunnel, thirteen trips daily.

Simplon: Brig-Iselle (Switzerland-Italy), 12.3-mile railway tunnel, fourteen trips daily.

Furka: Realp-Oberwald (Switzerland), 9.5-mile railway tunnel, fourteen trips daily.

Seelisberg: Beckenried-Seedorf (Switzerland), 5.7-mile car tunnel, no toll.

St. Gotthard: Goschenen-Airolo (Switzerland), 10.1-mile car tunnel.

St. Bernardino: Hinterrhein–San Bernardino (Switzerland), 4.1-mile car tunnel, no toll.

Pfander: Horbraty-Bregenz (Germany-Austria), 4.1-mile car tunnel, no toll.

Arlberg: Langen–St. Anton (Austria), 8.6-mile car tunnel.

Felbertauern: Mittersill-Matrei (Austria), 3.2-mile car tunnel.

Tauern: Flachau-Rennweg (Austria), 3.2-mile car tunnel.

Gleinalm: St. Michael–Peggau (Austria), 2.4-mile car tunnel.

National Auto Decals

Decals, usually black-and-white ovals, are attached to the rear of most European cars to indicate the country where they are registered. These abbreviations are also used as postal codes to indicate countries when writing addresses.

Andorra - AND	Monaco - MC
Austria - A	Netherlands - NL
Belgium - B	Norway - N
Bulgaria - BG	Poland - PL
Canada - CDN	Portugal - P
Czechoslovakia - CS	Romania - RO
Denmark - DK	San Marino - RSM

Finland - SF	Spain - E (sometimes SP)
France - F	Sweden - S
Germany - D*	Switzerland - CH
Great Britain - GB	Turkey - TR
Greece - GR	U.S.A. - USA
Hungary - H	U.S.S.R. - SU
Iceland - IS	Vatican City - SCV
Ireland - IRL	Yugoslavia - YU
Italy - I	
Liechtenstein - FL	Consular Corps - CC
Luxembourg - L	Diplomatic Corps - CD

* For postal codes, O (east) and W (west) will be used for a few years.

Visa Requirements

If you don't have a current passport, apply for one several months before your trip. Allow even more time if you need visas for countries that require long processing periods. *Always* use registered mail when sending your passport away for visas. If you have a passport, make sure that it won't expire during your journey. Many countries require that a passport be valid for up to six months after your entry, even if they do not require a visa. If your old passport is getting full of visa stamps, have your consulate or passport office add more pages before you go.

If you are going on a business trip, find out the requirements for doing business in the country you will visit. Business permits may be required by countries that do not require visas for tourists. Most countries limit stays to between thirty and ninety days. If you hold dual citizenship in the country you plan to visit, check with the consulate for special requirements that you may have to fulfill or difficulties you may encounter.

Visa requirements listed here are for tourist visits by citizens of the United States and Canada. Resident aliens are required by some countries to have visas (i.e., bearers of Philippine passports must have visas to enter Italy, Switzerland, etc.). Countries that do not require tourist visas for U.S. and Canadian citizens are not listed here. Changes in visa requirements for some East European countries are likely in the future; contact the consulates of these countries or your travel agent for the latest information. Some countries that require visas give group visas for package tours.

BULGARIA

U.S. citizens no longer need visas for Bulgaria. Canadians may get visas at border crossings or in advance.

Tourist: Valid thirty days, obtainable at Bulgarian Consulate, 1621 22nd Street, N.W., Washington, DC 20008, tel. (202) 387-7969, or 325 Steward Street, Ottawa, Ontario K1N 6K5, tel. (613) 232-3215. You must complete a visa form and turn in your passport (valid at least six months after your planned trip) along with one passport-size photo. Inquire for current cost, to be paid in cash or by money order. Send your passport by registered mail only, and include a self-addressed envelope plus $3 for its return. Some travel agents will take care of visa formalities for a fee.

Transit: Single- or double-entry visas available at the border for a fee, good for thirty hours in-country. Expiration dates are three months from date of issue.

HUNGARY

U.S. citizens no longer need visas for Hungary. The following information still applies to Canadians.

Tourist: Valid thirty days. Multiple-entry visas available for one year. Visa can be obtained at highway or airport crossings, but not on board trains or boats. Available in advance from Hungarian Consulate, 3910 Shoemaker Street, N.W., Washington, DC 20008, tel. (202) 362-6730, or 8 East 75th Street, New York, NY 10021, tel. (212) 879-4127, or 7 Delaware Avenue, Ottawa, Ontario K1N 6K5, tel. (613) 232-1711.

You must complete a visa form and turn in your passport (valid at least six months after your planned trip) along with two passport-size photos. Inquire for current cost, to be paid in cash or by money order. Send your passport by registered mail only, and include a self-addressed envelope plus $3 for its return. Processing takes four to six weeks; express service costs extra. Some travel agents will take care of visa formalities for a fee.

Transit: Cost is the same as tourist visa, so it is pointless. Sightseeing permit good for forty-eight hours available at the airport for 100 forints.

POLAND

Tourist: Visas issued only for the number of nights you will be staying (ninety days maximum), as determined by the number of pre-paid hotel nights you have booked. Visas are available from Polish Consulates at 2640 16th Street, N.W., Washington, DC 20009, tel. (202) 234-3800; 233 Madison Avenue, New York, NY 10016; 1530 Lake Shore Drive, Chicago, IL 60610; 1500 Pine Avenue West, Montreal, Quebec

H3G IB4; 2603 Lakeshore Boulevard West, Toronto, Ontario M8V 1G5. Inquire for current fee.

Send your passport by registered mail only, and include a self-addressed envelope plus $3 for its return. Processing takes about two weeks but can be done in twenty-four hours if you go in person. Some travel agents will take care of visa formalities for a fee.

You must complete a visa form and turn it in with your passport (valid at least six months from the planned end of your trip) and two passport-size photos. Anyone who plans to study there for a month or longer must provide a negative test for AIDS.

Transit: Valid forty-eight hours, single- or double-entry. The process is the same as for tourist visas.

Extensions: Available through the District Militia Office. Expect a long wait.

ROMANIA

Tourist: Valid sixty days; compulsory exchange of $10 per day of your stay. Available for a fee at the border or in advance from the Romanian Consulate at 1607 23rd Street, N.W., Washington, DC 20008, tel. (202) 232-4747, or 655 Rideau Street, Ottawa, Ontario K1N 6A3, tel. (613) 232-5345. No visa required for persons on package tours; instead, a "tourist card" is issued.

Transit: Single- or double-entry.

U.S.S.R.

Tourist: Valid thirty days; obtainable from Soviet Consulate, 1125 16th Street, N.W., Washington, DC 20036, tel. (202) 628-7551, or 285 Charlotte Street, Ottawa, Ontario K1N 8L5, tel. (613) 235-4341.

You must complete a visa form and turn in your passport (valid at least six months after your planned trip) along with three passport-size photos. Inquire for current charge, payable in cash or by money order. Send your passport by registered mail only, and include a self-addressed envelope plus $3 for its return. Processing takes several weeks. Travel agents will take care of visa formalities for a fee if they book you on a package tour.

Transit: Valid three days. Obtainable at border.

YUGOSLAVIA

Yugoslavia no longer requires visas for U.S. and Canadian citizens.

International Road Signs

Here is a selection of the most common international road signs. They may vary artistically from country to country, and there are a few localized signs—such as *elk crossing* in Sweden and *frog crossing* in Germany. (It's true: an endangered species of frog is especially fond of some roads in Germany during the mating season, and the residents want to protect it.)

Warning

Stop

Stop ahead

Crossroad

Road work

Signal ahead

Bumpy road

Left curve

Right curve

Winding road

Downhill gradient

Uphill gradient

Left lane narrows

Road narrows

Lowflying aircraft

Side winds

Two-way traffic

Danger

Drawbridge

Slippery road

Loose gravel

Falling rock

Cycle crossing

Cycle path

Pedestrian zone

Pedestrian crossing

Children

Cattle crossing

Deer crossing

Border

Barricaded RR crossing

Open RR crossing

Dead-end street

Parking

Expressway begins

Expressway ends

Directional signs

RR crossing ahead
80 160 240 meters

No entry

Enter city

Leave city

No horns

Speed limit

End speed limit

End restrictions

No left turn

No right turn

No U turn

Mechanic

Gasoline

Telephone

First aid

SHOPPING

Opening Hours

Shopping hours vary considerably from country to country. Times given here are approximate. Small shops may close for lunch and earlier on Saturdays, while large department stores remain open. Souvenir shops often open on Sundays, especially during high season. Shops, banks and sometimes museums close on holidays (note that most European countries take both December 25 and 26 for Christmas), so check before you go. Shops also close for national days and saints' days.

AUSTRIA
Weekdays: Open 8:00 A.M.–6:00 P.M. Small shops close for

lunch noon–2:00 or 3:00 P.M. Some close Monday morning.

Weekends: Open Saturday 8:00 A.M.–noon, except first Saturday of month to 4:00 P.M. Closed Sunday.

Banks: Open Monday–Friday 8:00 A.M.–12:30 P.M. and 1:30–3:00 P.M., on Thursday to 5:30 P.M.

BELGIUM

Weekdays: Open 10:00 A.M.–6:00 P.M., Friday to 9:00 P.M. Food shops open at 8:00 or 9:00 A.M. Some shops close for lunch, some close Monday morning.

Weekends: Open regular hours Saturday; a few open Sunday.

Banks: Open Monday–Friday 9:00 A.M.–4:00 P.M. Some close for lunch.

BULGARIA

Weekdays: Open 9:00 A.M.–1:00 P.M. and 2:00 P.M.–7:00 P.M. Food shops open 7:00 or 8:00 A.M.

Weekends: Open Saturday 9:30 A.M.–7:00 P.M. Some open Sunday.

Banks: Open Monday–Friday 8:00 A.M.–noon; Saturday 8:00–11:00 A.M.

CZECHOSLOVAKIA

Weekdays: Open 9:00 A.M.–7:00 P.M. Food shops open 7:00 A.M.–7:00 P.M. or 8:00 A.M.–6:00 P.M.

Weekends: Open Saturday 9:00 A.M.–1:00 P.M. Closed Sunday.

Banks: Open Monday–Friday 8:00 A.M.–4:00 P.M., Saturday 8:00 A.M.–noon.

DENMARK

Weekdays: Open 9:00 A.M.–5:30 P.M. Many stay open to 7:00 or 8:00 P.M.

Weekends: Open Saturday 9:00 A.M.–noon or 2:00 P.M. First Saturday is "long Saturday," open to 5:00 P.M. Closed Sunday.

Banks: Open Monday–Friday 9:30 A.M.–4:00 P.M.; Thursday to 6:00 P.M. Hours vary outside Copenhagen.

FINLAND

Weekdays: Open 9:00 A.M.–6:00 P.M. Some open 8:00 A.M.–8:00 P.M.

Weekends: Many shops open regular hours Saturday and Sunday. Those open on Sunday may close Monday.

Banks: Open Monday–Friday 9:00 A.M.–4:15 P.M.

Note: In Helsinki, an underground shopping center called *The*

Tunnel is open daily 10:00 A.M.–10:00 P.M. and Sunday noon–10:00 P.M.

FRANCE

Weekdays: Open 9:00 A.M.–7:00 P.M. Closed for lunch 1:00–3:00 or 4:00 P.M.

Weekends: Many shops open regular hours Saturday and Sunday. Those open on Sunday close Monday. Many markets open on Sunday.

Banks: Open Monday–Friday 9:00 or 9:30 A.M.–4:30 or 5:00 P.M. Some close for lunch noon–2:00 P.M. Hours vary outside Paris.

GERMANY

Weekdays: Open 10:00 A.M.–6:30 P.M.; Thursday to 8:30 P.M. Food shops and pharmacies may open at 8:00 A.M. Small shops may close noon–3:00 P.M.

Weekends: Open Saturday 8:00 or 10:00 A.M.–1:00 P.M.; first Saturday of the month, to 4:00 or 6:00 P.M. Closed Sunday.

Banks: Open Monday–Friday 8:30 A.M.–12:30 P.M. and 1:30–4:00 P.M.; Thursday to 6:00 P.M.

GREAT BRITAIN

Weekdays: Open 9:00 A.M.–5:30 P.M. In London, late shopping in Knightsbridge and Kings Road on Wednesday, in the West End on Thursday. In the Arab quarters, shops open daily into the late evening.

Weekends: Open Saturday 9:00 A.M.–5:30 P.M. Most close Sunday.

Banks: Open Monday–Friday 9:30 A.M.–3:30 P.M.

GREECE

Weekdays: Open Monday and Wednesday 8:30 A.M.–2:30 P.M. On Tuesday, Thursday and Friday 8:30 A.M.–1:30 P.M. and 5:00–8:00 P.M. Souvenir shops open 8:00 A.M–9:00 P.M. in summer; hours vary in winter.

Weekends: Open Saturday 8:30 A.M.–2:30 P.M. Souvenir shops open Sunday 9:00 A.M.–3:00 P.M. in season.

Banks: Open Monday–Friday 8:00 A.M.–2:00 P.M. Some open afternoons in Athens, Pátras, Thessaloníki and Piraeus.

HUNGARY

Weekdays: Open 10:00 A.M.–6:00 P.M.; Thursday to 8:00 P.M. Food shops open 7:00 a.m.–7:00 P.M. No lunch closing in main towns.

Weekends: Open Saturday 9:00 A.M.–1:00 P.M., to 3:00 P.M. in Budapest. Food shops to 2:00 P.M. Closed Sunday.

Banks: Open Monday–Friday 9:00 A.M.–5:00 P.M.; Saturday to 2:00 P.M.

ICELAND

Weekdays: Open 9:00 A.M.–6:00 P.M.; Friday to 7:00 P.M., some to 8:00 P.M. Weekends: Some open Saturday 9:00 A.M.–4:00 P.M. Closed Sunday.

Banks: Open Monday–Friday 9:15 A.M.–4:00 P.M. and 5:00–6:00 P.M.

IRELAND

Weekdays: Open 9:00 A.M.–5:30 P.M., varying greatly. Large shops and shopping centers open Thursday and Friday to 9:00 P.M.

Weekends: Open regular hours Saturday. Closed Sunday.

Banks: Open Monday–Saturday 10:00 A.M.–12:30 P.M. and 1:30–3:00 P.M.; Thursday to 5:00 P.M.

ITALY

Weekdays: Open 9:00 A.M.–1:00 P.M. and 3:30 or 4:00–7:30 or 8:00 P.M.; department stores 9:00 A.M.–6:00 P.M.

Weekends: Open regular hours. Some shops open half–day Sunday and close half-day during the week.

Banks: Open Monday–Friday 8:30 A.M.–1:30 P.M.

LIECHTENSTEIN

Weekdays: Open 8:00 A.M.–noon and 2:00–6:30 P.M.; in Schaan, Friday to 8:00 P.M.

Weekends: Open Saturday 8:00 A.M.–4:00 p.m. Closed Sunday.

Banks: Open Monday–Friday 8:00 A.M.–noon and 2:00–4:30 P.M.

LUXEMBOURG

Weekdays: Open 8:00 A.M.–noon and 2:00–6:00 P.M., though more and more remain open through lunch. Some close Monday morning. Shopping centers open 7:00 A.M.–8:00 P.M.

Weekends: Shopping centers open Saturday 9:00 A.M.–6:00 P.M. Closed Sunday.

Banks: Open Monday–Friday 8:30 A.M.–noon and 1:30–4:30 P.M.

MONACO

Weekdays: Open 9:00 A.M.–7:00 P.M.; closed for lunch 1:00–3:00 or 4:00 P.M.

Weekends: Many shops open regular hours Saturday and Sunday. Those open Sunday close Monday.

Banks: Open Monday–Friday 9:00 A.M.–noon and 2:00–4:00 P.M.

NETHERLANDS

Weekdays: Open Monday 1:00–6:00 P.M.; Tuesday–Friday 9:00 A.M.–6:00 P.M.; Thursday or Friday to 9:00 P.M. Some shops open Monday morning and close one afternoon during the week. In cities, a few shops open 4:00 P.M.–midnight.

Weekends: Open Saturday 9:00 A.M.–5:00 P.M. Closed Sunday.

Banks: Open Monday–Friday 9:00 A.M.–4:00 P.M.

NORWAY

Weekdays: Open 9:00 A.M.–5:00 P.M. Some shops open late in summer.

Weekends: Open Saturday 9:00 A.M.–2:00 P.M. Some shops open on Sunday in summer.

Banks: Open Monday–Friday 8:15 A.M.–3:00 P.M., Thursday to 5:00 P.M.

POLAND

Weekdays: Open 11:00 A.M.–7:00 P.M. Food shops open at 7:00 A.M. Department stores open 8:00 A.M.–8:00 P.M.

Weekends: Open first and last Saturday of the month; food shops every Saturday 7:00 A.M.–1:00 P.M. Closed Sunday.

Banks: Open Monday–Saturday 8:00 A.M.–noon and Monday–Friday 2:00–6:00 P.M.

PORTUGAL

Weekdays: Open 9:00 A.M.–12:30 P.M. and 3:00–7:00 P.M.; many stay open through lunch. Shopping centers open to midnight in Lisbon.

Weekends: Open Saturday mornings. Shopping centers open Saturday and Sunday in Lisbon.

Banks: Open Monday–Friday 9:00 A.M.–noon and 2:00–3:30 P.M.

ROMANIA

Weekdays: Open 8:00 A.M.–8:00 P.M. in summer, 9:00 A.M.–6:00 P.M. in winter.

Weekends: Open regular hours Saturday; Sunday 8:00 A.M.–1:00 P.M.

Banks: Open Monday–Friday 8:15 A.M.–1:30 P.M.; Saturday to 11:30 A.M.

Spain

Weekdays: Open 9:00 or 10:00 A.M.–1:30 or 2:00 P.M. and 4:00 or 4:30 P.M.–7:00 or 8:30 P.M.

Weekends: Open regular hours Saturday. Some shops in tourist areas open Sunday.

Banks: Open Monday–Friday 9:00 A.M.–2:00 P.M.; Saturday to 1:00 P.M.

Sweden

Weekdays: Open 9:30 A.M.–6:00 P.M. Some food shops open ten hours a day.

Weekends: Open Saturday 9:30 A.M.–2:00 P.M. Some food shops open Sunday. Large department stores open to 4:00 P.M. Saturday, 11:00 A.M.–2:00 P.M. on Sunday.

Banks: Open Monday–Friday 9:30 A.M.–3:00 P.M.

Switzerland

Weekdays: Open 8:00 A.M.–6:30 P.M.; some close for lunch; some close Monday morning; some open Thursday or Friday to 9:00 P.M.

Weekends: Open Saturday 8:00 A.M.–4:00 P.M. Some open Sunday in tourist areas.

Banks: Open Monday–Friday 8:30 A.M.–12:30 P.M. and 1:30–5:30 P.M. In Zurich, open 8:15 A.M.–4:30 P.M., Monday to 6:00 P.M.

Turkey

Weekdays: Open 8:00 A.M.–7:00 P.M.; lunch break usually 1:00–2:00 P.M.

Weekends: Many shops open Saturday as on weekdays. Closed Sunday, except food shops.

Banks: Open Monday–Friday 8:30 A.M.–6:00 P.M.; lunch break varies between noon and 1:30 P.M.

U.S.S.R.

Weekdays: Open 8:00 or 10:00 A.M.–8:00 P.M.

Weekends: Open regular hours Saturday; large stores open Sunday 8:00 A.M.–7:00 P.M.

Banks: Open Monday–Friday 9:00 A.M.–1:00 P.M.

Yugoslavia

Weekdays: Open 8:00 A.M.–noon and 4:00–8:00 P.M.; some open through lunch, especially in high season June 15–September 15. Food shops in cities open 6:00 A.M.–8:00 P.M.

Weekends: Open Saturday 8:00 A.M.–3:00 P.M. Food shops may open Sunday.

Banks: Open Monday–Friday 7:00 A.M.–7:00 P.M.; Saturday to 1:00 P.M.

National Handicrafts Shops

AUSTRIA

Heimatwerk shops are found in the provincial capitals: Linz, Salzburg, Innsbruck, Bregenz, Klagenfurt, Graz, Eisenstadt and Vienna.

Specialties: Ceramics, pewter, jade jewelry, wood carvings, wrought iron, cut glass, painted glass and wood, handwoven linens, lodencloth coats and suits.

BELGIUM

No national handicraft shops.

Specialties: Bruges and Brussels lace, Val St. Lambert crystal, copper, tin, chocolates, diamonds (Antwerp is one of the world's great diamond centers), carpets (machine-made only), linens, hand-crafted shotguns.

BULGARIA

Corecom shops are the hard-currency shops carrying both Bulgarian crafts and imported items. In Sofia, the big Corecom is at 8 Kaloyan Street; others are at 166 ul Rakovski, 125 Boulevard Dmitrov, 51 Boulevard Evtimii, 27 Boulevard Tolbukhin, 81 Boulevard Stamboliiski and in the large hotels. Check the selections in **Valentina** shops, the **Center of Novelty Goods and Fashion SBH** (Sajos na Balgarskitekudojnizi Zadruga ha Maistorite), the shops of the **Union of Bulgarian Artists** at 6 Russki Boulevard and 13 ul Rakovski, and **Magasin Narmag**. Vitosha Boulevard is a pedestrian zone and good shopping area.

Specialties: Pottery, embroidery, leather, furs.

The Bulgarian shop in East Berlin is on Unter den Linden. In Prague, it is at Nǎ Príkopĕ 6 at the end of Wenceslas Square. In Budapest, it is at Népköztársasag 7.

CZECHOSLOVAKIA

Tuzex shops are the hard-currency shops where everything from handicrafts to farm machinery is sold for Tuzex vouchers. Buy the vouchers at Tuzex or banks in-country or from Tuzex agencies abroad. Keep receipts for tax-free export; otherwise you may be subject to paying up to 100 percent of the purchase price in tax at the border. Limits are strictly enforced on amounts of some goods that can be exported. Inquire about current regulations *before* you buy. The Tuzex glass and china shop in Prague is at Zelezná 18; the antiques shop is on Národní Trida; the food shop is on Leninova Trida.

Czech and Slovak folk crafts are sold in Prague at **Česka Jizba**, Karlova 12; **Slovenska Jizba**, Vaclavske Nam 44 (Wenceslas Square); and **Kransna Jizba**, Národní 23. Several good crafts shops are located on Wenceslas Square and near Karlovy Most (Charles Bridge). Good selections can sometimes be found in the following department stores: **Druzhba**, Vaclavske Nam 21; **Kotva**, Republiky 8; **MAJ**, Národní Trida 26.

Specialties: Crystal and Bohemian glass, porcelain, painted eggs, pottery, handwoven rugs, embroidery. It is illegal to export musical instruments and glass (except that purchased in hard-currency shops). The Czech shop in East Berlin is on Leipzigerstrasse.

DENMARK

Den Permanente in Copenhagen has a large selection of work done by provincial craftspeople. A center of sixty craftspeople is open at Amagertov 1, Copenhagen. **Haandarbejdts Fremme**, the Danish Handicraft Guild, promotes cottage industries. A group of women living on the Faroe Islands has formed a cottage-industry cooperative that sells handknit items at the shop by the harbor in Thorshavn, the main town of Faroe.

Specialties: Embroidery, knitwear, ceramics, sleekly designed furniture, household utensils, jewelry, china.

FINLAND

Major towns have **Käsityöläiskauppa** shops.

Specialties: Furs, wood, glass, leather, hunting knives, Lapp crafts of reindeer leather and bone.

FRANCE

No national handicraft shops.

Specialties: Porcelain and crystal (in Paris, the Rue de Parides is lined with shops and manufacturers' outlets)—the Limoges area is famous for its fine porcelain and the crystal factories are concentrated in Lorraine. Santons (clay crèche figures) are a specialty of Provence. The village Betschdorf specializes in salt-glazed stonewear and neighboring Soufflenheim in earthenware; they are located in Alsace. Villedieu-les-Poêles in Normandy is the place to buy copper utensils.

GERMANY

In former East Germany, handicrafts can be found in *kunstwerk* or *kunstgewerbe* shops. No national handicrafts shops exist as such in the West, although there are many crafts and souvenir outlets.

Specialties: Wood carvings, candles and wax figures from Bavaria; tin figures from Franconia; cuckoo clocks from the Black Forest; loden cloth, dirndls and leather clothing, especially in the south; amber from the North Sea; pottery, china and crystal from Franconia; knives and scissors from Solingen; jewelry from Idar Oberstein; gold and watches from Pforzheim; gold and silver from Hanau; salt-glazed pottery from Höhr-Grenzhausen; ivory carvings and jewelry (from mammoth tusks found in Siberia) from Erbach; wooden figures from the Erzgebirge Mountains; glass Christmas tree ornaments from Thuringen; Sorbian etched Easter eggs; Meissen porcelain (considered by many to be the best in the world and the most expensive).

GREAT BRITAIN

The **Design Center** in London is the government-sponsored showcase for the best in British crafts at reasonable prices. **The Craftsmen Potters Shop** in the William Blake House, Marshall Street, London, sells work by members of the Craftsmen Potters Guild of Britain. The **Scotch House** in London's Knightsbridge has the largest selection of plaids in Britain. The **Wales Travel Center** at 34 Piccadilly in London has a good selection of Welsh products.

Weaving is an ancient Welsh craft, and mills that can be visited include the **Alfonwen Mill** near Mold, Clwyd, and the **Penmachno Wool Mill** near Betwys-y-Coed, Gwynedd. The **James Pringle** woolen firm has converted the railway station in Llanfairpwllgwyngyllgogery-chwyrndrobwllllantisiliogogogoch (the longest town name in the world) to a woolens showcase. (The town, located on the Isle of Anglesey, is known as Llanfair P.G. for short and means St. Mary's Church by the Pool of the White Hazel Trees near the Rapid Whirlpool by the Red Cave of the Church of St. Tysilio.) Pringle also has mill shops in Edinburg and Inverness, along with a computerized Clan Tartan Center where visitors can discover their Scottish "roots." The area around Stoke-on-Trent is famous for its fine potteries. **Royal Doulton, Minton, Wedgwood** and **Spode** have tours of the factories as well as factory-outlet shops.

GREECE

The **National Organization of Greek Handicrafts** has a display at 9 Mitropoleos Street, Athens. The items are not for sale, but provide a standard for quality and price. The **Greek Women's Institute**, 13 Voukourestiou Street, Athens, sells embroideries and handwoven items from the islands and reproductions of embroideries from the Benaki Museum collection. The **Lyceum of Greek Women**, 17 Dimokritou Street, Athens, sells weavings, embroideries, rugs, ceramics and jewelry. The **National Welfare Organization** has two shops stocked with copper, weavings, embroideries and rugs at 8 Karageorgi Servias Street and 24 Voukourestiou Street, Athens. The **XEN (YWCA)** at 11 Amerikis Street, Athens, has a small collection of embroidery for sale.

Specialties: Pottery, flokati rugs, furs, jewelry, and embroidery from Skyros, Crete, Lefkas and Rhodes. The town of Castoria specializes in making unique-model coats from bits and pieces of fur.

HUNGARY

The **Konsumtourist** shops in hotels and **Intertourist** shops in town sell souvenir and imported items for hard currency. The main Intertourist shop in Budapest is at Kígyo Útca 5. Handicrafts can be found in shops at **Folkart Hungary**, Váci Útca 14, and the **Cooperative of Folk Craftsmen**, Kecskeméti Útca 13. Other handicrafts shops are at Szent István Körut 26 and on Régiposta Útca and Károlyi Milháy Útca in Budapest. Craftsmen sell from stalls around the Matthias Church in Budapest. Department stores have a small selection of souvenir items; in Budapest, they are **Corvin Áruház** at Blaha Lujza Tér, **Luxus Áruház** on Vörösmarty Ter and **Skála Áruház** opposite the West railway station. A growing number of shops (jewelry, fur, etc.) are selling for hard currency.

Transylvanian women sell embroidery (and, in winter, Poles sell fur hats) along the Váci Útca and in the Astoria metro station. They disappear when the police walk by, but the police usually turn a blind eye to any who are a little slow in slipping away. Antique shops have handwoven and leather clothing and embroideries. Some art, antiques and postage stamps cannot be taken out of the country except with certificates from the shop. The artists' colony Szentendre, about 20 kilometers from Budapest, has several handicrafts shops.

Specialties: Embroideries, blue-dyed cloth, dolls in traditional costume, porcelain by Herend (quality comparable to Meissen), Hollma'za and Zsolnay, herdsmen's whips, black pottery, ceramics. The Hungarian shop in East Berlin is on Karl-Liebknecht-Strasse. In Prague, it is at Národní 22.

ICELAND

Handicrafts are found in **Minjagripaverslun Rammagerdin** and **Islenskur Heimilisidnadur** on Hafnarstraeti in Reykjavík. The airport shops also carry a good selection.

Specialties: Wool sweaters, sheepskin coats, ceramics.

IRELAND

The **Kilkenny Design Workshops** were founded by the government in the 1960s to support traditional crafts and design. The workshops at Kilkenny Castle can be visited and there is a large shop in Dublin on Nassau Street. Private craft shops can be found throughout the country. A working crafts center operates in the Powerscourt Townhouse Centre in Dublin.

Specialties: Woolens, pottery, baskets, handwoven cloth, crystal, silver and gold jewelry.

ITALY

ISOLA, the Sardinian Institute for the Organization of Handicrafts, has piloted cooperatives for selling crafts. Inquire at local tourist offices for other area cooperatives.

Specialties: Venetian glass (especially from the island Murano), Burano lace, papier maché Christmas figures from Puglia, *ollar* stone ornaments from Lombardy, linen from Umbria, Renaissance-style weavings from Tuscany, weavings and ceramics from Sardinia, mosaics and faience from Ravenna, inlaid wood from Sorrento, alabaster from Pisa, jewelry from Vicenza, pottery from Bassano del Grappa, cameos from Naples, lodencloth clothing and wood carvings from the South Tirol, hand-painted ceramics from Faenza and gold, leather and paper from Florence.

LIECHTENSTEIN

This tiny country has few handicrafts, unless one counts false teeth and postage stamps. One small firm, **Gebruder Haas** in Schann, produces handmade and hand-painted ceramics. Stamps are the country's third largest source of income. They are issued four times a year, with two themes for each issue. A collectors' shop is located in the post office complex in Vaduz.

LUXEMBOURG

No national handicraft shops. Crafts can be found at the flea market held alternate Saturdays in Luxembourg City.

Specialties: Villeroy & Boch pottery and miniature reproductions of cast-iron fireplace backs called *tak*.

NETHERLANDS

A number of wooden shoe factories sell wearable shoes as well as miniatures. Flower growers will ship bulbs to the United States with the health certificates required for importation. Amsterdam's Schiphol Airport has one of the largest selections of duty-free goods anywhere.

Specialties: Blue Delft ware (factories in Delft can be visited), diamonds in Amsterdam, silver, pewter, crystal and wooden shoes.

NORWAY

Husfliden (Norwegian Home Crafts) was established almost 100 years ago and flourishes with forty-three shops in major cities and tourist areas.

Specialties: Silver, jewelry, crystal, pottery, pewter, furs, handwoven textiles, woolen knits and winter sports equipment.

POLAND

Cepelia cooperatives are folk-art shops found in major cities; they accept both local and hard currencies. **Pewex** and **Baltona** are the hard-currency shops selling imported items, often at lower prices than in the West. **Orno** shops carry silverware and handmade jewelry; **Desa** stores sell art objects—both accept either local or hard currency.

Specialties: Glass and enamelware, amber and handwoven rugs. The Polish shop in East Berlin is on Karl-Liebknecht-Strasse. In Prague, it is on Jindřišská, just around the corner from Wenceslas Square.

PORTUGAL

No national handicrafts shops, but plenty of outlets for local and regional work.

Specialties: The polychrome Barcelos Cockerel (the country's symbol), baskets, leather, copper, filigree, embroidery (especially from Madeira), cork and fishermen's sweaters. Pottery and ceramics are found throughout the country, but designs vary considerably by region. The black pottery of Vila Real is hard to find even 25 kilometers away. The Barcelos area makes earthenware Christmas crèche figures. Aviero specializes in faience jugs. Azulejos (hand-painted tiles) decorate everything from bars to churches. You can take home a single tile or a whole motif. Originally blue, they now come in many colors; sets tell a story or illustrate history.

Romania

Artizanat shops sell handicrafts. In Bucharest, the shops are at Str. Academiei 25 and Bulevardue Balĕscu 30. Comturist are the hard-currency shops. **Galerie de Arta** shops are run by the Sculptors' Union. One such shop is **Horizont** opposite the Intercontinental Hotel in Bucharest.

Handicrafts are sold in Bucharest at **Artă Populară**, Calea Victoriei 118; **Săteanca**, Calea Victoriei 91; **Hermes**, Şepcari 16; and **Meşteri Făurari**, Strada Gabroveni 6. Department stores that may have crafts are **Cocurul**, Boulevard 1848-33; **Bucur**, Soseaua Colentina 2; **Victoria**, Calea Victoriei 17; **Unirea**, Piaţa Unirii 1; and **Bucureşti**, Bărăţiei 2. **Batarul Hanul cu tei**, a complex of little shops beside a restored inn, is in the Lipscani shopping district.

Specialties: Wood carvings, embroideries, ceramics and carpets.

Spain

Artespaña shops are found in each provincial capital.

Specialties: Leather, filigree jewelry, lace, carpets, *esparto* grasswork, damascene from Toledo, copper, terra cotta, knives, ceramics, pearls (Mallorca) and embroidery.

Sweden

Handverk or hemslöjds shops are operated by the Swedish handicraft society. They are expensive, but quality and selection are superb. One of the best is **Halländska Hemslöjdsföreningen** in Halmstad, a charming port town on the west coast. The Dalarna region is strong in folk tradition and has a good selection of regional crafts, but most shops also carry items from other parts of the country, including Lappland. Shops at the Royal Palace in Stockholm and at the Royal Residence on the island of Öland sell quality items bearing the three crowns motif—copies of the royal porcelain, silk scarves, ties, etc. Proceeds go to museum or park upkeep.

The **Glass Kingdom** is a cluster of about twenty glass companies in southern Sweden. They are open to visitors; the larger ones provide guided tours, while the smaller ones simply allow visitors to watch the glassblowers at work. All of them have shops, and each has a specialty. Among them are Orrefors, Kosta, Boda, Bergdala, Eneryda,

Johansfors, Lindshammar, Målerås, Nybro, Pukeberg, Rosdala, Sandvik, Sea, Skruf, Åfors and Älghult. A working handmade paper mill in the area is at Lessebo.

Specialties: Wood, baskets, handwoven linens and rugs, pottery, glass, porcelain, furs, jewelry, the Dalarna horse (a symbol on the order of Portugal's Barcelos Cockerel), sleekly designed furniture and household utensils. Furs are the specialty of Tranås.

SWITZERLAND

More than twenty **Heimatwerk** shops can be found in cities and tourist centers, with the largest concentration in the German-speaking two-thirds of the country. Criteria for goods sold in the shops are strict and specific. Most goods are produced by artisans working at home or by small factories with no more than twenty employees. Mass-produced souvenirs are primarily Swiss Army knives and some textiles.

Specialties: Traditional and modern pottery and ceramics from the Bernese Oberland, wood carvings from Brienz, intricate paper cuttings from the Pays d'Enhaut, pewter from the Valais, brass from Ticino, belts decorated with stamped-brass cows from Appenzell, embroidery and weavings from Graubünden, cowbells and music boxes. Swiss watches are found in jewelry stores, never in Heimatwerk shops. Cuckoo clocks are German, not Swiss.

TURKEY

The bazaars are the shopping centers of Turkey, and one of the best is the **Grand Bazaar** of Istanbul, the **Kapalí Çarşísí**. More than 4,000 stalls and shops make up the covered labyrinth; the most precious objects are in its center, the **Bedesten**. The **Egyptian Bazaar (Misir Çarşísí)** nearby is for food only and well worth exploring, as is the picturesque **Sahaflar Çarşísí**, the market of second-hand books. Ankara has no comparable bazaar, but the **Turkish Handicraft Association** has a shop at Selanik Cad.

Specialties: Meerschaum pipes and ornaments, gold, copper, brass, leather and carpets. Don't buy a carpet without at least basic knowledge of how to judge value; it is especially important to know the difference between real and artificial silk. Beware of "antiques." The penalty for unlicensed export of genuine antiques is imprisonment.

U.S.S.R.

Beriozka hard-currency shops are found in major cities and hotels. In Moscow, a good one for furs and lacquer boxes is at 9 Kutuzovsky Prospect and for books at 31 Kropotkinskaya. Major hotels also have souvenir stands which accept roubles. Sidewalk artists and craftsmen line Arbat Street (Moscow's only pedestrian zone) and Ostrovsky Square (facing Nevsky Prospect in Leningrad). Moscow's best-known "department store" GUM is undergoing extensive renovation and appears to be slowly turning into a showcase of Western goods for hard currency. TSUM is another Moscow department store. In Leningrad, the large department store is Gostinny Dvor.

Specialties: Lacquered papier maché boxes painted with scenes from fairy tales and legend (the most famous are from Palekh, Fedoskino, Mstiora and Kholui), matrioska dolls, balalaikas, chess sets, amber, ivory (not from endangered elephants, but from tons of ancient mammoth tusks found in Siberia), caviar, vodka, furs and handwoven carpets. Books and phonograph records are inexpensive, but English translations may not be the best and records may wear out quickly.

The Russian shop in East Berlin is called **Natasha** and is located under a pink awning just off Karl-Marx-Allee. The Soviet Book Store is on Unter den Linden. In Prague, the Soviet Folk Crafts Shop is at Železná 24, around the corner from the Soviet Kultur Dom. In Budapest, the Russian Shop is on Kossuth L. Útca, across from the Astoria Hotel.

Yugoslavia

Narodina Radinost handicrafts shops can be found in major cities and along the coast. Hotel shops carry some crafts; markets are a good place to find handmade baskets and other items.

Specialties: Handwoven carpets from Macedonia, pottery, wood carvings, items made from Brač stone, naivé paintings (especially on glass), embroidery, crochet and "Ohrid pearls," made from the scales of a rare fish that lives in Lake Ohrid. The nuns of the Benedictine Convent on the island Hvar make delicate lace from the agave plant (it's very expensive). The women of the village Sirogojno and its surroundings knit high-quality sweaters and coats depicting village and mountain scenes.

Tax Rebate Plans

Most West European and Scandinavian countries collect value-added tax—that is, a form of indirect sales tax paid on products and services at each stage of production or distribution, based on the value at that stage and included in the cost to the consumer. In 1988, Hungary became the first East Bloc country to charge a value-added tax; considering recent developments, other East European countries will probably follow suit in the foreseeable future.

In Britain, the tax is called VAT; in France, it is TVA; in Denmark, it is MOMS; in Turkey, it is KDV; in Germany, it is MWSt. By any name, it is hefty—it can be as much as 38 percent. While the process of getting a tax refund can be time-consuming, it is worthwhile for expensive purchases. Tax rebate plans vary from country to country, but many do provide relief for tourists. Sometimes the refund can be collected as the tourist leaves the country. In other cases, it is mailed or credited on the credit card bill. Usually the buyer must show her passport at the shop to receive the forms. Here is a run-down of how the plans work and countries where they are available.

Andorra

The entire country is duty-free. Shops carrying every luxury and brand name imaginable attract day-trippers from France and Spain; the peseta and French franc are accepted equally. Most shops take dollars and a wide range of credit cards.

Austria

The tax ranges from 32 percent on luxury goods, to 20 percent on items such as food, to 10 percent on books, cards and some art objects. Refunds are 24 percent, 17 percent and 9 percent, respectively, because of the handling fee. The minimum total purchase must be at least 1,000 schillings.

Two refunding processes operate in Austria. Some stores use a commercial agency called Heimig, which charges an extra handling fee that can amount to as much as 114 schillings per item. Because of complaints about this fee, the ÖAMTC (Austrian automobile club) has instituted its own service. A brochure in five languages, including English, is available from ÖAMTC, Mehrwertsteuerverrechnung, Schubertring 1-3, A-1015 Vienna. It explains exactly how to get the refund and warns shoppers that ÖAMTC handles only refund forms with the ÖAMTC headings. Don't get the wrong form. Stores that provide these forms display blue-and-yellow stickers on their doors or windows.

Form U-34 must be filled in completely. The goods, unused and unopened, must be taken out of the country within four weeks of purchase. When crossing the border, present the goods and forms to the customs officer. That means putting them in carry-on luggage for plane trips. For train travel, the opposite is true. The only way to have customs okay the forms is to send the items in checked luggage. The luggage offices of the Austrian Federal Railway will acknowledge exportation. The forms are either presented at the ÖAMTC clearing station at the border (the brochure lists these stations with opening hours) or mailed to ÖAMTC. The customer gives her bank name and account number and the refund is transferred to the account.

BELGIUM

The tax ranges from 18 to 25 percent. No explanatory booklet is in print, but refunds are available from most major stores. The store will fill out the form and stamp it, and customs agents will stamp it again at the border when you show the unopened goods. Mail the form to the shop and it will send you the refund.

DENMARK

The tax, called MOMS, is 22 percent. Shops participating in the tax-free service display a red Tax-Free symbol on their doors or windows. Refunds are available on purchases of more than 400 crowns, including tax. A handling fee is charged. To get the refund, get the export invoice from the shop and sign it. At the border, the customs officer will endorse the invoice when you show the unopened goods. Mail it in a Danish Tax-Free letterbox provided at the airport or border crossing. At Copenhagen's Kastrup Airport, a tax-free service is located both in the check-in and transit halls.

FINLAND

The tax is 16 percent on most goods, refundable except for a 5 percent service charge. Shops offering the service display a "Tax-Free for Tourists" sign. To get the refund, the customer must show her passport at the time of purchase. The shop clerk writes a Tax-Free Shopping Check, which the customer must fill out on the back. The cash refund is paid in local currency upon leaving Finland, even if the purchase was made with a credit card. The purchase must be unused and shown at the time the refund is made. The plan is available to all persons living outside the Nordic countries. Refunds are available at major airport transit halls (Helsinki, Turku, Tampere, Mariehamn, Vaasa, Roveniemi and Ivalo), on board ferries of the Finnject, Silja, Viking Lines and Vaasaferries (before the ship leaves the harbor) and at major land border crossings.

FRANCE

The French tax varies from 7 to 33 percent, with most goods carrying about 19 percent tax. Refunds are available on items costing more than 1,200 francs for persons living outside the European Economic Community countries and 2,000 francs for those living within the EEC. A passport must be shown at time of purchase. Refunds are given to persons over fifteen years old who have been in France less than six months.

The shop will fill out the form *Vente a l'Exportation,* which the customer must sign and show, along with unopened purchases, at the border. Mail the validated forms to the customs office for a refund or get a cash refund at the airport *detaxe* customs booth. Refunds may also be credited to charge cards. Many large department stores allow customers to total up all items purchased in the store and fill out one refund slip. A "Welcome to France" brochure available from the tourist office explains the system.

GERMANY

The tax is 14 percent and major stores offer the refund with a minimum 50 mark purchase. The form is filled out and presented with the unopened items at border crossings. Refunds may be mailed in German marks. At the Frankfurt Airport, refunds may be collected at the bank or at branches of some shops inside the international departure lounge. Refunds cannot be credited to charge cards.

GREAT BRITAIN

Most of the tax is 15 percent. Shops usually set a purchase minimum of 50 pounds, but sometimes it is higher. Harrods, for example, has a 100 pound minimum. At Harrods, customers with charge cards or store accounts have the refund credited to their balance. The shopper must go to the store's export office, fill out the VAT form and leave a self-addressed envelope so that the store can mail the refund check. A passport must be shown at the time.

The refund is offered on goods taken out of the country within three months. The unopened goods must be shown at the customs office upon departure and the form must be stamped and signed. The customer sends the form back to the shop in the stamped, self-addressed envelope the shop provided (mail it before leaving the country). When the shop gets the form, it will mail the refund or credit it to the charge card account.

HUNGARY

The tax ranges from 15 to 25 percent. A rebate (in forints only) is available on goods costing more than 25,000 forints, except art objects and antiques. The process is handled through banks; participating stores will have the forms.

ICELAND

Tax is 24.5 percent. Ask shops if they have tax rebate forms similar to those of Scandinavian countries.

IRELAND

Taxes vary from 8 percent on clothing to 23 or 35 percent on other items. Shops charge a handling fee of 2 Irish pounds for the refunds. To get a refund, the customer may have to show both passport and airline ticket. Goods must be taken out of the country unopened within two months of purchase. Invoices must show the customer's name and address and amount of VAT paid. Minimum purchase for non-EEC residents is 50 Irish pounds. The invoice must be stamped by the customs officer, who may ask to see the goods. It should then be sent back to the shop. Some shops will credit the refund to charge cards; others refund by check or money order. A brochure describing the procedure is available from Irish tourist offices. Some operational details are still being resolved.

ITALY

The tax generally ranges from 9 to 18 percent, but can be as much as 23 percent on some luxury goods. Officially, the tax is refundable to tourists who purchase goods worth a minimum of 250,000 lire in one shop. The system works slowly, however, and many shopkeepers prefer to offer discounts rather than be bothered with the formalities. For the insistent, tax-free forms should be requested from the store, filled out and presented with the unopened goods upon departure. The forms are mailed to the shops and refunds can take up to twelve weeks. Unless the customer asks for the form, there is little chance it will be offered.

LUXEMBOURG

The tax is 12 percent on most goods and minimum purchase is an 8,000 franc total purchase at each store. The shop gives the customer a form, which may be validated at a downtown Luxembourg City customs office, so the store may give the refund before departure if you go back and ask for it. Otherwise, the form is validated at the border crossing, where unopened goods must be shown. Mail the form to the shop or turn it in at the airport for the refund.

NETHERLANDS

The tax in the Netherlands is 18.5 percent. Minimum purchase is 300 guilders. Form OB-90, along with the unopened goods, is to be shown at the customs office at the border, where the form is stamped. The customer must send the form back to the shop, which sends it back to customs. After the shop gets the tax refund, it sends the refund on to the customer. Some shops are members of the Holland Tax-Free Shopping organization, which provides a special check that allows the refund to be paid at some border crossings. Refunds cannot be credited to charge cards.

NORWAY

The tax is 20 percent, of which 10 to 14 percent is refundable. A tax-free shopping plan operates in about 2,000 shops. The money is refunded at the airport or border crossing. Goods must be exported within one month. Travelers going through Sweden and Finland can also receive their Norwegian refunds in those countries. Shops participating display a red-and-blue sticker on their windows or doors. Minimum purchase is 300 Norwegian crowns. The shop issues a Tax-Free Check at time of purchase, which the purchaser must fill out on the back. The unopened goods must be presented at the border refund station. The purchaser must show her passport there, as well. Information is available by telephoning 02-50 18 80 in Oslo.

PORTUGAL

Tax is up to 22 percent. Ask shops if they cooperate in a rebate plan.

SPAIN

Spain has a 10 percent tax on most items. The tax refund system operates in major stores, with the minimum purchase usually 10,000 pesetas. The forms must be validated at the border and returned to the government office. Refund checks in pesetas are mailed to the customers. Refunds are not credited to charge cards.

SWEDEN

Sweden's tax is 23.46 percent and the Tax-Free Check system works the same as Norway's. Participating shops display a blue-and-yellow Tax-Free sticker. The shop fills out the check, then the customer fills out the back of the check and presents it with the unopened goods at the border crossing. The money is refunded in Swedish crowns on the spot. Goods must be exported within one week of purchase. Minimum purchase is 200 crowns. A booklet available from the tourist office lists the places where the checks can be presented by ferry and airline passengers. In some cases, refunds can be collected on board ship. At the Stockholm Airport, an office in the entry hall will validate the purchases before check-in, for those who wish to pack their purchases in luggage to be checked.

Additional Information

When and What to Drink

Here is a listing of drinking hours, minimum drinking age and a selection of national drinks.

AUSTRIA
No time restrictions; minimum age eighteen. National drinks: *obstler* (fruit brandy); *most* (new wine) found especially in Upper Austria; *schilcher*, rosé wine from Styria.

BELGIUM
Alcohol served 10:00 A.M.–1:00 A.M.; minimum age eighteen.

National drinks: beer, 300 kinds from 100 breweries; *genever,* a kind of gin found in more than 150 varieties.

Bulgaria

Alcohol served 10:00 A.M.–midnight; minimum age sixteen. National drinks: *rakia,* called *grozdova* when made from grapes, *slivova* when made from plums, *plodova* when made from mixed fruits; wines include *Warna Misket* (white), *Melnik Harsovo* (red) and *Gamza von Suhindol* (red); *ayryan,* beaten yogurt and mineral water (Bulgarian yogurt is superb).

Czechoslovakia

No time restrictions; minimum age eighteen. National drinks: beer (*Pilsner Urquell* and *Budvar* are considered some of the best in the world); *Becherovka,* a liqueur from the spa Karlsbad served in distinctive small blue glasses.

Denmark

No time restrictions; minimum age eighteen. National drinks: *aquavit* (it should be small, cold and hit like a hailstone!); beer.

Finland

Beer served from 9:00 A.M., wine and hard liquor from noon; bars close as early as 11:30 P.M. or as late as 2:30 A.M. National drinks: vodka; *lakka,* made from rare Arctic berries known as *Suomuurain moltebeere; mesimarja,* made from Arctic blackberries.

France

No time restrictions; minimum age eighteen. National drinks: wine; Champagne; Cognac; Armagnac; calvados; wide variety of *eau-de-vie* and liqueurs.

Germany

No time restrictions; minimum age eighteen. National drinks: beer; wine; schnaps, clear brandies; *digestifs,* thick brown liqueurs for the digestion; apple wine, in the Frankfurt a.M. area only.

Great Britain

Alcohol served 11:00 A.M.–11:00 P.M. (opening hours are voluntary, but a pub must open eight hours a day to keep its license, and late-opening licenses are available); minimum age eighteen. National drinks: malt whisky (Scotch); beer; stout; ale. England produces a tiny amount of wine!

GREECE

No time restrictions; minimum age eighteen. National drinks: *retsina,* white wine with a taste of turpentine; *ouzo,* aniseed-flavored liquor.

HUNGARY

Alcohol served from 9:00 A.M.; minimum age eighteen. National drinks: wine; *tokaji,* fortified wine; *barack,* apricot brandy; *cseresznye,* cherry brandy; *alma,* apple brandy; *körte,* pear brandy; *szilva,* plum brandy; *unicum,* a *digestif.*

ICELAND

Alcohol served noon–2:30 P.M. and 6:00 P.M.–3:00 A.M.; minimum age twenty. National drink: *brennivin,* Icelandic aquavit.

IRELAND

Alcohol served 10:00 A.M.–2:30 P.M. and 3:30–11:00 P.M., in summer to 11:30 P.M.; minimum age eighteen. National drinks: stout; Irish whisky.

ITALY

No time restrictions; minimum age eighteen. National drinks: wine; *sambuca,* served with a few coffee beans in it; *grappa; cynar,* artichoke liqueur; *campari;* many *digestifs* and liqueurs.

LIECHTENSTEIN

No time restrictions; minimum age eighteen. National drink: wine.

LUXEMBOURG

Cafes (which serve alcohol) open 7:00 A.M.–1:00 A.M.; discos open 8:00 P.M.–3:00 A.M.; minimum age seventeen. National drinks: wine, beer.

NETHERLANDS
No time restrictions, cafes (which serve alcohol) usually open 10:00 A.M.–1:00 A.M.; minimum age sixteen. National drinks: beer; *jenever,* a type of gin, either old or young, ideally served in a small glass filled to overflowing so that the first sip has to be taken without picking up the glass.

NORWAY
Alcohol served 3:00 P.M.–midnight; after midnight only in specially licensed bars. No hard liquor served on Sunday. Minimum age eighteen for beer and wine, twenty for hard liquor. National drinks: *aquavit*—Linje brand boasts that it is stored on ships traveling to Australia and back to improve the flavor.

POLAND
No time restrictions on beer and wine; hard liquor sold from 1:00 P.M.; minimum age eighteen. National drink: vodka.

PORTUGAL
No time restrictions; minimum age eighteen. National drink: Port, fortified wine.

ROMANIA
Alcohol served from 10:00 A.M.; minimum age eighteen. National drink: *tuica,* plum brandy available in varying strengths from 26 to 60 percent, served hot in winter.

SPAIN
Alcohol served 8:00 A.M.–midnight, later with special license; minimum age eighteen. National drinks: wine, beer, sherry, liqueurs, fruit brandies.

SWEDEN
Alcohol served noon–midnight; after midnight, a few clubs catering to tourists are open; minimum age twenty. National drink: *lättöl,* very light beer.

SWITZERLAND
No time restrictions, but most bars close at midnight; minimum age sixteen. National drink: wine.

TURKEY

No time restrictions; minimum age eighteen. National drink: *raki,* aniseed liqueur.

U.S.S.R.

Alcohol served 2:00–10:00 P.M.; minimum age eighteen. National drinks: vodka, which comes plain or in flavored varieties—*lemonnaya* (lemon), *vishnevka* (cherry), *pertsovka* (pepper), *zubrovka* (bison grass); sparkling wine and wine (both rather sweet).

YUGOSLAVIA

No time restrictions; minimum age eighteen. National drinks: *sljivovica,* plum brandy; *lozovaca,* made from grapes already pressed for wine after they begin to ferment; *maraschino,* cherry liqueur.

Tipping

The questions of tipping—when, to whom, how much—are eternal. Customs vary from country to country. In some places, a service charge is built into the bill; in others, it is added on at the bottom. If you are taking a guided tour, it is customary to tip the guide and the bus driver the equivalent of $1 to $2.50 per person per day each, depending on type of tour and quality of service. Tip in the currency of the country. If you must tip in dollars, use bills only—coins cannot be exchanged in other countries and are therefore useless. One cannot make hard and fast rules (tipping is, after all, a reward for service), but here are a few handy guidelines.

AUSTRIA

Hotels and restaurants: 10 percent to 15 percent is usually included in the bill, but giving an extra 5 percent is usual. Taxis: 10 percent. Railway porters: 10 schillings per bag. Chambermaids: 10 schillings per person per day. Hairdressers: 10 percent. Washroom attendants: 5 schillings.

BELGIUM AND LUXEMBOURG

Hotels, restaurants, taxis: included in bill. Skycaps: 30 francs per bag. Bellmen: 50 francs per bag. Washroom and cloakroom attendants: 10 francs. Hairdressers: 15 percent. Tipping is more common in French-speaking than in Flemish-speaking Belgium.

BULGARIA
Give 50 stotinki to 1 lev for all service.

CZECHOSLOVAKIA
Restaurants and taxis: 5 percent. Porters: 2 crowns per bag. Hairdressers: 5 crowns. Cloakroom charges are usually posted.

DENMARK
Tips are seldom given, except for small change to the toilet attendant and to the taxi driver who helps with the luggage—3 crowns per bag.

FINLAND
Hotels: 15 percent included in the bill. Restaurants: 14 percent on workdays, 15 percent on weekends and holidays, included in the bill. Taxis: 2 or 3 finnmarks. Porters: 2 finnmarks per bag. Cloakroom attendants: 2 finnmarks.

FRANCE
Hotels and restaurants: 15 percent included in the bill; leave an extra 5 percent for good service. Taxis: 10 percent to 15 percent. Chambermaid: 10 francs per night. Porters: 2 francs per bag. Cloakroom attendants: 5 francs per item. Washroom attendants: 5 francs. Gas station attendants: 1 franc. Hairdressers: 5 to 10 francs.

GERMANY
Hotels and restaurants: 10 percent to 15 percent included in bill; round off for good service. Taxis: 5 percent. Bellmen: 1 mark per bag. Hairdressers: 1 to 4 marks. Chambermaids: 1 mark per day for long stays. Gas station attendants: 1 mark for extra service.

GREAT BRITAIN
Restaurants: 10 percent to 15 percent, sometimes added onto bill. Taxis: 15 percent. Porters: 40 pence per bag. Doormen: 20 to 50 pence per bag. Chambermaids: 50 pence per person per day. Hairdressers: 1 pound.

GREECE
Hotels and restaurants: 15 percent usually included in bill, but giving additional 5 percent to 10 percent to the staff is usual. Taxi

drivers: 5 percent to 10 percent. Chambermaids: 140 drachmas per night. Porters: 10 drachmas per bag.

Hungary
Hotels: some add 15 percent. Restaurants: varies, but usually included; round off for good service. Taxis: 10 percent. Porters: 10 forints per bag. Cloakroom attendants: 5 forints. Hairdressers: 20 forints.

Iceland
Service is included in the bill. Many people are offended if offered a tip.

Ireland
Hotel: 15 percent usually included; if not, distribute among the staff. Restaurants: 10 percent to 15 percent, often not included. Taxis: 10 percent to 15 percent. Porters: 40 to 50 pence per bag. Washroom attendants: 50 pence. Hairdressers: 10 percent.

Italy
Hotels: included in bill. Doormen and chambermaids: 1,000 lire per day. Porters: 1,000 lire per bag. Waiters: 10 percent. Taxis: 10 percent to 15 percent. Hairdressers: 15 percent. Service station attendants: 1,000 lire for extra service, including giving directions.

Liechtenstein
Hotels and restaurants: included in bill, but an extra 5 percent to waiters for good service. Porters: 1 franc per bag. Cloakroom attendants: 1 franc. Taxis and hairdressers: 10 percent to 15 percent.

Monaco
Hotels and restaurants: included in bill. Taxis and hairdressers: 10 percent. Porters: 4 francs per bag.

Netherlands
Hotels, restaurants, taxis: included, but round off the amount. Porters: 1 guilder per bag. Cloakroom attendants: 1 guilder. Doormen: 2 guilders. Chambermaids: 2 guilders per night.

NORWAY
Hotels: 10 percent to 15 percent included in bill. Taxis: 1 crown. Restaurants: 12.5 percent included in bill. Porters: 2 crowns per bag. Cloakroom charges are posted.

POLAND
Taxis: 5 percent to 10 percent. Porters: 10 zloties per bag. Hairdressers: 10 zloties. Cloakroom attendants: 2 zloties.

PORTUGAL
Hotels and restaurants: included, but add 5 percent to 10 percent for good service. Taxis: 10 to 20 escudos. Porters: 10 escudos per person. Cloakroom attendants: 10 escudos.

ROMANIA
Hotels and restaurants: included, but small gratuities may be given. Waiters: 3 percent to 5 percent. Porters: 5 lei per bag. Taxis: 10 lei. Cloakroom attendants: 3 lei. Hairdressers: 10 lei.

SPAIN
Hotels and restaurants: included, but add 10 percent for good service in restaurants. Taxi drivers: 5 percent to 10 percent. Bellmen: 50 pesetas. Hairdressers: 20 percent. Cloakroom attendants: 10 pesetas. Porters' rates are posted.

SWEDEN
Hotels and restaurants: included. Taxis: 10 percent to 15 percent. Cloakroom attendants: 5 crowns per item. Porters: 5 crowns per bag. Hairdressers do not expect tips.

SWITZERLAND
Hotels and restaurants: 15 percent included. Taxis: 15 percent unless included. Porters: 1 franc per bag. Cloakroom attendants: 1/2 franc. Hairdressers: 15 percent.

TURKEY
Hotels and restaurants: included, but waiters get extra 5 percent for good service. Hairdressers: 20 percent. Hotel porters: 10 lire per bag. Airport porters: rate posted. Taxi drivers do not expect tips.

U.S.S.R.

Waiters: 10 percent. Hairdressers: 2 roubles. Cloakroom attendants: 1 rouble.

Yugoslavia

Hotels and restaurants: included, but extra 5 percent for waiter is customary. Taxis: 5 percent to 10 percent. Porters: 5 dinars per bag. Hairdressers: 10 percent. Cloakroom attendants: 5 dinars.

Currency Regulations

Many countries limit the amount of their currencies travelers can bring in or take out. Here is a survey, subject to change as East European economies change. The United States has no import or export limits, but more than $10,000 must be reported on Customs Form 4790. Canada has no import or export limits.

Some countries use the same name for their currencies, but the values are not the same. For example, several Scandinavian countries use the crown, but the Danish crown is not worth the same as the Swedish crown. The French, Swiss and Belgian francs, the Turkish and Italian lire and English and Irish pounds all have different exchange rates to the U.S. dollar. The exception is the Luxembourg franc, which has the same value as the Belgian franc. Belgian francs can be used in Luxembourg, but Luxembourg francs are not accepted in Belgium. The name of the currency is given, with the division into small change in parentheses.

> **Andorra:** French franc (100 centimes) and Spanish peseta are both official currencies.
> **Austria:** Schilling (100 groschen). No import limit; 15,000 schilling export limit.
> **Belgium:** Franc (100 centimes). No import or export limit.
> **Bulgaria:** Lev (100 stotinki). No leva may be taken into or out of the country. In an effort to discourage black marketing, tourists are offered a bonus of 200 percent above the official exchange rate at Balkantourist offices.
> **Czechoslovakia:** Koruna (100 halers). No koruna may be taken into or out of the country. Exchange rates are divided into official, tourist, tourist bonus and bank rates. The tourist rate is 4 percent better than the official rate. The bonus rate is

available through Čedok to pay for its services and is 36 percent above the tourist rate, but money cannot be changed back to hard currency at this rate. Visitors must change $10 per day unless they are on package tours or have pre-booked accommodations.

Denmark: Krone (100 ore). No import limit; 50,000 kroner export limit.

Finland: Markka (100 penni). No import limit; 10,000 markka export limit. Declaration advised for large amounts.

France: Franc (100 centimes). No import limit; 5,000 franc export limit. Declaration advised for large amounts.

Germany: Mark (100 pfennige). No limits.

Great Britain: Pound (100 pence). No limits.

Greece: Drachma. 3,000 drachma (in bills up to 500 drachma only) import and export limit. Declaration advised when bringing in more than $5,000.

Hungary: Forint (100 fillérs). 100 forints in coins import and export limit.

Iceland: Króna (100 aurar). 20,000 króna (in bills no larger than 1,000 króna) import and export limit.

Ireland: Pound (100 pence). No import limit; 100 pound export limit. Declaration advised.

Italy: Lire. 400,000 lire import and export limit. Declaration advised.

Liechtenstein: Swiss franc (100 centimes or rappen). No limits.

Luxembourg: Franc (100 centimes). No limits.

Malta: Lire (100 cents of 10 mils each). 50 lire import limit; 25 lire export limit.

Monaco: French franc (100 centimes). No import limit; 5,000 franc export limit. Declaration advised for large amounts.

Netherlands: Guilder (100 cents). No limits.

Norway: Krone (100 ore). No import limit; 5,000 kroner export limit. Declaration advised for large amounts.

Poland: Zloty (100 groszy). No zloties may be taken in or out. Amount of Western currency brought in must be declared at border (keep the form).

Portugal: Escudo (100 centavos). 5,000 escudo import and export limit. Declaration advised.

Romania: Leu (100 bani). No lei may be taken in or out. Compulsory exchange $10 per day except for those on package tours.

Spain: Peseta. 150,000 peseta import limit; 20,000 peseta export limit. Declaration advised for large amounts.

Sweden: Krona (100 öre). No import limit; 6,000 krona (in bills not over 1,000 krona) export limit.
Switzerland: Franc (100 centimes or rappen). No limits.
Turkey: Lire. No import limit; 300,000 lire export limit.
U.S.S.R.: Rouble (100 kopeks). No roubles can be taken in or out. No compulsory exchange.
Yugoslavia: Dinar (100 paras). At publication time, efforts were underway to make the dinar convertible. New bills are being printed, but old ones will remain in circulation for several years. When using old bills, place a decimal point four digits from the end of the number for the new value of the bill. For example, an old 100,000-dinar note is worth 10 new dinars.

Holidays and Summer Vacation Periods

Public holidays vary considerably throughout Europe, sometimes frustrating visitors who had planned a day of shopping or a business meeting. The main holidays are listed here, but you may wish to inquire from tourist offices about local or regional holidays. Shops generally don't take extra days before or after holidays to close for long weekends, but offices sometimes do.

The approximate main vacation periods are also given; within a country, states may stagger vacation time in an effort to alleviate congestion on the roads and at the resorts. Many shops, businesses, restaurants and even some factories close completely for two weeks to six weeks vacation. Trying to find a place to eat in Paris in August can be a major problem because of this practice.

In addition to the summer vacation, many Europeans have one or two weeks off during the Christmas and Easter seasons. Schools may have staggered autumn vacations of about a week. Carnival is celebrated in a number of cities all over Europe, but the exact day of the celebration varies.

AUSTRIA

January 1 (New Year's Day), January 6 (Epiphany), May 1 (Labor Day), August 15 (Assumption Day), October 26 (National Day), November 1 (All Saints' Day), December 8 (Immaculate Conception), December 25 (Christmas), December 26 (St. Stephen's Day). Movable: Easter Monday, Ascension Day, Whit Monday, Corpus Christi. Vacation: Mid-June to mid-September.

BELGIUM

January 1 (New Year's Day), May 1 (Labor Day), July 21 (National Day), August 15 (Assumption Day), November 1 (All Saints' Day), December 25 (Christmas). Movable: Easter Monday, Ascension Day, Whit Monday. Vacation: July and August.

BULGARIA

January 1 (New Year's Day), May 1 & 2 (Labor Days), May 24 (Saints Cyril and Methodius Day), September 9 & 10 (Revolution Days), November 7 (anniversary of October Revolution). Vacation: July to mid-September.

CZECHOSLOVAKIA

January 1 (New Year's Day), May 1 (Labor Day), May 9 (Liberation Day), December 25 (Christmas), December 26 (St. Stephen's Day). Movable: Easter Monday. Vacation: July and August.

DENMARK

January 1 (New Year's Day), May 1 (Labor Day—afternoon), June 5 (Constitution Day—afternoon), December 25 & 26 (Christmas). Movable: Maundy Thursday, Good Friday, Easter Monday, Prayer Day (fourth Friday after Easter), Ascension Day, Whit Monday. Vacation: Mid-June to mid-August.

FINLAND

January 1 (New Year's Day), May 1 (Labor Day), December 6 (Independence Day), December 25 & 26 (Christmas). Movable: Epiphany (Saturday nearest January 6), Good Friday, Easter Monday, Ascension Day (celebrated the following Saturday), Whitsun Eve, Midsummer (Saturday nearest June 24), All Saints' Day (Saturday nearest November 1). Vacation: June to mid-August.

FRANCE

January 1 (New Year's Day), May 1 (Labor Day), May 8 (Victory Day), July 14 (Bastille Day), August 15 (Assumption), November 1 (All Saints' Day), November 11 (Armistice Day), December 25 (Christmas). Movable: Easter Monday, Ascension Day, Whit Monday. Vacation: July to mid-September (August is the most popular).

GERMANY

January 1 (New Year's Day), January 6* (Epiphany), May 1 (Labor Day), August 15* (Assumption Day), October 2 (Day of German Reunification), November 1* (All Saints' Day), December 24 (Christmas Eve—afternoon), December 25 & 26 (Christmas). Movable: Good Friday, Easter Monday, Ascension Day, Whit Monday, Corpus Christi*, Day of Penitence. (*Only in certain states.) Vacation: Mid-June to mid-September.

GREAT BRITAIN

January 1 (New Year's Day), January 2 (in Scotland only), March 1 (St. David's Day, in Wales only), first Monday of May (May Day), last Monday of May (Spring Bank Holiday), first Monday of August (Summer Bank Holiday, in Scotland), last Monday of August (Summer Bank Holiday, in England and Wales), December 25 (Christmas), December 26 (Boxing Day). Movable: Good Friday, Easter Monday (in England and Wales). Vacation: July to September.

GREECE

January 1 (New Year's Day), January 6 (Epiphany), March 25 (Independence Day), May 1 (Labor Day), August 15 (Assumption Day), October 26 (St. Dimitrius Day, in Salonica only), October 28 (Ochi Day), December 25 (Christmas), December 26 (St. Stephen's Day). Movable: First Day of Lent, Good Friday, Easter Monday. Vacation: Mid-June to mid-September.

HUNGARY

January 1 (New Year's Day), April 4 (Liberation Day), May 1 (Labor Day), August 20 (Constitution Day), December 25 (Christmas), December 26 (St. Stephen's Day). Movable: Easter Monday. Vacation: Mid-June to August.

ICELAND

January 1 (New Year's Day), May 1 (Labor Day), June 17 (National Day), first Monday in August (Shop and Office Workers' Day), December 24 (Christmas Eve), December 25 & 26 (Christmas), December 31 (New Year's Eve). Movable: Maundy Thursday, Good Friday, Easter Monday, Summer Celebration (third or fourth Thursday in April), Ascension Day, Whit Monday. Vacation: July and August.

IRELAND

January 1 (New Year's Day), March 17 (St. Patrick's Day), first Monday of June (June holiday), first Monday of August (August holiday), last Monday of October (October holiday), December 25 (Christmas), December 26 (Boxing Day). Movable: Good Friday, Easter Monday. Vacation: June to August.

ITALY

January 1 (New Year's Day), April 25 (Liberation Day), May 1 (Labor Day), August 15 (Assumption Day), November 1 (All Saints' Day), December 8 (Immaculate Conception), December 25 (Christmas), December 26 (St. Stephen's Day). Movable: Easter Monday. Vacation: Mid-June to mid-September.

LIECHTENSTEIN

January 1 (New Year's Day), January 6 (Epiphany), February 2 (Candlemas), March 19 (St. Joseph's Day), March 25 (Annunciation), May 1 (Labor Day), August 15 (Assumption Day), November 1 (All Saints' Day), December 8 (Immaculate Conception), December 25 (Christmas), December 26 (St. Stephen's Day). Movable: Good Friday, Easter Monday, Ascension Day, Whit Monday, Corpus Christi. Vacation: July and August.

LUXEMBOURG

January 1 (New Year's Day), May 1 (Labor Day), June 23 (National Day), August 15 (Assumption Day), November 1 (All Saints' Day), November 2 (All Souls' Day), December 25 & 26 (Christmas). Movable: First Monday of Lent, Easter Monday, Ascension Day, Whit Monday. Vacation: Mid-June to mid-September.

MONACO

January 1 (New Year's Day), January 27 (St. Devote's Day), May 1 (Labor Day), August 15 (Assumption), November 1 (All Saints' Day), November 19 (National Day), December 8 (Immaculate Conception), December 24 (Christmas Eve—afternoon), December 25 (Christmas). Movable: Easter Monday, Ascension Day, Whit Monday, Corpus Christi. Vacation: July and August.

NETHERLANDS

January 1 (New Year's Day), April 30 (Queen's Birthday), December

25 & 26 (Christmas). Movable: Good Friday, Easter Monday, Ascension Day, Whit Monday. Vacation: Mid-June to August.

NORWAY

January 1 (New Year's Day), May 1 (May Day), May 17 (Constitution Day), December 25 & 26 (Christmas). Movable: Maundy Thursday, Good Friday, Easter Monday, Ascension Day, Whit Monday. Vacation: Mid-June to mid-August.

POLAND

January 1 (New Year's Day), May 1 (Labor Day), July 22 (National Day), November 1 (All Saints' Day), December 25 (Christmas), December 26 (St. Stephen's Day). Movable: Easter Monday, Corpus Christi. Vacation: July and August.

PORTUGAL

January 1 (New Year's Day), April 25 (National Day), May 1 (Labor Day), June 10 (Camoens Day), June 13 (St. Anthony's Day—Lisbon), June 24 (St. John's Day—Oporto), August 15 (Assumption Day), October 5 (Republic Day), November 1 (All Saints' Day), December 1 (Restoration Day), December 8 (Immaculate Conception), December 25 (Christmas). Movable: Good Friday, Corpus Christi. Vacation: July and August.

ROMANIA

January 1 & 2 (New Year's), May 1 & 2 (Labor Days), August 23 & 24 (National Days). Vacation: Mid-June to mid-September.

SPAIN

January 1 (New Year's Day), January 6 (Epiphany), March 19 (St. Joseph's Day), May 1 (Labor Day), July 25 (St. James' Day), August 15 (Assumption Day), October 12 (Columbus Day), November 1 (All Saints' Day), December 8 (Immaculate Conception), December 25 (Christmas). Movable: Good Friday, Easter Monday, Corpus Christi. Vacation: Mid-June to mid-September.

SWEDEN

January 1 (New Year's Day), January 6 (Epiphany), May 1 (Labor Day), December 25 & 26 (Christmas). Movable: Good Friday, Easter Monday, Ascension Day, Whit Monday, Midsummer (Saturday nearest

June 21), All Saints' Day (the Saturday between October 31 and November 6). Vacation: June to mid-August.

SWITZERLAND

January 1 (New Year's Day), August 1 (National Day), December 25 (Christmas Day), December 26* (St. Stephen's Day). Movable: Good Friday*, Easter Monday*, Ascension Day, Whit Monday*. (*Not in every canton.) Vacation: July and August.

TURKEY

January 1 (New Year's Day), April 23 (Children's Day), May 19 (Youth Day), August 30 (Victory Day), October 28 & 29 (Republic Days). Vacation: July to mid-September.

U.S.S.R.

January 1 (New Year's Day), January 7 (Orthodox Christmas), March 8 (International Women's Day), May 1 & 2 (Labor Days), May 9 (Victory Day), October 7 (Constitution Day), November 7 & 8 (anniversary of the October Revolution). Vacation: June to August.

YUGOSLAVIA

January 1 & 2 (New Year's), May 1 & 2 (Labor Days), July 4 (Veteran's Day), November 29 & 30 (Republic Days). Vacation: June and July.

Keeping in Touch in English

Here is a listing of English-language broadcasts, publications, theaters and movies.

AUSTRIA

Broadcasts: Österreich 1 FM has English news at 8:05 A.M. In Vienna, Blue Danube FM 102.2 has scattered English broadcasts between 7:00 A.M. and 8:00 P.M. daily.

Publications: *Austria Today, Vienna Live, Vienna Flair;* numerous "what's on" publications.

Theater: The English Theater, Josefsgasse 12, Vienna.

Movies: Usually dubbed, but in the cities English-language films can be found. Repertory movie houses often show movies in the original language.

BELGIUM

Broadcasts: Receives BBC radio and (on cable TV) BBC 1 and 2.

Publications: *Bulletin,* a weekly newspaper in Brussels. No Sunday papers are published in Belgium.

Theater: Some touring companies perform in English.

Movies: Original language.

BULGARIA

Broadcasts: May to September, programs for tourists are broadcast in several languages, including English, on Radio Varna on the Black Sea coast between 10:30 and 11:15 A.M.

CZECHOSLOVAKIA

Broadcasts: Interprogram Radio Prague, medium- and shortwave, 8:00 A.M. to 1:00 P.M.

Movies: Original language.

DENMARK

Broadcasts: News in English at 8:05 A.M. year-round on the First Program.

Publications: Large selection.

Theater: Mermaid Theater, Copenhagen.

Movies: Original language.

FINLAND

Broadcasts: News in English in summer only on radio and television.

Publications: Leading daily newspapers have English-language columns in summer.

Movies: Original language.

FRANCE

Broadcasts: In the North, it is possible to pick up BBC programs. Radio Canada broadcasts in English Monday–Friday 6:15–6:30 A.M., 6:45–7:00 A.M., 4:45–5:00 P.M. and 10:00–11:00 P.M.

Publications: *Passion, Paris Free Voice, City* and *Speakeasy* are among Paris publications in English.

Theater: In Paris, Galerie 55, 55 rue de Seine; Théatre Maubel, 4 rue de l'Armée-d'Orient; Act 4, rue de l'Orchidee; American Center, 261 Bd. Raspail.

Movies: Usually dubbed, but in Paris some are shown in the original language, especially along the Champs-Elysèes and in the Latin Quarter.

Germany

Broadcasts: American Forces Network has AM and FM radio, as well as television stations in Frankfurt a.M., Stuttgart, Munich, Karlsruhe and Berlin. Canadian Forces radio can be picked up in the the Black Forest; British Forces radio can be picked up in northern Germany. BBC can also be picked up in the north and on satellite programs.

Publications: *German Tribune,* weekly roundup of the German press; *Scala,* monthly magazine; events magazines in many cities.

Theater: Café Theatre, Hamburgerallee 45, Frankfurt a.M.

Movies: Dubbed. Repertory movie houses show films in the original language.

Greece

Broadcasts: Daily radio news 7:15–7:30 A.M. in English, French and German. American Forces Network.

Publications: *This Week in Athens* and similar *This Summer In ...* magazines for Hydra, Naxos, Ios, Mykonos, Thessaloníki, Messenia and Santorini.

Movies: Original language.

Hungary

Broadcasts: Ten minutes of news in English, German and Russian after the noon news on the Petöfi station.

Publications: *Daily News* newspaper. *Program* monthly events magazine.

Movies: Dubbed.

Iceland

Broadcasts: News at 5:00 P.M. daily in summer on AM radio includes weather forecast and report on road conditions.

Publications: *Timinn,* a daily newspaper, has one page in English. Monthly events magazines.

Movies: Original language.

ITALY

Broadcasts: Radio 1 OM has weather, road and emergency announcements at 1:55 P.M. in four languages, including English. American Forces Network broadcasts from the following towns on FM 106 and 107: Vicenza, Livorno, Sigonella (Sicily), Comiso, San Vito and Aviano.
Movies: Dubbed.

LIECHTENSTEIN

Movies: Original language.

LUXEMBOURG

Broadcasts: Radio Luxembourg has "Community Radio" in English from 2:00 to 5:30 P.M. and English broadcasts during the night.
Movies: Original language.

NETHERLANDS

Broadcasts: BBC and American Forces Network can be picked up.
Publications: *Amsterdam This Week* in four languages.
Theater: English cabaret in Amsterdam.
Movies: Original language. Television interviews are shown in original language.

NORWAY

Broadcasts: Mid-June to end of August, weather report on "Travel Radio/Nitimen" daily from 9:15 to 9:30 A.M.
Publications: *Aftenpost* daily newspaper has short reports and weather in English on back page. *Oslo This Week* events magazine.
Theater: Occasional touring companies in Oslo.
Movies: Original language.

POLAND

Broadcasts: Hourly news in summer between 9:00 A.M. and noon.
Publications: Events magazines.
Movies: Original language.

PORTUGAL

Broadcasts: Program 2 at 8:15 A.M. has English news.
Publications: *Algarve News, Mediera News, Lisbon Day & Night.*
Movies: Original language.

ROMANIA
Broadcasts: Hourly news 9:00 A.M. to 1:00 P.M. and 5:00–8:00 P.M. on medium-wave on the Black Sea coast.
Publications: *Lumea* (The Word) published weekly.
Movies: Original language.

SPAIN
Broadcasts: American Forces Network.
Publications: *Iberian Sun* daily newspaper; *Guidepost* weekly newspaper; *Lookout* monthly magazine.
Movies: Dubbed.

SWEDEN
Broadcasts: News on medium-wave in summer.
Publications: Many in English.
Movies: Original language.

SWITZERLAND
Publications: Events magazines in cities.
Theater: The Nestle company in Vevey sponsors English performances, especially Shakespeare. Geneva has three groups that perform in English: Little Theater of Geneva, Geneva English Drama Society and Calendar of the Year.

TURKEY
Broadcasts: In summer, news in English follows Turkish news two or three minutes after the hour (7:00 A.M.–1:00 A.M.) on Radio 3. Year-round, news roundup for tourists after the 7:00 P.M. news every Saturday. American Forces Network Radio.
Movies: Both dubbed and original language.

U.S.S.R.
Broadcasts: Radio Studio 8 broadcasts in English year-round. CNN and BBC can sometimes be picked up.
Publications: *Morning Star,* daily newspaper; *Sputnik,* monthly digest of Soviet press and literature; *Travel to the U.S.S.R.,* bimonthly magazine in English, French and German; *Moscow* magazine.

YUGOSLAVIA

Broadcasts: Radio Belgrade First Program, June 1–September 1 at 12:02 P.M. daily has thirty minutes of news in English, French and German (MW 493, UHF 88.9, 95.3 and 94.3).

Radio Zagreb, June 15–September 15, news at 11:00-11:30 A.M.

Radio Ljubljana 1st Program, May 1–September 30, news at 9:35-10:00 A.M. and "Tourist Information for Our Guests" in English, French and German daily 1:00–2:00 P.M. and 10:15–10:25 P.M., as well as nautical information at 6:35 A.M. and 9:55 A.M.

Radio Novi Sad, news in German and English daily except Sunday, 11:30 A.M.–noon.

Radio Yugoslavia broadcasts daily in ten languages year-round with news, sports and tourist information on UHF or FM 102.9. English programs at 3:30–4:00 P.M., 6:30–7:00 P.M., 8:00–8:30 P.M. and 10:15–10:30 P.M.

Publications: *Yugoslav Life* newspaper, *Yugoslav Review* magazine.
Theater: Touring companies perform in English.
Movies: Original language.

Telephone Codes

Four sets of numbers are needed to dial direct. First, dial the International Access Code of the country you are in, then dial the Country Code of the country you are calling. Third, dial the Area Code for the state or region: in Europe, this code often begins with 0, which usually—but not always—must be dropped when phoning from another country. Finally, dial the individual number.

For example, to dial New Orleans 523-0000 from West Germany, first dial 00 for Germany from the International Access Codes list. Then dial 1 for the United States from the Country Codes list. Then dial the Louisiana area code, 504. Last, dial the individual number, 523-0000. Altogether, you will dial 001 504 523-0000. Note that you can direct dial to some countries but cannot direct dial *from* them.

INTERNATIONAL ACCESS CODES

Austria 00[a]	Luxembourg 00
Belgium 00[b]	Malta 00
Canada 011	Monaco 19
Czechoslovakia 90	Neatherlands 09
Denmark 009	Norway 095

INTERNATIONAL ACCESS CODES (continued)

Finland 990	Poland 80
France 19	Portugal 07
Germany, East 06[c]	San Marino 00
Germany, West 00[c]	Spain 07
Great Britain 010	Sweden 009
Greece 00	Switzerland 00
Hungary 00	Turkey 99
Iceland 09	Vatican 00
Ireland 010	U.S.A. 011
Italy 00	Yugoslavia 99
Liechtenstein 00	

COUNTRY CODES

Andorra 33	Liechtenstein 41
Austria 43	Luxembourg 352
Belgium 32	Malta 356
Bulgaria 359	Monaco 33
Canada 1	Netherlands 31[b]
Czechoslovakia 42	Norway 47
Denmark 45	Poland 48
Finland 358	Portugal 351
France 33	Romania 40
Germany, East 37[c]	San Marino 39
Germany, West 49[c]	Spain 34
Great Britain 44	Sweden 46
Greece 30	Switzerland 41
Hungary 36	Turkey 90
Iceland 354	Vatican 39
Ireland 353	U.S.A. 1
Italy 39	Yugoslavia 38

[a] When dialing from Austria, the International Access Code plus the Country Code is 050 to Switzerland, 060 to Germany, 040 to Italy and 0432 to Luxembourg. To dial any other countries from Austria, follow the normal pattern.

[b] Wait for second dial tone after dialing this number.

[c] The phone codes will remain as they were for the two sections of Germany for some time to come.

AT&T USA Direct Service Numbers

A convenient and money-saving way to call the United States from Europe is with the USA Direct service offered by AT&T. It helps avoid language barriers and the rates you pay are AT&T's normal operator-assisted long-distance rates, rather than the much more expensive rates of European countries.

To reach an American operator, just dial the USA Direct access number from the following countries. (Note that these are special numbers which have nothing to do with the direct-dial codes listed above. These numbers simply put you in touch with the American operator, who places the call for you. You must give the operator the area code and individual number you are calling.) Before you leave home, check with your telephone office for additional countries where this service is offered, as the network is being expanded. If you are calling from a public phone, you must deposit coins or use a phone card to get a dial tone, except in Great Britain.

Austria: 022-903-011
Belgium: 11-0010
Denmark: 0430-0010
Finland: 9800-100-10
France: Dial 19, wait for second dial tone, then dial 0011
Germany: 0130-0010 (trial basis in Frankfurt a.M. only as of this
    writing)
Great Britain: 0800-89-0011
Hungary: 171-499 (limited availability)
Italy: 172-1011 (available in Rome and Milan only)
Netherlands: Dial 06, wait for second dial tone, then dial 022-9111
Norway: 050-12-011
Sweden: 020-795-611
Switzerland: 046-05-0011

In Italy, Spain and Great Britain, a few "designated telephones" are available that connect with the USA Direct operator simply by lifting the receiver. However, they are limited to U.S. military bases and a few telephone centers.

Tourist Offices

The national tourist promotion organizations of every country can provide maps, brochures and listings of events on request. The country's offices in the United States and Canada are listed first, followed by the headquarters in the country itself.

Andorra

Andorra Tourist Office, 120 East 55th Street, New York, NY 10022. Tel. (212) 688-8681. Fax (212) 688-8683.

Govern d'Andorra, Secretary General of Tourism and Sports, Principality of Andorra. Tel. 62-21234. Fax 62-60184.

Austria

Austrian National Tourist Office, 500 Fifth Avenue, Suite 2009-2022, New York, NY 10110. Tel. (212) 944-6880.

Austrian National Tourist Office, 11601 Wilshire Boulevard, Suite 2480, Los Angeles, CA 90025. Tel. (213) 477-3332.

Austrian National Tourist Office, 2 Bloor Street East, Suite 3330, Toronto, Ontario M4W 1A8. Tel. (416) 967-3381.

Österreich Information, Margaretenstrasse 1, A-1040 Vienna, Austria. Tel. 0222-57 57 14.

Belgium

Belgian Tourist Office, 745 Fifth Avenue, New York, NY 10151. Tel. (212) 758-8130. Fax (212) 355-7675.

Office de Promotion du Tourisme, rue Marché-aux-Herbes 61, B-1000 Brussels, Belgium. Tel. 02-518 12 11.

Bulgaria

Balkan Holidays, Bulgaria Center, 161 East 86th Street, New York, NY 10028. Tel. (212) 722-1110 or 7626.

Balkan Tourist, Boulevard Vitoscha 1, BG-1000 Sofia, Bulgaria. Tel. 02-43331.

Bulgarian Association for Tourism, Lenin Square 1, BG-1000 Sofia, Bulgaria. Tel. 02-84232.

Czechoslovakia

Čedok, 10 East 40th Street, New York, NY 10016. Tel. (212) 689-9720. Fax (212) 481-0597.

Čedok, Na Příkopě 18, CS-11135 Prague 1, Czechoslovakia. Tel. 02-12 71 11.

DENMARK

Danish Tourist Board, 655 Third Avenue, 18th Floor, New York, NY 10017. Tel. (212) 949-2333.

Danish Tourist Board, P.O. Box 115, Station N, Toronto, Ontario M8V 3S4. Tel. (416) 823-9620.

Scandinavian Tourist Office, 8929 Wilshire Boulevard, Beverly Hills, CA 90211. Tel. (213) 657-4808. Fax (213) 657-4686.

Scandinavian Tourist Office, 150 North Michigan Avenue, Suite 2110, Chicago, IL 60601. Tel. (312) 726-1120. Fax (312) 726-3774.

Danmarks Turistraad, Vesterbrogade 6d, DK-1620 Copenhagen, Denmark. Tel. 033-11 13 25.

FINLAND

Finnish Tourist Board, 655 Third Avenue, New York, NY 10017. Tel. (212) 949-2333. Fax (212) 983-5260.

Scandinavian Tourist Office, 8929 Wilshire Boulevard, Beverly Hills, CA 90211. Tel. (213) 657-4808. Fax (213) 657-4686.

Scandinavian Tourist Office, 150 North Michigan Avenue, Suite 2110, Chicago, IL 60601. Tel. (312) 726-1120. Fax (312) 726-3774.

Tourist Information, Unioninkatu 26, SF-00521 Helsinki, Finland. Tel. 90-40 30 11. Fax 90-40 30 13 33.

FRANCE

French National Tourist Office, 610 Fifth Avenue, New York, NY 10020. Tel. (212) 757-1125.

French National Tourist Office, 645 North Michigan Avenue, Suite 630, Chicago, IL 60611. Tel. (312) 337-6301.

French National Tourist Office, 9401 Wilshire Boulevard, Los Angeles, CA 90212. Tel. (213) 272-2661 or 6665.

French National Tourist Office, One Hallidie Plaza, Suite 250, San Francisco, CA 94102. Tel. (415) 986-4161.

French National Tourist Office, World Trade Center 103, 2050 Stemmons Freeway, P.O. Box 58610, Dallas, TX 75258. Tel. (214) 742-7011.

French National Tourist Office, 1981 McGill College Avenue, Suite 49, Montreal, Quebec H3A 2WG9. Tel. (514) 288-4264.

French National Tourist Office, 1 Dundas Street W, Suite 2405, Box 8, Toronto, Ontario M56 L23. Tel. (416) 593-4717.

France Tourist Information, 127 Avenue des Champs- Elysèes, F-75008 Paris, France.

GERMANY

German National Tourist Office, 747 Third Avenue, 33rd Floor, New York, NY 10017. Tel. (212) 308-3300.

German National Tourist Office, 444 South Flower Street, Los Angeles, CA 90071. Tel. (213) 688-7332.

German National Tourist Office, 175 Bloor Street East, Toronto, Ontario M4W 3R8. Tel. (416) 968-1570.

Deutsche Zentrale für Tourismus, Beethovenstrasse 69, W-6000 Frankfurt a.M. 1, Germany. Tel. 069-75720.

GREAT BRITAIN

British Tourist Authority, 40 West 57th Street, New York, NY 10019-4001. Tel. (212) 581-4700. Fax (212) 265-0649.

British Tourist Authority, 350 South Figueroa Street, Room 450, Los Angeles, CA 90071. Tel. (213) 628-3525. Fax (213) 687-6621.

British Tourist Authority, 625 North Michigan Avenue, Suite 1510, Chicago, IL 60611. Tel. (312) 787-0490. Fax (312) 787-7746.

British Tourist Authority, Cedar Maple Plaza, Suite 210, 2305 Cedar Springs Road, Dallas, TX 75201. Tel. (214) 720-4040. Fax (214) 871-2665.

British Tourist Authority, 94 Cumberland Street, Suite 600, Toronto, Ontario M5R 3N3. Tel. (416) 925-6326. Fax (416) 961-2175.

British Tourist Authority, Thames Tower, Black's Road, London W6 9EL, England. Tel. 081-846 90 00.

GREECE

Greek Tourist Office, 645 Fifth Avenue, Olympic Tower, New York, NY 10022. Tel. (212) 421-5777.

Greek Tourist Office, 611 West Sixth Street, Los Angeles, CA 90017. Tel. (213) 626-6696.

Greek Tourist Office, 168 North Michigan Avenue, National Bank of Greece Building, Chicago, IL 60601. Tel. (312) 782-1984.

Greek Tourist Office, 68 Scollars Street, Toronto, Ontario M5R 1G2. Tel. (416) 968-2220.

Greek Tourist Office, 1233 rue de la Montagne, Montreal, Quebec H3G 1Z2. Tel. (514) 871-1535.

National Tourist Organization of Greece, 2 rue Amerikis, GR-10672 Athens, Greece. Tel. 01-322 31 11.

HUNGARY

IBUSZ Hungarian Travel Company, 630 Fifth Avenue, Suite 520,

New York, NY 10020. Tel. (212) 582-7412.

IBUSZ Hungarian Travel Company, One Parker Plaza, Suite 1104, Fort Lee, NJ 07024. Tel. (212) 592-8585.

Hungarian Tourist Office, Vigado Útca 4, H-1051 Budapest, Hungary. Tel. 01-118 50 44.

IBUSZ—Hungarian Travel Bureau, Tanács Krt. 3/C, H-1075 Budapest, Hungary. Tel. 01-21 10 00.

ICELAND

Viking Travel, Gimli, Manitoba, Canada (a travel agency that concentrates on Iceland). Tel. (204) 642-5114.

Feroaskrifstofa rikisiins, Iceland Tourist Bureau, Reykjanesbraut 6, Reykjavík, Iceland.

IRELAND

Irish Tourist Information Office, 757 Third Avenue, New York, NY 10017. Tel. (212) 418-0800.

Irish Tourist Information Office, 10 King Street East, Toronto, Ontario M5C 1C3. (416) 364-1301.

Irish Tourist Information Office, 14 Upper O'Connell Street, Dublin, Ireland. Tel. 01-74 77 33.

ITALY

Italian Government Tourist Office, 630 Fifth Avenue, Suite 1565, New York, NY 10111. Tel. (212) 397-5293. Fax (212) 586-9249.

Italian Government Tourist Office, 360 Post Street, Suite 801, San Francisco, CA 94108. Tel. (415) 392-5266. Fax (415) 392-6852.

Italian Government Travel Office, 500 North Michigan Avenue, Suite 1046, Chicago, IL 60611. Tel. (312) 644-0990.

Italian Government Travel Office, c/o Alitalia, 120 Adelaide Street West, Suite 1202, Toronto, Ontario H3B 2E3. Tel. (416) 363-1348.

ENIT (Ente Nazionale Italiano per il Turismo), Via Marghera 2, I-00185 Rome, Italy. Tel. 06-49711.

LIECHTENSTEIN

Served by Swiss offices in the United States.

Liechtensteinische Fremdenverkehrszentrale, Postfach 139, FL-9490 Vaduz, Liechtenstein. Tel. 075-21443.

LUXEMBOURG

Luxembourg Tourist Office, 801 Second Avenue, New York, NY 10017. Tel. (212) 370-9850.

Office National du Tourisme, P.O. Box 1001, L-1130 Luxembourg. Tel. 40 08 08. Fax 40 47 48.

MALTA

Malta Tourist Information, 249 East 35th Street, New York, NY 10016. Tel. (212) 725-2345.

National Tourist Organization, Harper Lane, Floriana, Malta. Tel. 24444 or 28282.

MONACO

Direction du tourisme et des Congres de la Principaute de Monaco, 2A Boulevard des Moulins, MC-98030 Monte Carlo, Monaco CEDEX. Tel. 093-30 87 01.

NETHERLANDS

Netherlands Board of Tourism, 355 Lexington Avenue, New York, NY 10017. Tel. (212) 370-7367. Fax (212) 370-9507.

Netherlands Board of Tourism, 90 New Montgomery Street, Suite 305, San Francisco, CA 94105. Tel. (415) 543-6772. Fax (415) 495-4925.

Netherlands Board of Tourism, 225 North Michigan Avenue, Suite 326, Chicago, IL 60601. Tel. (312) 819-0300. Fax (312) 819-1740.

Netherlands Board of Tourism, 25 Adelaide Street East, Suite 710, Toronto, Ontario M5C 1Y2. Tel. (416) 363-1577. Fax (416) 363-1470.

Netherlands Bureau voor Toerisme, Vlietweg 15, NL-2266 KA Leidschendam, The Netherlands. Tel. 070-70 57 05.

NORWAY

Norwegian Tourist Board, 655 Third Avenue, New York, NY 10017. Tel. (212) 949-2333.

Scandinavian Tourist Board, 8929 Wilshire Boulevard, Beverly Hills, CA 90211. Tel. (213) 657-4808. Fax (213) 657-4686.

Scandinavian Tourist Board, 150 North Michigan Avenue, Suite 2110, Chicago, IL 60601. Tel. (312) 726-1120. Fax (312) 726-3774.

Norwegian Tourist Board NOTRA, Postboks 499 Sentrum, N-0105 Oslo 1, Norway. Tel. 02-42 70 44.

Poland

ORBIS—Polish Travel Bureau Inc., 500 Fifth Avenue, New York, NY 10036. Tel. (212) 391-0844.

Polish National Tourist Office, 333 North Michigan Avenue, Chicago, IL 60601. Tel. (312) 236-9013.

LOT Polish Airlines, International Aviation Square, 1000 Sherbrooke Street West, Suite 2220, Montreal, Quebec H3A 2W5. Tel. (514) 844-2674.

National Tourist Enterprise ORBIS, 16 Braca Street, PL-00028 Warsaw, Poland. Tel. 022-27 62 32.

Portugal

Portuguese National Tourist Office, 590 Fifth Avenue, 4th Floor, New York, NY 10036. Tel. (212) 354-4403. Fax (212) 764-6137.

Portuguese National Tourist Office, 2180 Yonge Street, Concourse Level, Toronto, Ontario M4S 2B9. Tel. (416) 487-3300. Fax (416) 487-3938.

Office National du Tourisme Portugais, 500 Sherbrooke West, Suite 930, Montreal, Quebec H3A 3C6. Tel. (514) 843-4623. Fax (514) 843-9328.

Instituto de Promocao Turistica, Rue Alexandre Herculano 51-2, P-1200 Lisbon, Portugal. Tel. 01-68 11 74.

Romania

Romanian Tourist Office, 573 Third Avenue, New York, NY 10016. Tel. (212) 697-6971.

Ministere du Tourisme, Magheru Boulevard 7, 7000 Bucharest, Romania. Tel. 0-14 51 60.

San Marino

Ufficio di Stato per il Turismo, Palazzo del Turismo, RSM-47031 Republic of San Marino. Tel. 549-99 21 01.

Spain

National Tourist Office of Spain, 665 Fifth Avenue, New York, NY 10022. Tel. (212) 759-8822.

Spanish National Tourist Office, Princesa 1 Torre de Madrid, E-28006 Madrid, Spain. Tel. 091-24 12 325.

SWEDEN

Swedish Tourist Office, 655 Third Avenue, 18th Floor, New York, NY 10017. Tel. (212) 949-2333. Fax (212) 697-0835.

Scandinavian Tourist Office, 8929 Wilshire Boulevard, Beverly Hills, CA 90211. Tel. (213) 657-4808. Fax (213) 657-4686.

Scandinavian Tourist Office, 150 North Michigan Avenue, Suite 2110, Chicago, IL 60601. Tel. (312) 726-1120. Fax (312) 726-3774.

Swedish Tourist Office, P.O. Box 7473, S-10392 Stockholm, Sweden. Tel. 08-789 20 00.

SWITZERLAND

Swiss National Tourist Office, 608 Fifth Avenue, New York, NY 10020. Tel. (212) 757-5944. Fax (212) 262-6116.

Swiss National Tourist Office, 105 North Michigan Avenue, Chicago, IL 60601. Tel. (312) 630-5840. Fax (312) 630-5848.

Swiss National Tourist Office, 222 North Sepulveda Boulevard, Suite 1570, El Segundo, CA 90245. Tel. (213) 335-5980. Fax (213) 335-5982.

Swiss National Tourist Office, 260 Stockton Street, San Francisco, CA 94108. Tel. (415) 362-2260. Fax (415) 391-1508.

Swiss National Tourist Office, 154 University Avenue, Toronto, Ontario M5H 3Y9. Tel. (416) 971-9734. Fax (416) 971-6425.

Schweizerische Verkehrszentrale, Bellairiastrasse 38, CH-8027 Zurich, Switzerland. Tel. 01-20 23 737.

TURKEY

Turkish Tourism and Information Office, 821 United Nations Plaza, New York, NY 10017. Tel. (212) 687-2194. Fax (212) 599-7568.

Turkish Embassy Information Office, 1714 Massachusetts Avenue, N.W., Washington, DC 20008. Tel. (202) 429-9409. Fax (202) 429-5649.

Ministry for Culture and Tourism, G.M. Kemel Bulvari 33, Ankara, Turkey. Tel. 41-29 29 30.

U.S.S.R.

Intourist, 630 Fifth Avenue, Suite 868, New York, NY 10111. Tel. (212) 757-3884.

Intourist, 1801 McGill College Avenue 630, Montreal, Quebec H3A 2A4. Tel. (514) 849-6394.

Intourist, Prospekt Marxa 16, SU-103009 Moscow, U.S.S.R. Tel. 095-203 69 62.

Sputnik, International Youth Travel Bureau of the U.S.S.R., Kosygin 15, SU-117946 Moscow, U.S.S.R. Tel. 095-139 86 65. Fax 095-41 10 49.

YUGOSLAVIA

Yugoslav National Tourist Office, 630 Fifth Avenue, Suite 280, New York, NY 10111. Tel. (212) 757-2801.

Turisticki Savez Jugoslavije, Mose Pijade 8, YU-11000 Belgrade, Yugoslavia. Tel. 011-33 53 67.

International Information Signs

Like international road signs, general information of use to the tourist (locations of phones, toilets, information booths, etc.) is often best expressed by symbols. Here are some of the more common symbols used in Europe.

Information

Toilet

Foreign exchange

Smoking

No smoking!

Customs

No entry

Telephone

Post office

Telegraph

First aid

Pharmacy

Lost and found

Escalator

Litter container

Taxis

To ferry docks

Bus

To the airport

Assistance or access for handicapped

Restaurant

Drinking water

Non-drinkable water

Washroom

Tickets

INDEX